Discourse De

MW01519746

This volume advances scholarly understanding of the ways in which discourse deixis underpins the workings of metafictional novels. Building on existing scholarship in the field, the book begins by mapping out key themes and techniques in metafiction, then puts forward a focused and theoretically coherent account of discourse deixis—language which points to a section or aspect of the discourse context in which that language is used—in written literary discourse, highlighting its inherent significance in metafiction specifically. Andrea Macrae takes readers through an exploration of discourse deixis as used within the techniques of metanarration, metalepsis, and disnarration, drawing on a mix of both well-established and lesser-known metafictional novels from the late 1960s and early 1970s by such authors as John Barth, Brigid Brophy, Robert Coover, John Fowles, Steve Katz, and B. S. Johnson. This comprehensive account integrates and develops a new approach to understanding discourse deixis and innovative insights into metafictionality more broadly. It will be of particular interest to scholars in literary studies, postmodern literature, narratology, and stylistics.

Andrea Macrae is a Principal Lecturer in Stylistics and in Student Experience at Oxford Brookes University, U.K. She is the co-editor of *Pronouns in Literature: Positions and Perspectives in Language*. She has published on deixis in several journals and edited collections.

Routledge Studies in Rhetoric and Stylistics
Edited by Michael Burke,
Christiana Gregoriou, and
Joe Bray

Stories, Meaning, and Experience
Narrativity and Enaction
Yanna B. Popova

From Conversation to Oral Tradition
A Simplest Systematics for Oral Traditions
Raymond F. Person, Jr.

Making Sense of Narrative Text
Situation, Repetition, and Picturing in the Reading of Short Stories
Michael Toolan

A Prosody of Free Verse
Explorations in Rhythm
Richard Andrews

Similes, Puns and Counterfactuals in Literary Narrative
Jennifer Riddle Harding

Rethinking Language, Text and Context
Interdisciplinary Research in Stylistics in Honour of Michael Toolan
Edited by Ruth Page, Beatrix Busse and Nina Nørgaard

Metaphor and Persuasion in Strategic Communication
Sustainable Perspectives
Federica Ferrari

Discourse Deixis in Metafiction
The Language of Metanarration, Metalepsis and Disnarration
Andrea Macrae

For more information about this series, please visit: www.routledge.com/
Routledge-Studies-in-Rhetoric-and-Stylistics/book-series/RSTYL

Discourse Deixis in Metafiction

The Language of Metanarration, Metalepsis and Disnarration

Andrea Macrae

Routledge
Taylor & Francis Group
NEW YORK AND LONDON

First published 2019
by Routledge
605 Third Avenue, New York, NY 10017

and by Routledge
2 Park Square, Milton Park, Abingdon, Oxon OX14 4RN

First issued in paperback 2020

Routledge is an imprint of the Taylor & Francis Group, an informa business

Library of Congress Cataloging-in-Publication Data
A catalog record for this book has been requested

ISBN 13: 978-0-367-72999-8 (pbk)
ISBN 13: 978-0-367-14124-0 (hbk)

Typeset in Sabon
by Apex CoVantage, LLC

Contents

List of Figures   vii
Acknowledgements   viii
Permissions   ix

1 Introduction   1
   1.1 Mapping Out Metafictionality 1
   1.2 Critical Studies of Metafiction 9
   1.3 Metafictional Techniques 18
   *1.4 Where Discourse Deixis Meets/Makes
       Metafiction 22*
   *1.5 Introducing Barth, Brophy, Coover, Fowles,
       Johnson, and Katz 25*
   1.6 The Chapters to Come 30

2 Discourse Deixis in Literature   35
   2.1 Introducing Discourse Deixis 35
   2.2 Defining Deixis 37
   2.3 Person, Spatial, and Temporal Deixis 40
   2.4 Deixis in Written Literature 45
   2.5 Discourse Deixis in Written Literature 49
   2.6 Conclusion 61

3 Discourse Deixis in Metanarration   64
   3.1 Defining Metanarration 65
   3.2 Metatextual Metanarration 73
   3.3 Metacompositional Metanarration 76
   3.4 Metadiegetic Metanarration 81
   3.5 Metanarrative Metanarration 85
   3.6 Metadiscursive Metanarration 91
   3.7 Conclusion 98

4 **Discourse Deixis in Metalepsis** 102

    4.1 Defining Metalepsis 103

    4.2 Metaleptic Awareness 115

    4.3 Metaleptic Communication 121

    4.4 Metaleptic Moves 138

    4.5 Conclusion 153

5 **Discourse Deixis in Disnarration** 159

    5.1 Defining Disnarration 160

    5.2 Discourse Deixis in Denarration 162

    5.3 Discourse Deixis in Alternarration 180

    5.4 Discourse Deixis in Negation and Hypothetical Focalisation 199

    5.5 Discourse Deixis in Narrative Refusal and the Antinarratable 211

    5.6 Conclusion 216

6 **Conclusion** 220

    Index 226

Figures

1.1   Scale of metafictionality   5
1.2   Functions of metafictionality   5
4.1   Levels of narrative   103

Acknowledgements

Thanks go to Peter Moss and Peter Stockwell for the inspiration and for opening up worlds for me and thousands of others. Thanks go to my parents for their patience, to Lucia Simon for Lanzarote and general loveliness, to Steve Berrisford for the laughter, and to Barley for the Booness. More than thanks go to Genevieve Dear for her keen editorial eye and for being my superhero every single day.

Permissions

1 Introduction

This book explores discourse deixis in metafiction, investigating how discourse deixis works within and contributes to metafictional effects. Discourse deixis has remained a problematic category of deixis, with scope for further untangling. Metafiction has been the subject of much scholarly attention, particularly in the 1980s, but its linguistic workings have as yet not been investigated in great depth. Several metafictional techniques rely heavily on discourse deixis to create their metafictional effects. This book explores the intersection of discourse deixis and metafiction to offer new insights into both literary discourse deixis and the linguistics of metafictionality.

This introductory chapter begins with an overview of metafiction, including its development and common themes (section 1.1). The second section (1.2) reviews leading studies of metafiction and discusses the groundwork laid in some of these texts for an investigation of how metafictional effects are created. The next section (1.3) presents three of the main metafictional techniques: metanarration, metalepsis, and disnarration. The fourth section (1.4) introduces discourse deixis and its significance and role in metafictionality, through a brief illustrative discussion of an example from Barth's *Lost in the Funhouse* (1988 [1968]). The fifth section (1.5) introduces the metafictional texts that will be explored in this book, and explains why these texts, in particular, have been chosen for this study of discourse deixis in metafiction. Finally, the last section (1.6) provides an overview of the book's forthcoming chapters.

1.1 Mapping Out Metafictionality

The term 'metafiction' became critical currency in the late 1960s, 1970s, and 1980s as a means of labelling a particular type of fiction. It was coined by William Gass in his essay 'Philosophy and the Form of Fiction', originally written for a collection edited by Robert Scholes (1970) and then included in Gass's own collection of essays, *Fiction and the Figures of Life* (1970). As Berry notes, Gass used it only once, to talk about the work of Jorge Luis Borges, John Barth, and Flann O'Brien (2012, p. 128). He used the term 'metafiction' to refer specifically to fiction "in which the forms of fiction serve as the material upon which further forms can be imposed" (Gass, 1970, p. 25). In later uses, as the term was adopted within literary scholarship, it came to mean fiction which overtly uses both its narrative form and its thematic content to explore the nature of fiction, and through it the nature of reality. As a descriptor, 'metafiction' is often applied to works like Muriel Spark's *The Comforters* (1963) [1957], Gilbert Sorrentino's *Imaginative Qualities of Actual Things* (1973), and Kurt Vonnegut's *Breakfast of Champions* (1973). These novels variably involve pseudo-authorial narrators who intermittently comment on their acts of composition, characterisation, etc. (a kind of 'metanarration'); characters or events which are presented as existing in the storyworld and then cancelled out in some way (a type of 'disnarration'); characters who are aware of their fictional status; and/or some kind of crossing of the conventional boundary between the 'level' of narration and the 'level' of the storyworld (this awareness and this crossing being forms of 'metalepsis'). One example of this unusual awareness and crossing of narrative levels is Spark's heroine in *The Comforters* being able to hear the sound of her creator typing as the novel is composed, the sections which she hears being repeated within the narration of her experiences. The identifying characteristic of metafiction is its being "in constant dialogue with its own conventions" (Currie, 1995, p. 1), that is, its focused confrontation of fictionality and the conditions through which fiction is brought into being. Critical self-consciousness is not an incidental or minor feature in metafiction: rather, metafiction is dominantly, demonstratively, and constitutively engaged with its own conditions of existence, its parameters, its complexities, and its paradoxes throughout.

Some metafiction is, sometimes unfairly, criticised for merely offering a kind of literary navel-gazing. As Timmer asks, in relation to David Foster Wallace's metafictional novella 'Westward the Course of Empire Takes Its Way', "what exactly could be the use of all this playing around with narrative structures for which postmodern literature is renown; is it just 'fun' for fun's sake, and devoid of any humanness?" (Timmer, 2010, p. 106). Most metafiction is in fact "fun" precisely for the sake of humanness: it uses its self-reflexivity to address broader philosophical, social, and political themes (Hutcheon, 1988; Onega and Ganteau, 2007; Waugh, 1984). Much mid- and late twentieth century metafiction uses its self-reflexivity to embody and parody postmodern concern with the constructed and dialogic nature of reality and of identity, and with the relation between the subject and object, and between the self and other (Hutcheon, 1980; Waugh, 1984). These fictions employ a variety of metafictional strategies as part of a systematic and thematically integrated endeavour to confront ontological and epistemological uncertainties. The fictional form becomes both the medium and the parodic model for this interrogation of the subjectively constructed nature of reality.

Metafiction did not arise only with postmodernism, though. Miguel de Cervantes' *Don Quixote* (2003) [1605–1615] and Laurence Sterne's *The Life and Opinions of Tristram Shandy, Gentleman* (2003 [1759–1767]) are often heralded as the earliest examples of literature that is intensely metafictional. The birth and early development of the novel in the eighteenth century naturally saw a brief flourish of critical reflexivity, hence *Tristram Shandy, Shamela, A Sentimental Journey Through France and Italy*, etc.—works which demonstratively prioritise the medium of literary narrative as a thematic concern, albeit (like postmodernist metafiction) within a broader philosophical and socio-political context. These texts tend to interrogate the possibilities, impossibilities, and paradoxes of fictive narrative constructions at the same time as satirically exploring Enlightenment understanding of the self and social relations. For example, the eponymous narrator of Sterne's *Tristram Shandy* ruminates—at surreal and satirical length and in a faux autobiographical fashion—on the influences upon his personality and identity, archly mocking the science and psychology of the day. Simultaneously, he also playfully subverts conventions of plot arcs and narrative progression, and frequently and explicitly comments on his failure in this regard, at one point even drawing line illustrations of the circles and swirls of digressions he has made over preceding chapters.

As the novel form became more established, its value began to be determined in its potential as a vehicle for social observation. Throughout the late eighteenth and nineteenth century, the novel was developed according to more conventionally mimetic strategies. Within texts of this era, metanarrative commentary still occurred, but only occasionally, and often contributing to didactic or ironic social commentary and/or affirmation of the illusion of narratorial insight into the story (thereby paradoxically supporting the mimetic illusion of the reality of the characters). Consider, for example, the following quotes from works by George Eliot:

> Let me take you into that dining room [. . .] We will enter, very softly [. . .] the walls you see, are new. [. . .] He will perhaps turn around by and by and in the meantime we can look at the stately old lady.
> (*Adam Bede*, 2008 [1858], pp. 49–50)

> One morning, some weeks after her arrival at Lowick, Dorothea—but why always Dorothea? Was her point of view the only possible one with regard to this marriage? I protest against all our effort at understanding being given to the young skins that look blooming in spite of trouble. [. . .] In spite of the blinking eyes and white moles objectionable to Celia, [. . .] Mr. Casaubon had an intense

consciousness within him, and was spiritually a-hungered like the rest of us.

(*Middlemarch*, 1994 [1871–1872], p. 230)

In the first quote, from *Adam Bede*, the pseudo-authorial narrator addresses the reader directly as "you". Here, the narrator implies that she and the reader are both present together as quiet, discrete witnesses within the fictional scene. That "he" will "perhaps" turn around suggests that this pseudo-authorial narrator is observing, rather than creating and in control of, this scene. Ontologically impossible though this 'presence' is, this passage enhances the illusion of immediacy and the potential for a sense of immersion.

The metafictionality of the second quote, from *Middlemarch*, is more subtle and more complex. One the one hand, the (again) pseudo-authorial narrator appears to interrupt herself, affirming the illusion of her authorial role and power in her proclaimed proactive 'refusal' to focus on Dorothea's viewpoint. The ensuing words could be read as a broader reference to and critique of marriage in fiction always being portrayed as the concern of the female characters, as in Austen's novels, Richardson's *Pamela*, etc. Read as such, it draws attention to the fictionality of this text while making a comment on gender politics in literary art. On the other hand, the implication that other characters, beyond Dorothea, have "view[s]" supports the impression that they are real beings, with histories and perspectives. This implies that the pseudo-authorial narrator is merely relaying, rather than creating, these views, which in turn affirms the illusion of mimesis.

These quotes illustrate three important points. Firstly, metafictionality, as a quality of fiction, is scalar rather than binary. Alter and others have argued that all fiction bears the trace of its construction, reveals its fictionality, and undermines its own realism and conditions of believability and being. Alter goes so far as to suggest that "the realistic enterprise" of fiction, "from Renaissance Spain to contemporary France and America", has been informed, "complicated and qualified by" the awareness of the illusory and even contradictory nature of literary realism and the ontology of the novel (Alter, 1978 [1975], p. x). Critical reflection within fiction upon the narrative medium can be traced through the Western tradition of narrative mimesis as far back as Euripides' parody of the conventions of Greek tragedy (Alter, 1978 [1975], p. xi), and up to and through the 'realist' novels of the nineteenth and twentieth centuries. A reflexive awareness of literariness is therefore not particular to metafiction, but rather underscores much of the tradition of the novel as a mimetic form (see Figure 1.1). Secondly, metafictionality can serve sometimes to bolster, and sometimes to break, the 'fourth wall'—and sometimes, paradoxically, can do both simultaneously. Thirdly, metafictionality can be used for commentary beyond 'metacommentary': that is, it can be used to

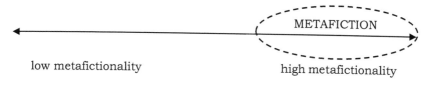

Figure 1.1 Scale of metafictionality

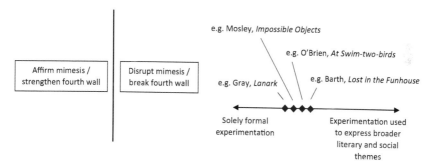

Figure 1.2 Functions of metafictionality

reflect beyond (though via) that particular book to broader literary and socio-political contexts and concerns (see Figure 1.2).

Metafictionality is, then, neither rare in literature nor uniform in function. Metafiction 'proper', however, appears more rarely across the Western canon than incidental metafictionality. Metafiction is not merely occasionally self-reflexive, but *dominantly* so. It frequently and strategically breaks the fourth wall to disrupt and call attention to the illusion of mimesis and the nature of fictionality. Following the initial wave of reflexivity soon after the birth of the novel form, metafiction proper did not begin to flourish again until the late modernist and postmodernist eras. Woolf's *Orlando* (1928) and O'Brien's *At Swim-two-birds* (1939) are examples of late modernist metafictional novels. Both of these novels exploit metafictionality partially for socio-political agendas distinct to their eras, but both are also precociously infused with the pressing ontological and epistemological concerns that came to drive the metafiction of the postmodern era.

Western metafiction arguably peaked in the 1950s to 1980s. These were decades in which socio-ideological conditions imbued a hyper-awareness of the self and her/his relation to reality and the other, a crisis of faith in enlightenment systems of rationalisation and totalisation, scepticism of histories and master-narratives, anxiety over the mediating role of consciousness, and philosophical questioning of the possibility of communication and a shared 'reality'. Metafiction is arguably the quintessential expression of postmodernism (Hutcheon, 1984, 1988; McHale, 1987; Waugh, 1984). The neatness of the marriage of metafiction and postmodernism is perhaps because the thematic concerns of the metafictional novels of the mid to late twentieth century are largely indistinguishable from the thematic concerns of postmodernism more broadly. Alternatively, it is potentially because metafiction's textual and narrative modes afford it a uniquely concentrated self-reflexivity and critical enactment of these concerns. Hutcheon suggests that postmodern self-reflexive art

> is perhaps a matter of finding an aesthetic mode of dealing with modern man's experience of life as being unordered by any communal or transcendental power—God or myth—and his new skepticism that art can unproblematically provide a consolatory order.
>
> (1984 [1980], pp. 18–19)

She argues that "the formal and thematic self-consciousness of metafiction [. . .] is paradigmatic of most of the cultural forms of [. . .] our 'postmodern' world" (p. xii).

One of the dominant themes within metafictional and postmodernist discourses is the dichotomy between the tendency, in narrative, theory, and human psychology, towards positivistic and comprehensive closure on the one hand, and the inevitably discursive, context-bound, pluralistic nature of meaning on the other. Postmodernism is marked by an undermining of the possibility and validity of a systematising master-narrative. Postmodernist theorists such as Lyotard (1983, 1984) state that there can be no valid claim of an ultimate truth or master-narrative, and take care to assert the contextually situated, constructed, and provisional nature of their own theoretical narratives (Hutcheon, 1988, p. 13, p. 20). However, they also note the internal paradox within any anti-totalising theoretical dogma: even the claim that there can be no ultimate truth is itself an implicit claim to a resolving cohesion and 'truth' of sorts, and therefore is an act complicit with the construction of totalising master-narratives. Metafictional novels both walk this tightrope and shine a spotlight on it, by problematising the ways in which fictional narrative can suggest the possibility of an author providing an ordered, cohesive, "totalizing scheme of explanation" (Hutcheon, 1988, p. 55) when this 'explanation' and meaning is entirely dependent on the reader's context-bound subjective interpretation. Metafiction enacts the postmodern literary-theoretical exploration of meaning-value and the referent, of the proactive, retrospective construction of coherence, and of how far the author or text can manipulate, constrain, assist, obstruct, or disown interpretation.

Hutcheon observes that postmodernism "acknowledges the human urge to make order, while pointing out that the orders we create are just that: human constructs, not natural or given entities" (1988, pp. 41–42). The central paradox of postmodernism and of metafiction likewise is that its act of exploring and deconstructing orders, systems, and narratives is enmeshed within, and inevitably affirms and newly creates, orders, systems, and narratives. The paradoxical and provisional nature of narrative systems is not stultifying: the confrontation of construction does not paralyse the act of creating or engaging with narratives. Instead, this paradox, and its inevitability, is flaunted. As Hutcheon writes, "the contradictions of both postmodern theory and practice are positioned within the system and yet work to allow its premises to be seen as fictions or as ideological structures". The self-reflexive critique works to expose "the tracks of the signifying systems that constitute our world—that is, systems constructed by us in answer to our needs" (p. 13).

A related theme commonly explored through both metafiction and postmodernism is the discursive nature of historiography. Many postmodern discourses recognise history as plural—as histories—and acknowledge these histories as fundamentally discursive constructs: the past is constituted by whichever versions of it are created and embedded within the discourses of the present. In historiographic metafiction, self-referentiality, problematisation of the author-function (as the determiner of the 'true' version of events), and confrontation of the processes of production and reception are used to explore historiography, truth, and reference, and the narrativisation of the subject (that is, both of subjective experience, and, dependent upon this, of a subjective sense of selfhood).

Again, though, this exploration does not destroy the totalising narratives that form histories: the conventions of historiography are at least partially retained—even reaffirmed—in the process of exposing them. Historiographic metafiction demonstrates histories as social texts, 'real' history being traceable only through this mediation, the sum of these mediations being all that 'remains' (see White, 1987, 1994). Hutcheon writes "we cannot know the past except through its texts" (1988, p. 16), and the same is true for the present, hence the Derridean observation that there is no outside-text from which we can 'know': we are parts of the texts through which we derive reality. Postmodern interrogation, through the insights of theorists such as Derrida (1981), LaCapra (1985), and de Certeau (1975), shifts the analysis of history to its crossovers with the enunciative and receptive conditions of fiction: each "imposes meaning on the past" and does so by (amongst other acts equally necessary to totalising interpretation) "postulating an end (and/or origin)" (Hutcheon, 1988, p. 97). Though these concerns are the dominant foci of historiographic metafiction in particular (see Cornis-Pope, 1994, pp. 411–416), confrontation of the inevitably illusory simplification and totalisation in the act of narrativisation, the situatedness of narrative within a discursive context, and the processes of production and reception are concerns central to metafiction more broadly.

A further concern central to both metafiction and postmodernism is the functioning of the referent. The investigation of historiography confronts aspects of the displacement of 'truth' and the inevitability of the situatedness of discourse within particular mediating socio-historical contexts. The impossibility of objective and transparent representation is directly addressed and problematised. This recognition of the significance of subjective positioning in the act of enunciation foregrounds the discursive context-dependence of the signifying process itself (Benveniste, 1971 [1966]). In asserting the pragmatics of meaning-generation in textual communication, theorists such as Foucault (1972), Barthes (1977 [1967]), and Bakhtin (1981) have in different ways challenged the notion of a closed, holistic, and universal interpretation. Again, however, postmodern discourses can only interrogate from within, utilising and endorsing signifying processes, often explicitly indicating reliance on the conventional communicative principles upon which textual direction can be expected to guide reader-reception, only to demonstratively question the referential relationship upon which the communication of this very questioning depends. Metafiction overtly epitomises this problem. It directly confronts the enunciative act of communication that constitutes the discourse of fiction, and brings to the fore the conditions of production and reception that uphold this act (Hutcheon, 1984, p. xiii). At the same time, it necessarily utilises and reaffirms these conditions and the stable communicative meaning-value of the sign. Metafiction at once creates and problematises mimesis, "spoil[ing] the simple geometry of the mirror held up to nature" (McHale, 1987, p. 29), invokes and destabilises narrative representation, and directs and contests interpretative closure.

Finally, 'self'-reflexive awareness of, and commentary upon, its processes of production and reception is an essential element of the explorations within metafiction. The notion of self-reflexivity is, however, internally problematic, and these problems become a further part of those explorations. Currie asks of the conventional definition of metafiction: how can fiction be self-conscious? Who is the 'self'? (Currie, 1995, pp. 1–2). Is the same self at once conscious, referred to, and conscious of being referred to? The self-consciousness of metafiction is part of overt interrogations of the ontological parameters and functioning of the text, the author, and the reader. With the textual manifestation of the conditions of production comes a confrontation of the designed nature of the fiction, the presence of the maker inscribed in the text. Intertwined with this is a problematisation of the notion of the sign, and, more broadly, of narrative, as both discursively determined and stable enough for communicative value, and thereby implicitly under the control of the author.

The reader of metafiction is made hyper-aware of the pragmatics of the text's communicative meaning and of the directed act of interpretation, and in turn is kept overtly conscious of her own constructed reading subjectivity. The act of enunciation requires a receptive reader in order to be realised: the author, reader, and text are effectively brought into being *as* text, author and reader in that encounter. Again, the alignment with postmodernism is apparent, for it is

> the concept of process that is at the heart of postmodernism: whether it be in fiction [. . .] or film. [. . .] it is the process of negotiating the postmodern contradictions that is brought to the fore, not any completed and closed product that results from their resolution.
>
> (Hutcheon, 1988, p. xi)

The significance of "process" is perhaps greater still than Hutcheon's words suggest, and is more acutely captured by McHale when he writes

> 'Postmodernist'? The term does not even make sense. For if 'modern' means 'pertaining to the present', then 'postmodern' can only mean 'pertaining to the future', and in that case what could postmodernist fiction be except fiction that has not yet been written?
>
> (1987, p. 4)

Metafiction is fiction which flaunts its ontological dependence—its reliance for a presence, the presence of its past, and its future presence—upon the discursive encounter, the dynamic, and performative processing of its enunciation and reception.

This section has offered a brief overview of metafiction, metafictionality, and metafiction's common themes, with reference to the dense and entangled postmodernist concerns with which they largely align. The next section of this chapter reviews the leading studies of metafiction, draws out their main contributions to theoretical understanding of the genre, and discusses some of the ways in which these texts pave the way for an investigation of how metafictional effects are linguistically created.

1.2 Critical Studies of Metafiction

The mid twentieth century proliferation of Western metafiction provoked several extended critical studies. These works make great strides in unravelling the complex themes of metafiction, often through useful and varied taxonomies of different types of metafiction. With the exception of McHale (1987), these works tend not to address language or form closely, nor examine the relationship between language, form, and effect. Nonetheless, all of them contribute to the beginnings of work in this area, and demonstrate a concern with form and language, signalling the fundamental importance of form and language to metafictionality.

Alter's *Partial Magic: The Novel as a Self-Conscious Genre* (1978 [1975]) provides a chronological study of manifestations of metafictionality, and of the relation between literary realism and self-consciousness

in the novel, from Renaissance Spain onwards and across Western literature. Alter's study reveals the ubiquity of metafictionality throughout the
evolution of the novel and offers penetrating discussions of the different
ideological uses to which metafictional techniques are put within particular Western historical contexts. This offers a valuable contribution
to a future platform for the exploration of any variation in the form of
metafictional techniques correlative to socio-historical contexts and uses,
though Alter does not himself analyse the formal constitution of these
techniques.

In *Fabulation and Metafiction* (1979), Scholes begins an exploration
of the theoretical and ideological structural and thematic underpinnings
of North American 1960s and 1970s self-reflexive fiction. Scholes identifies four basic emphases within this range of metafiction: philosophical,
formal, behavioural, and structural. What he categorises as 'structural'
metafiction primarily critiques "the essential [. . .] ideas common to all
fiction" (p. 112), these essential ideas being bound up in myth and folk-
lore. He perceives a type of metafiction that explores the ways in which
these ideas "inform fictional structure and the laws that preside over the
order of fiction" (p. 113). 'Formal' metafiction explores generic patterns
and changes in these patterns over time. This process is prototypically
played out through a fiction of forms which "imitates other fiction"
through derivation to the point of atrophy and decay or elaboration to
the point of intolerable complexity, romance, and parody being related
to both (p. 108). 'Behavioural' metafiction comments upon social reality
via a critically reflexive representation of observable human behaviour.
Lastly, 'philosophical' metafiction is "concerned with the deep structure
of being". It explores the essential "ethical ideas and absolutes of value"
that "inhere to the experience of fiction" within the combined content
and form of the work (p. 110, p. 113), often necessarily employing
"behaviouristic embodiment" (i.e. a specific fictive social scenario rather
than generic allegory) to test relative values against these philosophical
ideals (p. 110).

Scholes provides four brief, dense, and interconnected descriptive explorations of Barth's (1988 [1969]) *Lost in the Funhouse*, Barthelme's (1970) *City Life*, Gass's (1968) *In the Heart of the Heart of
the Country*, and Coover's (1969) *Pricksongs and Descants* as examples
of fiction demonstrating each of these four emphases, concluding with
the following:

> Beast and princess are not phoney symbols for Coover but fictional
> ideas of our human essences. Barth and Barthelme are chroniclers of
> our despair: despair over the exhausted forms of our thought and
> our existence. [. . .] Coover and Gass are reaching through form and
> behaviour for some ultimate values, some true truth.
>
> (p. 123)

This "true truth" is unmediated reality, human essence and existence without the discursive "mess of fabulation and deception" (p. 209), the representation of which metafiction self-consciously paradoxically both seeks and exposes as impossible.

Scholes's assessment of the overall plight of metafiction aligns with that of Waugh (1984) and Hutcheon (1984), while his identification of four major themes offers a more detailed account of its concerns. As with Alter, however, there is no analysis of the forms of metafictional techniques, nor of any correspondence between his categories and particular forms.

Hutcheon's *Narcissistic Narrative: The Metafictional Paradox* (1984, reprinted, with an additional foreword, after the 1980 edition) describes metafiction as "fiction that is [. . .] in some dominant and constitutive way, self-referring or autorepresentational: it provides, within itself, a commentary on its own status as fiction and as language, and also on its own processes of production and reception" (p. xii). Hutcheon claims to be the first to provide "an examination of the formal types of self-reflexivity found in contemporary metafiction", to demonstrate heretofore absent "analytical and descriptive work on the texts themselves" (p. 4), to "investigate the modes, forms and techniques of narrative narcissism" (p. 155), and to explore the "possibility of categorizing the many types of modern textual self-consciousness in the interests of clarity and discussion" (pp. 5–6).

Like Scholes, Hutcheon's approach is built upon her identification of a select few concerns prominent within postmodern metafiction. Hutcheon explores the metafictional revision of the concept of mimesis to include mimesis of process, a new reckoning of the author-text-reader relationship, and the 'metafictional paradox' mentioned in her subtitle.

Hutcheon's categorising framework promises to be of value to any analysis of the functioning of metafictional techniques. She distinguishes two different foci within metafictional texts: the 'diegetic' and 'linguistic'. Each of these concerns can be addressed within a metafictional text 'overtly' or 'covertly'. She uses the term 'diegetic' to refer to the narrative process. Diegetic metafiction thematises the narrative process of constructing a fictional world, shifting the reader's focus from the fictional world to the narration (p. 23). Among the techniques Hutcheon mentions in her discussion of novels which focus on diegetic metafiction are direct address of the reader, flaunting of the dynamic nature of the interpretative process, parody of genre-specific forms, *mise en abyme*, allegory, metaphor, typographical blanks, elision, and misleading arrangement of cues. 'Linguistic metafiction' thematises "the creative functioning of language" (p. 14), its limits and its powers, and the relationships and agents involved in textual representation and readerly actualisation through techniques such as parody of genre-specific styles, metanarrative commentary, pun, grammatical deviation, etc. Exploring either of these areas 'overtly' involves explicit self-consciousness and self-reflection through thematisation, allegorisation, or "narrative metaphor [of] or even narratorial commentary" upon the narrative process or the functioning of language (p. 23). In 'covert' metafiction these matters are "structuralized, internalized, actualized". She adds that 'covertly' metafictional texts are "self-reflexive, but not necessarily self-conscious" (p. 23).

Again, like Scholes, Hutcheon notes the degree to which narrative and linguistic self-consciousness are intertwined: linguistic play emphasises the narrative process, and narrative play is necessarily constituted through language, and, furthermore, often confronts the ontological status—the relative fictionality or reality—of the signified, hence the unavoidably overlapping nature of her categories. Her identification of some of the more common metafictional operations is valuable, and provides a useful key of sorts to test and build on. She quotes examples from texts manifesting use of one or two particular devices (such as linguistic pun, or direct address of the reader) to clarify and affirm her own identification of these techniques, and by way of categorising these novels. She prioritises explication of the theoretical significance of metafiction through exploration of the genre's range of forms, rather than the workings of metafiction through close analysis of the language of these texts. Hutcheon does, however, provide a comprehensive literary-theoretical exploration of metafiction and offers a formal categorising basis from which a more literary-linguistic analytical approach could be developed.

Waugh's (1984) *Metafiction: The Theory and Practice of Self-Conscious Fiction* offers a broad study of metafiction, its social and ideological contexts, its thematic concerns, and its means of literary experimentation. Waugh's work provides a useful survey of themes, motifs, and authors approached through Russian Formalist ideas of literary development, socio-political contextualisation, the more far-reaching branches of subjective idealism, and frame analysis (Goffman, 1974). Waugh sees metafiction as a rebellion against the modes of being and experiencing reality rooted in socio-economic Western cultural hegemonies and inscribed in literary conventions. For Waugh, metafiction is an authorial or textual 'practice': she sometimes acknowledges the role of the reader in actively engaging with and conceptually realising the text, but more often portrays the book as agent and implies that the reader is a passive recipient of the text.

McHale's (1987) *Postmodernist Fiction* investigates the techniques of Western experimental fiction from the mid to late twentieth century. Though metafiction is not his primary focus, the techniques he addresses, while featuring sporadically in postmodernist fiction more broadly, are those which, when employed in a concentrated fashion, constitute most metafiction.

McHale is the only critic among those reviewed here to address metafictional texts in terms of formal features over and above, though still very much in relation to, thematic features. He investigates foregrounding of and experimentation with fictional world-building, and the ontological statuses, boundaries between, and interrelations of these worlds. He explores the various means by which these worlds, once constructed, can be deconstructed, their realities split and/or ceased, etc., and discusses examples of foregrounding of and metaleptic transgression across ontological hierarchies. He studies the role of play with language in constructing fictional worlds, considering exploitation of tension between the different ontological statuses of the literal and metaphorical frames of reference embedded in metaphor, and playfulness with polysemantics, allegory, grammatical deviation, overlaid voices, and so on. He also explores graphological and structural experimentation. His study ends with a discussion of the relationship constructed between the reader and the text, particularly through the use of narratorial direct address of the reader, and experimentation with closure.

McHale's focus upon the ontological levels within fiction and the boundaries between them provides a useful basis for the analysis of the operation of metafictional techniques within and across these levels. His investigation addresses the thematic significance of these techniques specifically in relation to their form. He demonstrates each technique with a wealth of apt examples, including works by Beckett, Gass, Federman, Vonnegut, Spark, Brophy, Fowles, and many more, discussing them in variable detail but with much more granular attention to form than Hutcheon or Waugh. However, close analysis of language is not McHale's priority. While he does discuss, for example, pronouns and demonstratives within some quotations on occasion, these discussions are not grounded in and do not make reference to deictic theory, and the attention to language is not consistent. McHale's discussion of quotations tends to be illustrative at a higher level of formal and thematic analysis, as part of a rich and broad survey-style discussion of his topics.

Together these works provide a detailed definition of postmodern metafiction, an outline of its literary-historical context, an exploration of its chief concerns, some investigation of form in a broad sense (i.e. subtypes of the genre), and some samples of techniques (most prevalently in McHale). They also each draw attention to aspects of the role of language in underlying and generating some of metafiction's main themes. They do not, however, aim to provide a systematic analysis of the stylistic functioning of metafictional techniques.

Two issues seem to underlie these five studies. One is that while most of these works attempt to organise the range of Western metafictional texts into distinct categories or systematic taxonomies, their systems of organisation vary, and in most cases the categories are slightly overlapping, signalling that metafiction does rather evade such capture. This is a natural and inevitable consequence of the entangled and multidimensional concerns of metafiction and the multifarious and multifunctional nature of metafictional techniques.

The second, more significant, issue is that most of these texts seem to either background the role of the reader in the functioning of metafictional techniques, or have an ambiguous, ambivalent or otherwise ill-defined concept of the relationship between the reader and the text. This, too, is partly a symptom of the subject at hand, as metafiction inherently problematises the role of the reader in three respects: it problematises the act of interpretation (e.g. in terms of authorial control); it undermines the possibility and plausibility of coherence and closure (in the sense of an authoritative version of events); and it challenges the very concept of reference (in the sense of a word having a stable referential value, vs., for example, many potential, subjectively determined meanings).

Lawson (1985) argues that the reflexivity of postmodernism is so extensive and catastrophic in its abandonment of reason and the empirical that it undermines its ability to say anything meaningful at all: the logical conclusion of its argument is the impossibility of meaning and communication. To attempt to examine the interpretative implications of a metafictional novel as a whole or the interpretative effects of its parts, in the techniques it employs, can therefore seem antithetical. This tension seeps through some of the works described above.

Hutcheon's stance is a case in point. Her focus is only latterly reader-oriented. She occasionally discusses the functioning of the relationship between textual cues, the reader's use of the conventions and implicit communicative contracts that facilitate interpretation of those textual cues, and imaginative actualisation of the fictional worlds. More often, she exaggerates the freedom of the reader in the process of imaginative actualisation of the text, and, in turn, the liberating ramifications of metafiction with regard to the reader's relations with reality.

Both metafiction and postmodernism do problematise reference, authorial intention, ideal readings, and the possibility of interpretative closure, and do so consciously, formally, and thematically. They do, nonetheless, still rely on the concept of authorship, and on reference and interpretation (and knowingly play with that paradox). Some extreme metafictional and postmodern texts very overtly resist interpretative closure through side-stepping or breaking the literary conventions through which novels have historically produced meaning (or, to be more precise, the conventions both authors and readers assume are in place and rely upon as codes of interpretation). Most metafictional texts, however, walk the tightrope between explicitly problematising the notions of an ideal reading and reader (Iser, 1978), authorial direction and interpretative closure, and inherently also relying on implicit codes and conventions of interpretation and meaning-making. As discussed in the first section of this chapter (1.1), this paradox does not in any way destroy meaning-making; rather, it draws attention to the processes of meaning-making. Far from it being impossible to analyse the techniques of metafiction, these techniques are in fact exposed specifically as part of an invitation for reflection on their workings. Metafiction breaches the conventions of narrative radically and demonstratively, but inevitably does so from within those conventional narrative paradigms, setting up and maintaining the prototypical schemas, challenging them at intervals but never ceding them entirely. As Margolin argues, "through its use of nonstandard, often strongly deviant or deficient manners of narration, literature makes us aware *ex negativo* of the default clause, the standard or normal mechanisms and patterns of information processing" (2003, p. 279).

This foregrounding of processes—this "discursive exposition" (Alter, 1978, p. x)—also involves exposure and attention to the reader's role in these processes, dynamically following and comprehending the text and imaginatively conceptualising the story. Part of the work of self-reflexive fiction is that of overtly "keeping alive a reader (without whom the notion of a story that is ultimately written cannot be realised) [. . .] who therefore exists in a symbiotic, rather than hierarchical relationship with the author" (Wicomb, 2005, pp. 149–150). Metafictional techniques frequently highlight the 'heteronomy' of the text. This is neatly explained by Rimmon-Kenan as follows:

> Ingarden (1973) distinguishes between autonomous and heteronomous objects. While autonomous objects have immanent (i.e. indwelling, inherent) properties only, heteronomous ones are characterized by a combination of immanent properties and properties attributed to them by consciousness. Thus heteronomous objects do not have full existence without the participation of consciousness [. . .]. Since literature belongs to this category, it requires "concretization" or "realization" by a reader.
>
> (2002, p. 119)

Metafiction consciously confronts the conventions and discourse roles and relationships which facilitate the reader's realisation of fiction. These include the tacit communicative assumptions involved; the ontological levels of, and relationships between, the story and its narration; the role and function of the narrator and narration in framing, focalising, and directing the reader's engagement, processing, and imaginative conceptualisation; and the ontological dependence of all of these factors upon the active participation, imaginative realisation, conceptual immersion, and textual manipulation of the reader. The discursive and dynamic relationship between the text and the reader is thus central to metafictional concerns, explorations, and effects.

A relatively new strand of narrative theory—unnatural narratology—takes a different approach to metafiction and its techniques, one which is more oriented towards how readers process texts and make them meaningful. Definitions of 'unnatural narrative' vary. Fludernik defines 'unnatural narrative' as "the logically or cognitively impossible" (2012, p. 362). She includes within her definition "the discourse of postmodernist [. . .] transgression and metafiction" (p. 363). Alber, Iversen, Nielsen, and Richardson (2012), meanwhile, outline their various slightly different perspectives as follows: Alber defines unnatural narrative as "physically, logically, or humanly impossible scenarios or events" and differentiates between the 'conventionalized' unnatural (e.g. in fantasy) and "the unnatural in postmodernism, which still strikes us as disorienting or defamiliarizing"; Iversen discusses as 'unnatural' narratives which contain clashes or inconsistencies which are irresolvable (such as a single kind of antirealism in an otherwise realist text); and Nielsen uses the term to define "a subset of fictional narratives that—unlike many realist and mimetic narratives—cue the reader to employ interpretational strategies that are different from those she employs in non-fictionalized, conversational storytelling situations" (p. 373). Richardson defines unnatural narratives as those involving "significant antimimetic events, characters, settings, or frames" and uses 'antimimetic' to refer to "representations that contravene the presuppositions of nonfictional narratives, violate mimetic expectations and the practices of realism, and defy the conventions of existing, established genres" (2015, p. 3). For Richardson, the 'nonmimetic' refers to works which do not mimic real-world conditions but which nonetheless follow established narrative conventions specific to genre, such as science fiction. Richardson argues that conventional nonmimetic works are not unnatural narratives, proposing that "antimimetic texts [. . .] go beyond nonmimetic texts as they violate rather than simply extend the conventions of mimesis" via "intentional transgression" (pp. 4–5). He therefore finds his definition of unnatural narratives "more restricted" than those of his colleagues (p. 10). As examples of unnatural narratives he offers "narratives that collapse different consciousnesses together or denarrate events" (p. 13).

Some strands of unnatural narratology thus far have focused on proposing approaches to the analysis of those narratives or features of narrative which are deemed unnatural. Alber's scholarship investigates the challenges unnatural narratives pose to readers' conventional interpretative schemas and the strategies through which readers may resolve those challenges (2009). These strategies are summarised by Wolf as

(1) "reading [unnatural] events as internal states" (e.g. dreams); (2) understanding them as an aesthetic device to "foreground [. . .] the thematic" or (3) as a form of allegory; (4) [. . .] blending [the unnatural] with "pre-existing frames" [or schemas] or (5) by "stretch[ing existing] frames [or schemas]".

(Wolf, 2013, p. 118, citing Alber, 2009, pp. 80–83)

Richardson is also interested in the nature of the transgressions and the challenges unnatural narratives pose to narrative conventions, to dominant narratologies, and to readers in the act of interpretation. However, Richardson, with Phelan (1996), argues that such unnatural narratives are irresolvable (and that readers accept them as such). Richardson argues that dominant narratologies are based on mimetic narratives, and often therefore cannot address unnatural features of narrative—coming, as these narratologies do, from a contrary set of assumptions, such as the distinction between fabula and sjuzhet (2015, p. 28). He aligns his position with Abbott's emphasis on "rest[ing] in that particular combination of anxiety and wonder that is aroused when an unreadable mind is accepted as unreadable" (2014, p. 124), and with Phelan's concept of "the stubborn" (1996, pp. 173–189), which Richardson defines as "significant moments of narrative recalcitrance that defy a single, unified, overarching interpretation along conventional lines" (2015, p. 20), and that have "instability and utterly irresolvable tensions" (2015, p. 31). Richardson's focus, rather than being on interpretative strategies for cognitive resolution or 'naturalisation' of the unnatural, is instead on the 'creative play' of the unnatural (2015, p. 20).

Beyond work on the possibility or impossibility of 'naturalisation', some scholars in unnatural narratology have produced studies of the techniques which reoccur in metafiction. Strangely, the term 'metafiction' rarely explicitly arises within unnatural narratology, and yet metafiction does fall within some definitions of unnatural narrative (though outside of others, because it arguably has a set of conventions, including the transgression of conventions). Three individual metafictional techniques investigated in this book were mentioned briefly previously and are discussed in detail next—metanarration, metalepsis, and disnarration. Of these, metalepsis is arguably most unnatural according to most definitions, given that it cannot occur in real life or in non-fictional storytelling. Consequently, perhaps, of the three techniques, metalepsis has received the most critical attention within unnatural narratology (e.g. Bell and Alber, 2012; Thoss, 2015, 2011; Wolf, 2013, 2005). Disnarration and metanarration fall within some definitions of unnatural narrative, and outside others, partly because both occur in everyday storytelling, albeit not usually in the foregrounded, thematically significant and integrated ways in which they are used in metafiction. Notable work within unnatural narratology on disnarration and metanarration include Richardson (2001) and Wolf (2009), respectively.

Most of these theoretical works focus on typologies of unnatural narratives and/or unnatural narrative techniques, and so, as with the five texts more closely dedicated to metafiction, described previously, the linguistic constitution of techniques tends to remain neglected. These typologies are nonetheless useful in breaking down the various subtypes of the techniques, which then facilitates a more systematic investigation of the discourse deixis in those subtypes. Some of these works also include useful concepts to consider in relation to discourse deixis. Where relevant, therefore, these works inform the explorations of the three techniques in the chapters which follow.

This section has outlined the most significant texts in theory of metafiction, and has highlighted the significance attributed by some of these works to language and formal techniques in the creation of metafiction's meaning and effects. This review has also outlined some of the work these texts have begun in exploring metafictional techniques via detailed formal and, with less concentration, linguistic investigation. This section has raised some issues around interpretation, reference, textual cues, and readerly processing which are fundamental to the workings of metafictional techniques. Lastly, this section has introduced the relevance of unnatural narratology to the study of metafiction, and has reviewed the role of this subfield in contributing to understanding.

The three techniques of metanarration, metalepsis, and disnarration recur again and again across metafiction, and constitute the central means by which metafictionality and metafiction's common themes, such as those outlined in section 1.1, are expressed and explored. Hence, these three techniques are discussed again and again in the critical works described previously. The next section (1.3) describes these three techniques in detail, and the following section (1.4) begins the principal work of this book, in starting to draw out the role of discourse deixis in how these techniques work and in how metafictionality is cued, processed, and realised.

1.3 Metafictional Techniques

Metafictionality can be created in a variety of ways. Some of these ways are explicit and some are implicit. One implicitly metafictional technique, for example, is metafictionality by metaphor or analogy. Coover's short story 'Quenby and Ola, Swede and Carl' is an example of a story which is arguably metafictional only in a metaphorical sense. The narration is non-linear, and one strand of the narrative is possibly relayed in reverse chronological order (though other non-temporally anchored and less chronologically organisable segments are interwoven with this strand). This non-linearity and potential partial reverse chronological ordering arguably draws attention to—that is, elicits in some, perhaps most, readers a consideration of—the conventions of narrative ordering, and, in turn perhaps draws attention to other aspects of the implicit conventional communicative contract of storytelling, by its flouting of those conventions. Similarly, texts which can be read as metaphors or allegories of, for example, the fiction-making process, are arguably implicitly metafictional.

Coover's method in 'Quenby and Ola, Swede and Carl' could be regarded as a form of structural-pragmatic foregrounding through deviation (i.e. deviating from the novelistic structural conventions of a retrievable and coherent chronology). Another example of implicit meta-fictionality through foregrounding is overtly parodic use of novelistic conventions (such as epigraphs, or the specific conventions of a particular genre), drawing attention to and sometimes satirising those conventions. Overt intertextual reference, and sometimes outright 'borrowings' of, for example, characters from other books (McHale, 1987, p. 58), can be used in the service of metafictionality, to expose the nature of the text as a "tissue of quotations" (Barthes, 1977 [1967], p. 146), repeating and interpreted through its broader discourse context. Demonstratively play-ful polysemantics in fiction can have a related effect, foregrounding the linguistic craftedness of the text, and the multiple interpretable meanings of a word, phrase, novel, etc.

Some of the methods just described can be considered forms of implicit 'metanarration', specifically. Metanarration is the first of the three meta-fictional techniques which will be investigated in this book. Broadly speaking, metanarration is commentary within fictional discourse on an aspect of the "composition, constitution and/or communication" of the narrative (Macrae, 2010, p. 119). The following quote, from Field-ing's *Joseph Andrews*, is an example: "As we cannot therefore at present get Mr. Joseph out of the inn, we shall leave him in it, and carry our reader on after Parson Adams" (1977 [1742], p. 104). Metanarration can include explicit narratorial reference to novelistic conventions; narra-torial or character reference to the construction, act, or role of the char-acters, narrator, reader, and author; narratorial or character reference to the construction of the storyworld, or to the discourse situation, the discourse context and its influence; and character rebellion against nar-ratorial direction, novelistic conventions, etc. Nünning (2005) presents a full taxonomy of the wide variety of ways in which a narrative can be commented on from within.

The effects of metanarration, and indeed the effects of any metafictional technique, vary with the particular linguistic construction of its form and the nature of its specific context (Macrae, 2010, p. 128). That said, broadly speaking metanarration within metafiction tends to enhance or "create the illusion of a 'teller', a personalized voice serving as the narrator" (Nün-ning, 2005, p. 18), whilst, in one, several or many ways, disrupting the suspension of disbelief and any sense of mimesis or immersion in a fictional world. Metanarration serves to foreground the mediating role of the teller, and of the reader as interpreter, to destabilise the reliability of any one ver-sion or interpretation of events, and to expose and confront the conditions of the discourse of the novel by which fiction creates its artifice.

Some metanarration, as part of foregrounding the role of the reader as interpreter, involves narrators directly addressing readers. While all narration is fundamentally addressed to readers, the narrator's acknowledgement of the reader as reader, the impression of direct communication from the narrator to the reader, and the impression of the immediacy of that communication can be more or less foregrounded. Sentences presented as narratorial 'asides' to the reader, or interjections or interruptions within the flow of the main business of the narration (i.e. developing the story) can seem like a more explicit and 'conscious' form of address than the co-textual and more conventional narration. Some narratorial address of the reader in metafiction is yet more overt, sometimes including explicit terms of address (such as 'you' or 'reader').

Narratorial address of the reader, whilst often involved in metanarration, can also be explored as a type of 'metalepsis'. This is the second metafictional technique to be explored in this book. Metalepsis is the crossing of the different ontological levels of fictional narrative (McHale, 1987, pp. 121–130). In its simplest ontological structure, the levels of a fictional novel are the level of the story (the diegesis), at which the characters exist; the level of the narration (the extradiegesis), at which the narrator exists (in past tense and/or third-person narration); and the level of the real, at which the real reader and author exist (Genette, 1980, 1988). The diegesis and extradiegesis are equally fictional in contrast to the reality of the world in which the book is read. The very aim of mimesis is to create the contrary impression—portraying the storyworld as real. Yet, this impression is often created via presenting the teller as 'more' real than the storyworld characters, or at least more proximal to and intimate with the reader (e.g. presenting the narrator as the author her/himself, a person rather than a mere textual construct, blurring the boundary between the extradiegesis and reality). Metaleptic address from the narrator to reader, as illustrated in the examples from Eliot, can serve this blurring, mimetic effect. However, it can also be used for the contrary purpose, and/or for drawing attention to the reader as reader of a work of fiction, and to the impossibility and illusory nature of this seeming direct communication between a real (i.e. non-textual) person and a single, individual, identifiable reader.

Metaleptic communication is most commonly in the form of a narrator explicitly addressing the reader, but it also occurs in the form of, for example, exchanges between characters and the narrator in circumstances in which the narrator has thus far been presented as an extradiegetic narrator. This kind of metaleptic exchange can also involve not just metaleptic communication but metaleptic 'moves'. Metaleptic movement by a narrator is the crossing of narrative levels by that narrator, so that she/he 'appears' at a narrative level different to the level at which she/he has so far resided. One famous example is the narrator of Fowles's *The French Lieutenant's Woman* (1996 [1969]), who is throughout most of the narrative explicitly given to be writing from a point one hundred years later than the story occurred. The narrative is in the past tense, and the narrator has a degree of omniscience conventional to third-person narratives. Nonetheless, at two points in the novel, the narrator appears within the storyworld, silently observing his character, Charles.

Not only narrators, but also characters, readers, editors, and authors can be portrayed as involved in this "violation of ontological boundaries" (McHale, 1987, p. 226). In Federman's *Take It or Leave It* (1976), a delegation from the narrative audience twice manifests within the storyworld. The first "interferer" appears suddenly in the passenger seat of the protagonist's car, describes himself to the protagonist as "one of your potential listeners", and insists he is just there to take notes (Chapter XVII, titled "A visitor from above") (np). He is replaced in the next chapter by another 'potential', this one named Claude, who compliments the story's hero on his storytelling panache, and goes on to seduce him, leading to a passionate sexual encounter in a hotel. In O'Brien's *At Swim-two-birds* (1939), one of the strands of the pseudo-authorial narrator's tale involves a character-narrator, Dermot Trellis, who tells a story about a set of characters within a further embedded story, one of whom he metaleptically rapes, producing a child, Orlick, who then leads a rebellion in overthrowing Dermot's narration. In novels with multiple levels (e.g. stories within stories) the opportunities for narrator and character metalepsis are rife.

As McHale argues, such migration across fiction's ontological boundaries serves to display the boundaries as not impermeable, but rather as "semipermeable membrane[s]" (1987, p. 34), foregrounding and destabilising "ontological boundaries and ontological structure" (p. 35). The logical end point of this fracturing of the boundaries between the fictive and the real is the quintessentially postmodern undermining of the privileging of reality as more 'true' and stable than other discourses.

The third and final metafictional technique to be introduced here often has a related effect. 'Disnarration' is a term coined by Prince (1988, p. 2) to describe events which are narrated in the negative or hypothetical mode, so that their existence within the ontology of the storyworld, though potentially transiently affirmed, is ultimately uncertain or denied. McHale cites a pithy example from Pynchon's *Gravity's Rainbow* (1973, p. 667), "Of course it happened. Of course it didn't happen", along with a more complex and ambiguous instance from Beckett's *The Unnamable* (1979 [1959/3], p. 330): "The slopes are gentle that meet where he lies, they flatten out under him, it is not a meeting, it is not a pit, that didn't take long, soon we'll have him perched on an eminence" (McHale, 1987, p. 99, p. 101; see Macrae, 2010, for a discussion of the latter example).

There are several kinds of counter-linear, mutually exclusive and indefinite narrative modes which can constitute forms of disnarration, the effect of which is described by McHale as a kind of ontological "flickering" (1987, p. 100). Through disnarration, the stability of the storyworld's ontology is disturbed, exposing the illusory conditions and logic of that ontology. Disnarration also undermines the reliability of the narrative, and in turn of the narrator, foregrounding and threatening the implicit communicative contract of fictive narration. The reader's role in dynamically conceptualising that which is narrated is also often brought to the fore. The impossibility of a reader undoing, by narratorial direction, any imaginative conceptualisation of the story in retrospect—the inevitable perpetual trace of the erased within reader's holistic interpretation—makes disnarration troubling for notions of authorship and ownership of fictional worlds, and of ethical responsibility for the imagined. Hence, disnarration is an ideal tool in the postmodern metafictional armoury against both the 'author-god' and a reliable and resolving truth.

This section has introduced the metafictional techniques of metanarration, metalepsis, and disnarration. Most metafiction involves some or all of these techniques, and even a short extract of metafiction might employ several simultaneously. They can overlap with regard to their functioning and the aspects of fiction they foreground, confront and/or problematise. All three are essentially concerned, to varying extents, with the ontological structure of fiction, the interrelationships between the participants of fiction (that is, the author, reader, narrator, and characters) within and across that ontological structure, and the dynamic reading process.

Each of these three metafictional techniques tends to rely heavily on discourse deixis. Discourse deixis is but one linguistic feature of metafictionality, and some metafictionality can be created without its use. However, discourse deixis is particularly prevalent within these three techniques, not least because the 'work' of discourse deixis engages directly with their essential concerns: the ontological structure of fiction, the relationships between its participants, and the dynamic reading process. The following section presents a short introduction to discourse deixis and its role in the functioning of metafiction and the creation of its effects.

1.4 Where Discourse Deixis Meets/Makes Metafiction

'Deixis' is the name given to a set of words which are used to 'point to' something or someone from a particular perspective. Deictic words are words such as 'I' and 'you', 'this', 'now', and 'here'. The word 'I', along with all those other words listed (and many more), does not have a relatively stable referential value in the way that the word 'seaside' consistently refers to a place where the sea meets land. The referent of the word 'I' depends on and varies according to the context of the utterance—that is, according to the source of the utterance; who is saying 'I'. This referential value changes with every person's use of the word 'I'. Deictic words are unusual in that they can be interpreted only in relation to the context in which they are being used. Their meaning-value is therefore bound up with the origin of the utterance (the person/place/time etc. by/at/from which it is being uttered) and the relation it is signalling (of person, or spatial, temporal, etc.).

Discourse deixis is a subcategory of deixis (along with person, spatial, temporal, and social deixis). Discourse deixis is used to refer to aspects of the communication (verbal, textual, etc.) and/or the context of communication in which that deixis occurs. It remains a complex area of deictic theory. Chapter 2 is devoted to a fuller discussion and outline of discourse deixis in literature, but the brief discussion that follows serves as an introduction to its role in metafiction.

Both discourse deixis and metafiction are concerned with discourse and the processing of discourse. Discourse deixis can be used within metafiction to 'point', from a particular juncture within the text, to aspects of the fictional discourse (and fictionality more generally). For the purposes of metafictionality, discourse deixis can be used to point to the physical text (the lines on the page, the book, etc.), the narrative discourse (the developing plot, characterisation, etc.), the author's (or seemingly the pseudo-authorial narrator's) act of creating the narrative discourse, the reader's processing and imaginative conceptualisation of the discourse, and the broader discourse situation (including the conventions of literary fiction, the reader and narrator as discourse participants, etc.). While not all metafictionality involves discourse deixis (and much discourse deixis does not involve metafictionality), the three metafictional techniques described earlier often rely heavily on discourse deixis for their effects. This area of overlap—the use of discourse deixis in metafiction—is the focus of this book.

The following extract from Barth's (1988 [1969]) short story 'Lost in the Funhouse' (from his collection of the same name) illustrates some aspects of discourse deixis in metafiction.

> The function of the *beginning* of a story is to introduce the principal characters, establish their initial relationships, set the scene for the main action, expose the background of the situation [. . .], plant motifs and foreshadowings [. . .] and initiate the first complication or whatever the "rising action." [. . .] So far there's been no real dialogue, very little sensory detail, and nothing in the way of a *theme*. And a long time has gone by already without anything happening; it makes a person wonder. We haven't even reached Ocean City yet: we will never get out of the funhouse.
>
> (p. 77, italics in the original)

The first sentence in this extract (ending with "rising action") is metafictional, as it is a narratological comment, within a story, on the beginning of stories. However, it is not discourse deictic, as the reader's interpretation of this sentence does not rely on her relating this passage to its particular context within the progression of the discourse (at least, no more than the meaning of every utterance is grounded in its particular discourse context). That is, this sentence is meaningful, and is valid as a general description of the beginning of a story, irrespective of its positioning here at this particular juncture of the story.

The three following sentences are discourse deictic in that they are metanarrational commentary on this story specifically and in relation to this distinct juncture in its progression. These sentences also illustrate how discourse deixis co-opts other subcategories of deixis. "So far" and "A long time has gone by already" are both temporal deictic references, referring either to the duration and passing of the story time (the hours of trip already described) or the "time" it has taken for the narrator to relate the narrative up to this point (five pages worth of text, up to this point). The 'yet' of "We haven't even reached Ocean City yet" is similarly ambiguously either a reference to this point in the progression of the physical journey within the storyworld, or this point in the textual and/or temporal progression of the narrating discourse.

The person deixis in the use of the first-person plural pronoun "we" here troubles the ontological distinction between story and discourse: "we" could implicitly position the narrator and reader with the characters inside the storyworld journey (in the first reading of the phrase) or could implicitly position (only) the narrator and reader together in relation to the progression of the narrative discourse. The last sentence troubles this distinction further, as the funhouse is a physical reality within the story, but at this point in the story the funhouse is also beginning to be revealed to be a possible metaphor for the story (and all stories, and, later, all subjective views on/versions of reality). The spatial deixis of "get out of" implicitly positions the reader and narrator with the characters inside the physical funhouse within the ontological reality of the storyworld, and/or positions the reader with the narrator metaphorically 'within' the narrative discourse. To be 'in the middle' of or 'at the end of a story' is a more conventional way of spatially or, metaphorically, temporally conceptualising a reader's journey through a story. To be 'inside of' and get "out of" a story suggests a more literally physically immersive, or even entrapping, experience of reading and of narrative. As Ambrose, his brother, and Magda have not yet, in the progress of the narration, encountered or entered the funhouse, this last phrase in fact provides the 'foreshadowing' mentioned in the first sentence, and so doubly suggests the metaphorical value of the narrative as a funhouse.

Arguably, the latter sentences, and in particular the metaphorical implications of the narrative as funhouse, allow a retrospective reinterpretation of the first sentence of this extract as discourse deictic. Initially interpretable as a general commentary on storytelling, it becomes apparent that this first sentence is an implicit critique of what is lacking in *this* story—a critique ironically undermined by the extract's last phrase.

Literary discourse deixis is complex, particularly in its pragmatic intricacies, subcategorical borrowings, and blurred boundaries. Chapter 2 works through some of these complexities, and proposes a comprehensive account of literary discourse deixis capable of shedding light on its workings in metafiction, as a platform for the studies in the rest of this book. The brief exploration of a metanarrative extract from Barth here, though, is indicative of some of the ways in which discourse deixis can function to serve metafictionality. Close analysis of the discourse deixis inherent to extracts of metanarration, metalepsis, and disnarration will form the mainstay of this book. The following, penultimate section of this chapter outlines the fictions from which these extracts will be drawn, and why.

1.5 Introducing Barth, Brophy, Coover, Fowles, Johnson, and Katz

In investigating metafiction, Scholes drew on four collections of short stories published in 1968 and 1970 as prototypical examples of the form. This book takes a slightly broader view, bringing together four novels and two collections of short stories published between 1968 and 1973. These texts can arguably be regarded as examples of 'high metafiction'. 'High' is here being used in the sense of 'peak', as in high modernism: Western metafiction seems to peak between 1968 and 1973. Indeed, Groes describes 1969 as an *annus mirabilis* (2016, p. 173), and a 15-year rise beforehand and fall afterwards can be traced. The six works of fiction selected from this peak period are briefly introduced next.

Section 1.1 included a scale representing the functions of metafictionality (in Figure 1.2), moving from texts which are often accused of being esoteric and purely 'navel-gazing' in their experimentation on the left to texts which exploit metafictionality as a vehicle through which to express broader literary and social, philosophical, political, and ideological themes on the right. While there are many texts to choose from within this period of peak metafictionality (e.g. Gass, 1968; Sukenick, 1969; Pynchon, 1973; Vonnegut, 1973), the six works selected here can all be located between the mid-point of the scale and its right-hand pole; that is, they all use metafictionality as an integrated part of thematic engagement with some of the social, philosophical, etc. issues of the time. Between them, they also include varied examples of the three main metafictional techniques, and so collectively provide a rich range of extracts through which to explore the functioning of discourse deixis in these techniques.

John Barth's *Lost in the Funhouse* (1988 [1968]) and Robert Coover's *Pricksongs and Descants* (2011 [1969]) are collections of short stories just to the right of the mid-point on the scale. Barth's *Lost in the Funhouse* loosely hangs together around the 'Life-Story' (a title of one of the stories) of Ambrose. The book opens with the well-known 'Frame-Tale' (an instruction to cut, from the side of the first and second page, a strip on which is written "Once upon a time there was a story that began", and with it to create a Möbius strip). The next story echoes (amongst many other texts) the opening of Sterne's seminal metafictional work, *Tristram Shandy*, published three centuries earlier, in following the journey of a sperm to the point of conception. The next, less metafictional and more conventional story introduces Ambrose (which continues the echoing of *Tristram Shandy*, while also referencing *Moby Dick*). From then on, the stories shift between those more explicitly about (or seemingly in the voice of) Ambrose and metaphorical versions of the same stories and ideas in retellings and subversions of Greek epic tales (such as the story of Helen of Troy and Odysseus in 'Menelaiad').

Barth's stories are linked by themes and motifs such as textual marks (vs. for example, transitory oral sound) and meaning, the message in the bottle, endless regress and echoing, agency and lack thereof, self-alienation and alienation from the other, construction of the self and of the other, and desire. Though originally published between 1963 and 1968 (Gillespie, 1975, p. 224), these stories all express some of the ideas Barth explored in his essay 'The Literature of Exhaustion', published in 1967. The stories vary in the intensity or concentration of metafictional techniques. While some may seem more esoteric and superficial in their self-reflexive play than others, when placed within the context of the whole collection the deeper significance of the metafictionality, in relation to the network of broader themes, becomes apparent. The stories published originally between 1967 and 1968 are more densely metafictional, and so it is a selection of these which are discussed in detail in this book.

Robert Coover's *Pricksongs and Descants* (2011 [1969]), the second collection of short stories, has a different kind of cohesion: the dominant theme is the plurality of truths, paths, and realities. As with Barth, stories of old are reworked and recycled—this time folktales and biblical stories—and new stories are told, revised, and retold. It is this plurality and re-versioning that dominates critical responses (e.g. Evenson, 2003; Gordon, 1983). There is a coldness, an emptiness and a brutality to some of the stories; a postmodern glare of superficiality and commodification. The fabrication is surreal, and sometimes nightmarish. As well as darkly disrupting the security of linear narratives, origins, and ends, and a dominant or final interpretation, Coover's stories transgress the accepted ontological boundaries separating the figures of the author, narrators, and characters (and, in 'Panel Game' and 'The Leper's Helix', also the reader). Whereas in Barth we have the funhouse, in Coover we have the game, a fractured puzzle resisting solution, and a feeling of not knowing the rules. Coover flaunts his skill in storytelling, exploiting and flouting its conventions and rules to express sometimes despair, and sometimes resignation, in the face of the chaos of life.

Steve Katz's *The Exagggerations* [sic] *of Peter Prince* (2017 [1968]) shares Coover's surrealism, forked paths, and revisions, but in novel form, and in a work which touches upon "some of America's rawest contemporary nerves" (Bamberger, 2007, p. 36). Through extensive formal and graphological deviation, Katz takes Peter Prince through a journey made up of atemporal, often suddenly ceasing and disnarrated moments—all searching yet aimless. The narrative traverses through a surreal, dystopian castle bordered by heaps of wreckage (the story's starting point), a co-op apartment in Queens, captivity in Ethiopia, a police cell in Egypt, a river cruise in Europe, anonymous corporate meeting rooms, and more, mapping out some of 1960s America's suspicious, paranoid, and aggressive relations with the world. The global meanderings always start from and return to America, which is portrayed as a soulless place of dangerous plastic superficiality, of decay and anonymity. The American anxieties of the post–World War 2 era, the Cold War, and the Vietnam war—guilt, alienation, fear, and chaos—underscore every move in the novel, and every loose end.

The traversals are not only across the world of the disjointed story, but also all over the page, in a multimodal foray anticipating the likes of *House of Leaves* (Danielewski, 2000), and also upwards and downwards through the ontological levels of the fiction. The most radical metaleptic instance is perhaps when one of the characters, Philip Farrel—who is himself occasionally in the same storyworld as Peter Prince but more often at a higher narrative level and in a relationship of pseudo-authorial control—is drawn to a meeting to listen to the President of an anonymous company discuss possible product placement in the story. The seemingly highest level pseudo-authorial narrator, meanwhile, "look[s] on [. . .] fainting with nausea" (1968, p. 181).

Brigid Brophy's *In Transit: An Heroi-Cyclic Novel* (2002 [1969]) is described by Sweeney as "a post-Joycean anti-novel" and a " 'difficult', experimental text" (2018, p. 301). Perhaps because of this kind of perception, the novel has received limited critical attention. A 1995 special edition of *Review of Contemporary Fiction* is dedicated to her work, and a few articles and interviews can be found elsewhere (e.g. Kilian, 2007; Lawrence, 1998). A flurry of articles in a 2018 issue of *Contemporary Women's Writing,* along with Sweeney's article in *Textual Practice* in the same year, though, suggests a small critical resurgence.

Brophy herself describes *In Transit* as "about a series of disintegrations of the rulebook", expressed not least in the novel's progressive descent into the kind of chaos and surrealism with which *The Exagggerations of Peter Prince* begins. Again, though, this is a motivated chaos: the airport in which the novel is set is subject to a (chiefly) feminist industrial revolution, through which the story rejects the linearity of a hero's journey, resists cohesion and conclusion, and withholds any final answer to the dominating question of the sex of the protagonist. The novel's metafictionality is part of a trend of "women writers resist[ing] existing heteronormative and phallocentric ideologies", traceable in the contemporaneous works of Brooke-Rose, Carter, and Spark, amongst others (Groes, 2016, p. 68), though Brophy's text is particularly "Irish-inflected", riddled with intertextual references to Joyce, and overtly positioning the Irish as at a poignant juncture amidst mid twentieth century "transculturation" (Lawrence, 1998, p. 37). The airport in which the novel is set is itself explicitly a site of anonymity, to the point of identity loss: a site of transition, of freedom and containment, of newly overwhelming global transfer and mixing of languages and subjectivities. As with Katz and to an extent Johnson (see page 29), the page itself becomes a site of multimodal boundary-pushing, here incorporating operatic scores, diagrams, columns, and typographic play. Also as in Katz, ontological boundaries are disturbed, as when the previously first-person narrator switches to becoming a character referred to in the (temporarily gender-able) third person. Furthermore, the narrative is interrupted by intrusions from a higher level pseudo-authorial narrator. The novel also has other similarities with the short story collections in embedding and parodying particular genres (e.g. opera), including what McHale describes as sensationalist "sub-literary genres" (here erotica and detective fiction) (McHale, 1987, p. 102). *In Transit* is perhaps first and foremost, though, concerned with language, reference, and interpretation. It begins with rumination on the interlocutor, moves on to polylingualism and propositional logic, and is riddled with punning and wordplay throughout. At the core of the novel is the narrator's realisation that "the structure which [. . .] has been transporting all my thoughts and experiences all these years"—structures of language, gender, and understanding—might be merely "an arbitrary convention" (Brophy, 2002 [1969], p. 222; cf. Lawrence, 1998, p. 39).

Whereas the novels by Brophy and Katz are anti-conventional in various ways, the metafictionality of John Fowles's *The French Lieutenant's Woman* (1996 [1969]) is contained within a parody of the Victorian realist novel. Fowles's book is the most popular, and most studied, of the six (see, for example, Hutcheon, 1984; Kaplan, 1972; Onega, 1989; Waugh, 1984). It tells the story of an affair between a middle-class Darwinist, Charles, and the mysterious Sarah, the figure of the title. Though often adhering to popular narrative modes of feigned historical realism and omniscient third-person narration, the novel is interspersed throughout with metafictional techniques. The novel's metafictionality serves its interrelated themes of narrativisation, narratorial control, and responsibility; identity, self-determinism, and free will; the relativity of perspectives upon reality, and the impossibility of a traceable and narratable, underlying 'truth'; and, at each narrative level, the constructive and objectifying nature of the gaze.

Acheson (1998), Onega (1989), and Waugh (1984) are among many critics of Fowles who appreciate and further explicate the thematic significance of the novel's metafictional aspects, recognising the parody of Victorian realism as the overarching strategy of this self-reflexivity, though others misunderstand this self-reflexivity as lacking in purpose (Evarts, 1972) and as "a big boring herring" (Allen, 1970, p. 67). Onega and Waugh both point out that, just as the self-reflexivity is strategic, so too is the choice of Victorian realism. The latter is not a mere vehicle for retrospective postmodern pastiche: the relationship between Victorian and postmodern understanding and representations of reality—the affinities, their causes, rationales, and consequences—is at the heart of Fowles's existentialist and ontological explorations (cf. Buchberger, 2012; Marias, 2014).

Lastly, we have *Christie Malry's Own Double-Entry*, by B. S. Johnson (2001 [1973]). Though subjected to puritan readings (Parrinder, 1977) and psychoanalytic readings (Zouaoui, 2011), most critics foreground the novel's metafictional satire and radical commentary on industrial relations (e.g. Coe, 2004; Mengham, 2014; Tredell, 2000). The organising system of this novel is double-entry bookkeeping, which Lanchester, in his foreword to the book, describes as "the invention which made modern accounting techniques, and therefore all of modern business life, and therefore the whole structure of capitalism and the organization of contemporary society, possible", and so it is "one of the fundamental pillars of the given order" (2001 [1973], pp. 3–4). The strain of satire on the penetrating pervasiveness and brutality of capitalism which appears in Coover's stories such as 'The Elevator' and 'The Hat Act', in Katz's product placement, in the choice of Fowles's Darwinist protagonist between old money and systems of order, and new, comes to the fore in Johnson. The hero, Christie, working in accounting (as Johnson himself had), registers the mind- and soul-lessness of profit and loss, combined with the unjust chaos of life, and responds to his circumstances in kind, marking personal profit and loss on ledgers spread across pages. "Christie" is also an allusion to Christ; the grand narrative of Christianity is sat alongside the grand narrative of capitalism for similar darkly humourous lambasting (c.f. Crews, 1994). The creative construction of the narrative discourse (as fiction) is flaunted frequently, and is directly commented on by various characters. The pseudo-authorial narrator interjects, and occasionally joins Christie by his bedside for weighty and intimate conversations. This is the most linear and least interpretatively ambiguous of the six texts, pursuing consequence and cause and effect, rather than conditionality and plurality, through the narrator's and Christie's intertwined explorations of power and powerlessness, freedom and fatalism. Within this, metafictionality is exploited at every turn.

These texts form the focus of most of the forthcoming chapters. They have been selected because they were published at the peak of postmodern metafiction; because they sit towards the more broadly 'meaningful' end of the scale of functions of metafictionality (Figure 1.2); and because together they provide rich examples of the three main metafictional techniques examined in this book, and, within these examples, an illustrative array of the workings of discourse deixis in creating metafictionality. Where there is substantial criticism on some of these texts, little or none of that criticism explores quite how the metafictional effects involved are achieved, and none mentions discourse deixis. The exploration of the metafictionality of these texts presented in this book is not exhaustive: each text offers too many examples to allow for a coherent, comprehensive study of that text. Rather, examples from the novels and from selected stories from Barth and Coover have been chosen and organised in order to provide a comprehensive demonstration of discourse deixis in metafiction.

1.6 The Chapters to Come

This chapter has introduced metafiction and provided an overview of the three most common metafictional techniques. It has introduced the role of discourse deixis in metafictional techniques, and has presented a survey of the most important theoretical work on metafiction. Together these works foreground metafiction's concern with language, reference, and interpretation, and begin to discuss the role of language in metafiction's effects. Lastly, this chapter has introduced the six texts which form the touchstones of this book as it moves through an analysis of discourse deixis in the three main metafictional techniques.

In what follows, Chapter 2 provides an in-depth discussion and outline of discourse deixis, and draws out the unique aspects of its functioning which make it an ideal linguistic resource for metafictional techniques. Chapters 3, 4, and 5 are extended explorations of the role discourse deixis plays in the functioning of the main metafictional techniques, presenting illustrative analysis of extracts from Barth, Brophy, Coover, Fowles, Johnson, and Katz. Chapter 3 explores discourse deixis in metanarration, while Chapter 4 investigates discourse deixis in metalepsis. Chapter 5 studies discourse deixis in types of disnarration (such as denarration, alternarration, negation, and narrative refusal). While Chapter 4, on metalepsis, explores disruptions of the vertical ontological hierarchies of fiction, and Chapter 5, on disnarration, studies metafictional experimentation with horizontal conceptualisations and other aspects of linearity and paths in fiction, the discussion of metanarration, in Chapter 3, involves both vertical and horizontal kinds of play, intertwined. Finally, Chapter 6 presents a brief conclusion to the book, and suggests avenues for future research.

References

Abbott, H. P. (2014). *Real Mysteries: Narrative and the Unknowable*. Columbus, OH: Ohio State University Press.

Acheson, J. (1998). *John Fowles*. Houndmills, Basingstoke: Palgrave Macmillan.

Alber, J. (2009). "Impossible storyworlds—and what to do with them". *Storyworlds* 1. 79–96.

Alber, J., Iversen, S., Nielsen, H. K. and Richardson, B. (2012). "What is unnatural about unnatural narratology? A response to Monika Fludernik". *Narrative* 20.3. 371–382.

Allen, W. (1970). "The achievement of John Fowles". *Encounter* 25.2. 64–67.

Alter, R. (1978) [1975]. *Partial Magic: The Novel as a Self-Conscious Genre*. Berkeley, CA: University of California Press.

Bakhtin, M. (1981). *The Dialogic Imagination: Four Essays by M. M. Bakhtin*. Ed. M. Holquist. Trans. C. Emerson and M. Holquist. Austin, TX: University of Texas Press.

Bamberger, W. C. (2007). *43 Views of Steve Katz*. Rockville, MD: The Borgo Press.

Barth, J. (1967). "The literature of exhaustion". *The Atlantic Monthly* (August). 29–34.

Barth, J. (1988) [1968]. *Lost in the Funhouse: Fiction for Print, Tape, Live Voice*. New York: Doubleday.

Barthelme, D. (1970). *City Life*. New York: Farrar, Straus Giroux.

Barthes, R. (1977) [1967]. "The death of the author". In *Image-Music-Text*. Trans. S. Heath. London: HarperCollins. 142–148.

Beckett, S. (1979) [1959/3]. "The Unnamable". In *The Beckett Trilogy*. London: Pan Books. 293–418.

Bell, A. and Alber, J. (2012). "Ontological metalepsis and unnatural narratology". *Journal of Narrative Theory* 42.2. 166–192.

Benveniste, E. (1971) [1966]. *Problems in General Linguistics*. Trans. M. E. Meek. Coral Gables: University of Miami Press.

Berry, M. (2012). "Metafiction". In *The Routledge Companion to Experimental Literature*. Eds. J. Bray, A. Gibbons and B. McHale. London: Routledge. 128–140.

Brophy, B. (2002) [1969]. *In Transit: An Heroi-Cyclic Novel*. Chicago, IL: Dalkey Archive Press.

Buchberger, M. P. (2012). "John Fowles's novels of the 1950s and 1960s". *The Yearbook of English Studies* 42. 132–150.

Coe, J. (2004). *Like a Fiery Elephant: The Story of B. S. Johnson*. London: Picador.

Coover, R. (2011) [1969]. *Pricksongs and Descants*. New York: New American Library.

Cornis-Pope, M. (1994). "From cultural provocation to narrative cooperation: Innovative uses of the second person in Raymond Federman's fiction". *Style* 28.3. 441–413.

Crews, B. (1994). "*Christie Malry's Own Double-Entry*: B. S. Johnson's oppositional discourse of unbelief". *Revista Alicantina de Estudios Ingleses* 7. 55–66.

Currie, M. (Ed.). (1995). *Metafiction*. London: Longman.

Danielewski, M. Z. (2000). *House of Leaves*. New York: Random House.

de Certeau, M. (1975). *L'Ecriture de L'Histoire*. Paris: Gallimard.

de Cervantes Saavedra, M. (2003) [1605–1615]. *The Ingenious Hidalgo Don Quixote de la Mancha*. Trans. J. Rutherford. London: Penguin Books.

Derrida, J. (1981). *Positions*. Trans. A. Bass. Chicago, IL: University of Chicago Press.

Eliot, G. (2008) [1858]. *Adam Bede*. Oxford: Oxford World's Classics.

Eliot, G. (1994) [1871–1872]. *Middlemarch*. Ware, Hertfordshire: Wordsworth Editions Limited.

Evarts, P. Jr. (1972). "Fowles' *The French Lieutenant's Woman* as tragedy". *Critique: Studies in Contemporary Fiction* 13.3. 57–69.

Evenson, B. (2003). *Understanding Robert Coover*. Columbia, SC: University of South Carolina Press.

Federman, R. (1976). *Take It or Leave It: An Exaggerated Second-Hand Tale to be Read Aloud Either Standing or Sitting*. New York: Fiction Collective.

Fielding, H. (1977) [1742]. *Joseph Andrews*. London: Penguin Books.

Fludernik, M. (2012). "How natural is unnatural narratology; Or, what is unnatural about unnatural narratology?" *Narrative* 20.3. 357–370.

Foucault, M. (1972). *The Archaeology of Knowledge and the Discourse on Language*. Trans. A. M. Sheridan Smith. New York: Pantheon.

Fowles, J. (1996) [1969]. *The French Lieutenant's Woman*. London: Vintage.

Gass, W. H. (1968). *In the Heart of the Heart of the Country*. London: Jonathan Cape.

Gass, W. H. (1970). *Fiction and the Figures of Life*. Boston, MA: David Godine.

Genette, G. (1980). *Narrative Discourse*. Trans. J. E. Lewin. Ithaca, NY: Cornell University Press.

Genette, G. (1988). *Narrative Discourse Revisited*. Trans. J. E. Lewin. Ithaca, NY: Cornell University Press.

Gillespie, G. (1975). "Barth's *Lost in the Funhouse*: Short story text in its cyclic context". *Studies in Short Fiction* 12. 223–230.

Goffman, E. (1974). *Frame Analysis: An Essay on the Organization of Experience*. Cambridge, MA: Harvard University Press.

Gordon, L. (1983). *Robert Coover: The Universal Fictionmaking Process*. Carbondale, IL: South Illinois University Press.

Gray, A. (1981). *Lanark*. Edinburgh: Canongate.

Groes, S. (2016). *British Fictions of the Sixties: The Making of the Swinging Decade*. London: Bloomsbury.

Hutcheon, L. (1984) [1980]. *Narcissistic Narrative: The Metafictional Paradox*. Revised edn. London and New York: Methuen.

Hutcheon, L. (1988). *A Poetics of Postmodernism: History, Theory, Fiction*. London: Routledge.

Ingarden, R. (1973). *The Literary Work of Art: An Investigation on the Borderlines of Ontology, Logic and Theory of Literature*. Trans. G. G. Grabowicz. Evanston, IL: Northwestern University Press.

Iser, W. (1978). *The Act of Reading: A Theory of Aesthetic Response*. Baltimore, MD: Johns Hopkins University Press.

Johnson, B. S. (2001) [1973]. *Christie Malry's Own Double-Entry*. London: Picador.

Kaplan, F. (1972). "Victorian modernists: Fowles and Nabokov". *Journal of Narrative Technique* 3. 108–123.

Katz, S. (2017) [1968]. *The Exagggerations of Peter Prince*. Singapore: Verbivoracious Press.

Kilian, E. (2007). "Discourse ethics and the subversion of gender norms in Brigid Brophy's *In Transit*". In *The Ethical Component in Experimental British Fiction Since the 1960s*. Eds. S. Onega and J-M. Ganteau. Cambridge: Cambridge Scholars Publishing. 31–49.

LaCapra, D. (1985). *History and Criticism*. Ithaca, NY: Cornell University Press.

Lawrence, K. R. (1998). "*In Transit* from James Joyce to Brigid Brophy". In *Transcultural Joyce*. Ed. K. R. Lawrence. Cambridge: Cambridge University Press. 37–45.

Lawson, H. (1985). *Reflexivity: The Post-Modern Predicament*. London: Hutchinson.

Lyotard, J-F. (1983). *Le Différend*. Paris: Minuit.

Lyotard, J-F. (1984). *The Postmodern Condition: A Report on Knowledge*. Trans. G. Bennington and B. Massumi. Minneapolis: University of Minneapolis Press.

Macrae, A. (2010). "Enhancing the critical apparatus for understanding metanarration: Discourse deixis refined". *Journal of Literary Semantics* 39.2. 119–142.

Margolin, U. (2003). "Cognitive science, the thinking mind, and literary narrative". In *Narrative Theory and the Cognitive Sciences*. Ed. D. Herman. Stanford, CA: CSLI Publications. 271–294.

Marias, M. (2014). "'I am infinitely strange to myself': Existentialism, the Bildungsroman, and John Fowles's *The French Lieutenant's Woman*". *Journal of Narrative Theory* 44.2. 244–266.

McHale, B. (1987). *Postmodernist Fiction*. London: Routledge.

Mengham, R. (2014). "Antepostdated Johnson". In *B. S. Johnson and Post-War Literature*. Eds. J. Jordan and M. Ryle. Houndmills, Basingstoke: Palgrave Macmillan. 121–135.

Mosley, O. (1985). *Impossible Object*. Chicago, IL: Dalkey Archive.

Nünning, A. (2005). "On metanarrative: Towards a definition, a typology and an outline of the functions of metanarrative commentary". In *The Dynamics of Narrative Form: Studies in Anglo-American Narratology*. Ed. John Pier. Berlin and New York: Walter de Gruyter. 11–57.

O'Brien, F. (1939). *At Swim-Two-Birds*. New York: Plume.

Onega, S. (1989). *Form and Meaning in the Novels of John Fowles*. Ann Arbor, MI: U.M.I. Research Press.

Onega, S. and Ganteau, J.-M. (2007). "Introduction". In *Ethics and Trauma in Contemporary British Fiction*. Amsterdam: Rodopi. 7–20.

Parrinder, P. (1977). "Pilgrim's progress: The novels of B. S. Johnson (1933–1973)". *Critical Quarterly* 19.2. 45–59.

Phelan, J. (1996). *Narrative as Rhetoric: Technique, Audience, Ethics, Ideology*. Columbus, OH: Ohio State University Press.

Prince, G. (1988). "The disnarrated". *Style* 22.1. 1–8.

Pynchon, T. (1973). *Gravity's Rainbow*. New York: Viking.

Richardson, B. (2001). "Denarration in fiction". *Narrative* 9.2. 168–175.

Richardson, B. (2015). *Unnatural Narrative: Theory, History and Practice*. Columbus, OH: Ohio State University Press.

Rimmon-Kenan, S. (2002). *Narrative Fiction: Contemporary Poetics*. 2nd edn. London: Routledge.

Scholes, R. (1970). *The Philosopher-Critic*. Tulsa, OK: University of Tulsa Press.

Scholes, R. (1979). *Fabulation and Metafiction*. Urbana, IL: University of Illinois Press.

Sterne, L. (2003) [1758–1767]. *The Life and Opinions of Tristram Shandy, Gentleman*. London: Penguin Books.

Sukenick, R. (1969). *The Death of the Novel and Other Stories*. New York: Dial Press.

Sweeney, C. (2018). " 'Groping inside language': Translation, humour and experiment in Christine Brooke-Rose's *Between* and Brigid Brophy's *In Transit*". *Textual Practice* 32.2. 301–316.

Thoss, J. (2011). "Unnatural narrative and metalepsis: Grant Morrison's *Animal Man*". In *Unnatural Narratives—Unnatural Narratology*. Eds. J. Alber and R. Heinze. Berlin: De Gruyter. 189–209.

Thoss, J. (2015). *When Storyworlds Collide: Metalepsis in Popular Fiction, Film and Comics*. Leiden: Brill Rodopi.

Timmer, N. (2010). *Do You Feel It Too? The Post-Postmodern Syndrome in American Fiction at the Turn of the Millennium*. Amsterdam: Rodopi.

Tredell, N. (2000). *Fighting Fictions: The Novels of B. S. Johnson*. Nottingham: Pauper's Press.

Vonnegut, K. (1973). *Breakfast of Champions, or Goodbye Blue Monday*. New York: Delacorte Press/Seymour Lawrence.

Waugh, P. (1984). *Metafiction: The Theory and Practice of Self-Conscious Fiction*. London and New York: Routledge.

White, H. (1987). *The Content of the Form: Narrative Discourse and Historical Representation*. Baltimore, MD: Johns Hopkins University Press.

White, H. (1994). *The Names of History: On the Poetics of Knowledge*. Minnesota, MN: University of Minnesota Press.

Wicomb, Z. (2005). "Setting, intertextuality and the resurrection of the postcolonial author". *Journal of Postcolonial Writing* 41.2. 144–155.

Wolf, W. (2005). "Metalepsis as a transgeneric and transmedial phenomenon: A case study of the possibilities of 'exporting' narratological concepts". In *Narratology Beyond Literary Criticism: Mediality, Disciplinarity*. Ed. J. C. Meister. Berlin: De Gruyter. 83–108.

Wolf, W. (2009). "Metareference across media: The concept, its transmedial potentials and problems, main forms and functions". In *Metareference Across Media: Theory and Case Studies*. Ed. W. Wolf. Amsterdam: Rodopi. 1–85.

Wolf, W. (2013). " 'Unnatural' metalepsis and immersion: Necessarily incompatible?" In *A Poetics of Unnatural Narrative*. Eds. J. Alber, H. Skov Nielsen and B. Richardson. Columbus, OH: Ohio State University Press. 113–141.

Woolf, V. (1928). *Orlando*. London: Hogarth Press.

Zouaoui, K. (2011). " 'It is about frustration': Desire and creation in B. S. Johnson's Novels". *Critical Engagements: A Journal of Criticism and Theory* 4.1/4.2. 129–146.

2 Discourse Deixis in Literature

Note to Reader before proceeding further: Before proceeding further, the Reader is respectfully advised to refer to the Synopsis or Summary of the Argument on Page 60.

(O'Brien, 1939, p. 103, italics in the original)

How the hell did you manage to pass from the level of the present to the level of the past? From outside to inside this very personal recitation? This doesn't make sense! Normally such transfers are not permitted. They go against the logic of traditional narrative techniques!

(Federman, 1976, Chapter xvii [np])

2.1 Introducing Discourse Deixis

Discourse deixis is language which points to a section or aspect of the discourse context or co-text in which that language is used. Each of the above quotations employs discourse deixis (as does the part of this sentence preceding this parenthesis, as does that last clause, as does this clause here). As mentioned in section 1.3, 'deixis' is the name given to a subset of words which can be used as 'pointing' expressions. Unlike most words, the referential value of deictic words does not carry a set of relatively stable characteristics (as is the case for, for example, the noun 'table', or the adjective 'happy'). Deixis, instead, includes words like 'I', 'it', 'here', 'above', and 'soon'. Each of these words has a referential value which changes with every instance of use and which can only be resolved in relation to the context of that use (Bühler, 1934). Discourse deixis is the use of these 'pointing' expressions to refer to an aspect of the discourse or discourse situation.

Discourse deixis often works in tandem with general references to, or otherwise foregrounding of, aspects of fictional discourse and/or the fictional discourse situation. Such metafictional reference and foregrounding might be, for example, through a narrator discussing storytelling conventions in general, or through overt intertextuality, and can have such effects as 'breaking the fourth wall', disrupting the reader's sense of immersion in the story and heightening her awareness of her extrafictional position as reader. Discourse deixis shares many of the same effects, but has the distinguishing feature of requiring the reader to recourse to, reflect on, or re-cognize the context of the utterance, including her deictic centre within the discourse situation, as part of the act of processing and resolving the meaning of the discourse deictic referent. Compare, for example, a narrator within a story stating 'stories are hard to tell' and 'this story is hard to tell'. The core meaning of the former example, 'stories are hard to tell', does not substantially change if spoken by a different narrator, or if occurring in a different story or in discourse of a different type (e.g. non-literary discourse). Even if the identity of the speaker changes, further inferable meanings such as 'the speaker of the utterance believes the proposition entailed in the utterance to be true' hold fast. The meaning of the latter example, 'this story is hard to tell', requires the reader to reflect on the discourse context to resolve the specific reference of 'this story'—that is, which story, in particular is being referred to—and that referent would be different if the statement were lifted out of this context and into a different story. While general metafictional references to and foregrounding of aspects of literary discourse and/or the literary discourse situation are intertwined with many metafictional uses of discourse deixis, and will therefore be part of the discussions in the chapter that follow, it is delineating discourse deixis in particular which is the focus of this chapter.

   Though discourse deixis was not explicitly discussed, or labelled as such, in the seminal work on deixis by Bühler (1934, an edited translation of which was published in 2011), it came to be regarded, in the work of Lyons (1977) and Benveniste (1971 [1966]), as a significant subcategory of deixis. The nature of discourse deixis, and its relationship to the other subcategories, remains contentious, however. This chapter begins with an overview of deixis (section 2.2) and an outline of its three main subcategories: person, spatial, and temporal deixis (section 2.3). The chapter then discusses some of the theoretical issues within previous explorations of deixis in the context of written communication (section 2.4). Through these theoretical reflections, and the points and principles which arise, the chapter proposes a description of discourse deixis in written literary communication, drawing on some examples of discourse deixis within metafiction as test cases (taken from within and beyond the six metafictional texts that the rest of this book focuses upon in detail) (section 2.5). This description is narrower in scope than some previous models, and adopts a particular stance on the nature of deixis, in the service of presenting a principled and coherent account of the functioning of discourse deixis in literature and its role in metafiction. This account aims to offer further progress to the ongoing development of linguistic accounts of deixis.

2.2 Defining Deixis

The term 'deixis' is derived from the Greek word for 'pointing'. Deictic words are unusual in that they straddle the symbolic and indexical functioning of language. As Rauh explains, "symbolic expressions like *man* or *woman, room* or *house, hour* or *day* characterise properties of their potential referents which are not expressed by deictic terms like *I* or *you, here* or *there* and *now* or *then*" (1983, p. 10). 'Indexical' expressions, conversely, have been broadly identified, within linguistic philosophy, as pointing to features of the communicative context (Jakobson, 1960; Lyons, 1977; Peirce, 1955). Indices, according to Peirce's classification of signs, "stand in a relationship of proximity or causality with their referents" (Semino, 1997, p. 32). Deixis designates the relationship between (usually) the speaker and the referent, through consideration of the parameters of the context of the utterance. That is, the referential value of deictic expressions depends upon the "disambiguation of the context of use" (Semino, 1997, p. 33), and necessarily varies "from case to case" (i.e. from one use to another) (Bühler, 1982, p. 12).

As Semino (1997, pp. 31–32) and Burks (1948) argue, the term 'indexical symbolic' therefore captures the function of deictics most accurately: their indexical functioning may be the most interesting thing about them, but, though they characterise little about the referent, deictic expressions do carry symbolic meaning in terms of the precise nature of the relationship thereby signalled between the deictic centre (usually the speaker, in their particular spatio-temporal context of utterance) and the referent. For example, 'tomorrow' designates a temporal relation of specifically up to but fewer than 48 hours later than the instance of utterance (i.e. if I say 'I'll finish reading tomorrow' at 00:01 on a Monday, I am indicating that I will finish reading at some point up to 23:59 on Tuesday, the following day). It is through their combined indexical and symbolic functioning that deictic terms gain referential value.

The speaker and her locus within the context of communication are described as the 'perceptual *origo*', or 'deictic centre'. The deictic centre serves as the anchor point for deictic referents: unlike other relational expressions, deictic expressions are subjectively oriented in direct relation to a perceptual origo. Bühler originally used the deictic terms 'here, now, I' to identify the deictic centre in terms of the speaker and her spatio-temporal coordinates in the act of utterance. As described by Lyons,

> by deixis is meant the location and identification of persons, objects, events, processes and activities being talked about, or referred to, in relation to the spatiotemporal context created and sustained by the act of utterance and the participation in it, typically of a single speaker and at least one addressee.
>
> (1977, p. 637)

Lyons contrasts the expressions "The church is on the other side of the town hall from where I am looking" and "The church is on the other side of the town hall from the road". Here only the former "involv[es] a deictic point-of-observation" which he paraphrases as "seen from here", whereas the latter involves relational but non-deictic orientation in that it is not anchored to a particular perceptual origo (1977, p. 700).

To summarise, the two chief characteristics of deixis which distinguish it from the purely symbolic field are: i) deictic reference is anchored to a perceptual origo, and in turn, ii) interpretation of deictic terms depends upon the addressee relating the deictic terms to one or more dimensions of the context of the utterance—for example, spatial, temporal, or person (i.e. participant relations). What Lyons describes as "relation to the spatiotemporal context created and sustained by the act of utterance and the participation in it" has been further specified here as relation to one or more aspects of the context of utterance, as in some cases only one dimension is relevant to and required for identification of the referent (e.g. the addressee's knowledge of who the speaker is, when the speaker uses 'I', may not require reference to the spatio-temporal aspects of the context).

A third characteristic might be proposed: iii) in most cases, deictic terms tend to take on a different referential value each time they are used. The qualification within the third characteristic warrants explanation. Within my own discourse, when I use the term 'I', unless quoting someone else I am consistently referring to the same identity (Andrea Macrae). In a local context, 'I' might be regarded as the deictic term most 'stable' in referential value. We can consider, also, a circumstance in which, for example, two parents are talking to their child, and both using 'you' with the same referential value (i.e. to refer to and address the child). Within a particular local discourse context, then, some prototypically deictic terms therefore do not consistently satisfy this third condition. However, the proportion of my own use of the word 'I' on any one day (for example), and its referential value as referring to (this) 'Andrea Macrae', is minute in comparison to the total number of times the word 'I' is used globally on any one day. The potential number of different referential values of 'I' effectively correlates with the number of English-speaking individuals at any one time. Even within a local discourse context, two participants in discourse will use 'I' to refer differently, in that each uses it to refer to her/himself. The presence of the third characteristic as a determining feature of deixis is a source of some differences of opinion within accounts of deixis, and in particular the inclusion or exclusion of definite referring expressions, as will be discussed below.

Certain nouns have different meaning-values when used by different people in different contexts, for example 'home', and 'work' (e.g. 'I'm leaving to go to work now'), and so can be seen as sharing the characteristics of deixis. However, in such uses, 'home' is used and understood as 'my home', 'work' as 'my [place of] work', etc., and it is the combination of deictic personal pronoun plus noun which creates the deictic quality and which makes resolvable the deictic referential value.

Deixis can be considered from two angles: Fillmore describes deixis as items that "*are controlled by* certain details of the interactional situation" (my italics), and writes

> there are two general ways in which one speaks of deixis [. . .]: first, in terms of the manner in which the socio-spatio-temporal anchoring of a communication act *motivates the form*, or *provides material for the interpretation*, of the utterance that manifests the act; and second, in terms of the grammatical and lexical systems in the language which *serve to signal or reflect such anchoring*.
>
> (1982, p. 35, my italics)

The two "ways" Fillmore is describing deixis here seem to cross-cut his organisation of them: the first seems to be the ways in which the form of deixis is "controlled" or "motivate[d]" by "the socio-spatio-temporal anchoring", and the second seems to be the ways in which deixis "signal[s] or reflect[s] such anchoring", while this second 'way' is actually the means by which deixis "provides material for the interpretation [. . .] of the utterance". Though the two "ways" of thinking about deixis are interdependent, it is the second, interpretative element which is of key interest in this account of deixis. The interpretative mechanics of deixis—specifically, that deixis foregrounds the particular positioning of the speaker and addressee in the context of utterance—is in effect its fourth characteristic.

This effect of foregrounding the positioning of the discourse participants within the discourse context—the fourth characteristic—is particularly interesting in the context of metafiction, in that it coalesces with metafiction's thematic explorations of the positioning and role of the reader and author, as discourse participants, in the act of the construction of the story, of stories in general, and of reality as [a] story.

The discourse context of the construction of a story has distinct conditions. For example, in literary fictional discourse, the actual 'speaker' (the author) is superseded by the textual figure of the narrator in the primary 'speaking' role. These conditions have implications for the nature and functioning of deixis in literature. Within the traditional account of deixis, deictic reference is conventionally assumed to be anchored primarily to the locus of the (actual, original) speaker of the utterance, and the spatio-temporal context of the utterance is generally assumed to be shared by both the speaker and hearer. This is described as the 'canonical situation-of-utterance' (Lyons, 1977; Rauh, 1983): a situation in which the speaker and hearer are in the same space at the same time. A short-hand paraphrase might be 'face-to-face spoken exchange' (though the participants need not actually be face-to-face). Deixis within this situation is often what Bühler talks of as *demonstratio ad oculos*—pointing or gesturing towards something visible in the shared physical surroundings. Deixis within the canonical situation-of-utterance and *demonstratio ad oculos* has occupied much of the traditional account of deixis (e.g. Lyons, 1977) (though with the growth of discourse through communicative mediums such as the internet and mobile phone, if canonical in this phrase ever meant 'standard', 'conventional', or 'dominant', spoken face-to-face discourse is arguably less canonical than it was in Bühler's time). The context of the construction of a story, though, additionally involves what Bühler describes as *deixis am phantasma* (deixis of the imagination) and, more specifically, as identified by others, *deixis im vorstellungsraum* (deixis in the realm of invention), and *deixis in textraum* (deixis in the realm of the text), which carry further complexities that will be discussed below. However, the traditional account of deixis, and the three core categories of deixis which it tends to focus on—person, spatial, and temporal—are an important starting point for looking at deixis in literature.

2.3 Person, Spatial, and Temporal Deixis

Before the three core categories of deixis are outlined, it is worth noting that, though there has been a wealth of investigation into various deictic terms, deixis resists a rigid taxonomy. This is partly because the deictic referential quality of a word is often a matter of that word being used deictically rather than that word being inherently (and in all uses) deictic. Levinson and Lyons demonstrate that terms which are prototypically used deictically can be used non-deictically: Levinson compares the use of "that" in the sentences "That's a beautiful view" and "Oh, I did this and that" (1983, p. 66; see also Green, 1995). Furthermore, expressions which are, taken as a whole, deictic in quality are often constituted by a combination of prototypically deictic terms and non-deictic terms. Levinson makes the point that many complex time adverbials involve an interaction of calendrical terms or some other non-deictic name or unit of measurement of time, such as 'day', 'season', 'year', etc., or the names of specific months, and deictic modifiers, such as 'this', 'last', and 'next', to create deictic expressions such as 'this week' and 'next month' (Levinson, 1983, p. 73; see also Lyons, 1977, p. 678). Many spatial locative expressions follow similar patterns, using the same deictic modifiers but in combination with non-deictic geographic or locative referents or spatial units of measurement (e.g. 'the next town', 'the last 15 miles'). Deixis should be considered functions: words can function deictically or not, and words which can function deictically may be able to function as spatial deixis, or as person deixis, etc. Words considered to belong to specific subcategories of deixis are words which can function as that type of deixis but which may additionally belong to and function as another. Also, deixis varies across languages. For example, spatial prepositional phrases involving deixis can vary in their metaphorical value and in their frequency in different languages (cf. Hanks, 1990, 2009; Jungbluth and Da Milano, 2015). Lastly, deixis has been explored within many fields within linguistics and language study, including philology, transformational grammar, child language acquisition, pragmatics, and cognition. Each of these lenses on deixis has slightly different priorities and perspectives. The following account is most informed by aspects of pragmatics and cognition. It is, nonetheless, not a pragmatic or cognitive account of deixis, in that it does not attend to some of the pragmatic or cognitive dimensions of deixis, though it aims to be of use to those fields. Even within what has retrospectively been called 'the traditional account' (loosely and variably including Lyons, Benveniste, Rauh, and Fillmore) there are minor variations, some of which are indicated in the following pages. With these caveats in mind, the three core categories of deixis in English can be outlined as follows.

Person deixis includes personal pronouns such as 'I', 'you', 'they', 'his', and 'it'; possessive and reflexive pronouns; demonstrative pronouns ('this', 'that', 'these', and 'those'); and the definite article (and therefore also definite referring noun phrases, e.g. 'the hotel') (Lyons, 1977, pp. 574–575, 646–657; Stockwell, 2002, p. 45). The pronouns 'I' and 'you' are central to the deictic inventory, together with other first- and second-person pronoun forms, in referring to the discourse participants who are occupying the roles of speaker and addressee. Though in the traditional account, third-person reference is often considered derivative (Benveniste, 1971 [1966], pp. 200, 218–221; Lyons, 1977, p. 638), sometimes perceived as lacking explicit anchoring to the speaker, third-person reference does involve an indexical relation to the speaker and her deictic centre.

The definite article is considered deictic in what Lyons identifies as its second component (the first being pronominal, functioning to inform the addressee that something or someone is being referred to). The second component of the definite article, in Lyons' view, is its function as "the adjectivalized deictic adverbial 'there', interpreted in its neutral sense (cf. Thorne, 1972)" (Lyons, 1977, p. 655). This function "instruct[s] or invit[es] the addressee to find the referent in the environment" and presupposes that the referent is identifiable without further information (pp. 655–656). Lyons's argument may seem a little ambiguous, in that he asserts that the definite article is "unmarked for proximity" (p. 647), that it does not point the addressee "to any particular region of" the environment (p. 656), and that it correlates with 'there' only in the "neutral" sense of 'there', in relation to which he refers to Thorne (1972). Thorne, however, upholds a specifically "localist theory of the definite article" (Thorne, 1972, p. 564). According to Thorne, the definite article can be taken to mean "which is there" (p. 563), 'there' signalling, for Thorne, the local spatial context or nearby co-text (p. 564). Therefore, 'she's at the hotel' has deictic referential value in the sense of implying that the hotel being referred to is the nearest (geographically) to the deictic centre, and/or is the hotel which has been mentioned most recently within the discourse between the speaker and addressee(s).

The deictic quality of the definite article is, like other words in this deictic category and other deictic categories, a matter of use: the definite article can be used deictically or non-deictically. In its non-deictic use, the definite article, in its "adjectivalized adverbial component [. . .] will inform the addressee that he will find a satisfying description somewhere [not necessarily anywhere 'local' within the discourse context], and the presupposition is that the addressee has all the information he needs in order to find it" (Lyons, 1977, p. 656). The indefinite article is non-deictic in that it merely refers to something (and presupposes its existence), without a signalling that the referent can be found within the environment (e.g. the local spatial context or nearby co-text), and without presupposing that the addressee has all the information she needs in order to identify a specific referent.

The inclusion of the definite article, and thereby definite referring expressions, within deixis has logical implications for the analogous inclusion of locative expressions (as will be discussed below, within consideration of spatial deixis) and for proper names. Proper names are included in the category of person deixis by some theorists (e.g. Stockwell, 2002), and are arguably deictic in two ways. Stockwell explains his inclusion of names from the cognitive viewpoint that "reference is [understood as] to a mental representation and is a socially located act and is therefore participatory and deictic" (Stockwell, 2002, p. 45). An alternative but related explanation for categorising proper names as deictic is in considering them as, or as an extension of, definite referring expressions. Assuming a name (e.g. 'Ms. Reeves') is not preceded by an introductory clause containing a deictic element (i.e. 'This is Ms. Reeves') or accompanied by a similar implicit gesture (e.g. pointing), mention of the name 'Ms. Reeves' effectively means 'the particular Ms. Reeves most relevant and retrievable in relation to the context-of-utterance', the Ms. Reeves most 'proximal' to us, the one which is identifiable from or within the context of the spatio-temporal environment and/or preceding discourse. However, in practice, the referential value attached to proper names, more so than many definite referring expressions, tends not to change in different contexts of use within a relatively local discourse community, the function of a name being, after all, to serve as a unique identifier. If we take the view that the referent of a proper name is the same whether that name is mentioned by one person or another, on one day or the next, a proper name is an example of the caveat required within the third characteristic of deixis previously described (i.e. in most cases, but not all cases, deictic terms tend to take on a different referential value each time they are used).

The sense outlined here in which proper names can be considered deictic is effectively by analogy to the use of definite and indefinite articles in their co-referential function (i.e. to signal given/new information and anaphoric and cataphoric co-reference). Proper names may function to introduce a referent as newly included within the discourse (though note the referent of a proper name may potentially have been referred to beforehand via an anticipatory pronoun, on which see, for example, Emmott, 1997). Whether or not anaphoric and cataphoric reference is properly deictic is discussed in section 2.4.

Use of a proper name also has a significant pragmatic and/or social indexical function in that the speaker has chosen to use the name instead of a pronoun, nickname, role title, etc. This may potentially be as a result of and/or to signal a particular social relationship (e.g. degree of familiarity) or an interaction between relationship and context (e.g. close friends may address each other using role titles and surnames in professional public contexts but may address each other using only first names outside of that environment) (Brown and Yule, 1983, pp. 44–45). Lyons tries to distinguish social relations and deictic relations (1977, pp. 574–575), though this is difficult in practice. (For more on the social pragmatic functions of proper names, and the broader, thornier issue of what has been called 'social deixis', see Macrae in Sorlin, forthcoming). Put briefly, though, the kinds of words and phrases which have been discussed under the heading of social and/or empathetic deixis are, firstly, not grounded in or referential via a deictic centre in the same way as person, spatial, temporal, and discourse deixis are, and secondly, as indicated in relation to proper names, they are bound up with pragmatics in ways which are often difficult to disentangle.

To return to person deixis, on this basis one could perhaps argue that there is a scale of deictic quality within this category. Personal and demonstrative pronouns are wholly and inherently deictic in function, while the definite article and definite referring expressions are more occasionally and/or partially deictic in function, followed by proper names which are yet more rarely and/or minimally deictic in function.

Spatial deixis includes spatial adverbs such as 'here' and 'there', 'nearby' and 'beyond'; the demonstrative pronouns 'this', 'that', 'these', and 'those'; and verbs of motion such as 'come', 'go', and 'bring' (Stockwell, 2002, pp. 45–46). Locative expressions such as 'in the valley' are included by some, which can be justified on the grounds of involving a definite referring expression (though some theorists consider such expressions to be non-deictic: cf. Fillmore, 1982).

As explained by Herman (2001, 2002), spatial deictic expressions can interact with figure and ground relations, whereby the deictic centre serves as the ground in relation to which the system of orienting co-ordinates moves (Fillmore, 1982; Langacker, 2008; Talmy, 2000). Spatial deictic expressions can also interact with concepts of regions, landmarks, and paths (Landau and Jackendoff, 1993; Talmy, 2000), and with topological structures (the inherent geometric properties of object) (Frawley, 1992, pp. 250–293). For example, the statement 'Steve is stood in front of the house' may mean that Steve is stood between the speaker and the house, and is therefore in front of the house from the speaker's perspective. In this case, the 'ground' is the speaker's deictic centre, and the expression is deictic. Alternatively, Steve may be stood outside of the front of the house (usually conceived as the particular side of a house which includes its main—or indeed 'front'—door). In this case the statement is drawing upon the perceived geometric properties of the object, and the 'ground' is that object, the house, rather than the speaker's deictic centre. This sentence is not deictic, in that it is not related to the speaker's perspective from her deictic centre: it could be equally 'true' and mean the same thing if the speaker was saying this from several different positions, for example while standing at the opposite side of the house to Steve, or while standing next to Steve at the 'front' of the house. The deictic quality of some spatial statements such as this may therefore occasionally be ambiguous, and those other factors (topological structures, etc.) may need to be considered in order to discern their deictic quality in each instance of use.

Temporal deixis includes tensed verbs; temporal adverbs such as 'now', 'today', 'yesterday', 'tomorrow', 'soon', and 'later'; and prepositions such as 'beyond', 'with', and 'over' when used in combination with non-deictic terms such as calendrical terms or temporal units of measurement, as in "after three weeks" (Stockwell, 2002, p. 46; see also Levinson, 1983, pp. 73–79; Lyons, 1977, p. 678; Ryan, 2001, pp. 136–137). Temporal expressions such as 'in the morning' are included, again often on the grounds of the deictic value of definite referring expressions. Demonstrative pronouns are used in this category as well as the spatial category, and prepositions which are prototypically used to refer to spatial relations are also often used metaphorically to express temporal relations (e.g. 'an hour behind').

Apart from some minor variations, the inclusion of the items listed earlier in an account of person, spatial, and temporal deixis in the case of *demonstratio ad oculos* and in the canonical situation-of-utterance is broadly theoretically agreed upon. Further theoretical entanglements arise, however, and accounts of categories diverge, when *demonstratio ad oculos* (and indeed reference in general) is considered from a cognitive perspective; when the possibility (and frequency) of deictic orientation from an other's perspective (i.e. not the speaker's perspective) is acknowledged, which is known as 'deictic projection'; and when communication is not within the canonical situation-of-utterance, as is the case in most instances of written communication. This is where an account of discourse deixis begins.

2.4 Deixis in Written Literature

So far, this chapter has defined deixis and its three core categories. Temporal deixis is used to refer to a point in time via the temporal relation between that point and the temporal locus of the deictic centre. Spatial deixis is used to refer to a point in space via the spatial relation between that point and the spatial locus of the deictic centre. Person deixis is used to refer to people or objects via the slightly more abstract, and sometimes metaphorical, 'person relation' between the person or object and the deictic centre. For what purposes, then, is discourse deixis used? What kinds of things does discourse deixis refer to, and what is meant by 'discourse relations'?

One critical factor to start with is the nature of the 'discourse' in question. As mentioned, person, spatial, and temporal deixis have predominantly been explored in the context of the canonical situation-of-utterance—that is, when a speaker is speaking to an addressee, and the two share the same spatio-temporal context (i.e. the speaker is speaking to the addressee while they are in the same place at the same time). Discourse deixis focuses attention on the discourse situation itself, and, relatedly, on different types of discourse. This book is interested in the discourse type of written literature, specifically. Fowler (1986, p. 90) argues that literary deixis constitutes 'unnatural' use of deixis in its departure from the canonical situation-of-utterance. Rauh (1983), Green (1992), and Semino (1997), however, identify literary deixis as situated along a continuum of uses relative to particular discourse types.

So what happens to deixis when it is used not in the canonical situation-of-utterance but rather in the context of written literary communication? In this situation-of-utterance, the encounter between the reader and the text can be centuries after the author wrote that text; the author and reader may perform their respective acts of authoring and reading the text continents apart; the reader is but one of many potential addressees; and a narrator and often various other fictional voices are additionally involved in acts of utterance. This section explores theoretical viewpoints on deixis in the discourse situation of literary communication, and the implications for what discourse deixis, in this situation, can involve.

Though deictic theory has chiefly focused on the canonical situation-of-utterance, Bühler's original account does include the use of deixis to discuss imagined or remembered scenes. Bühler describes *deixis am phantasma* as follows:

> When Mohammed feels displaced to the mountain, his present tactile body image is connected with an imagined optical scene. For this reason, he is able to use the local deictic words *here* and *there* [. . .] and the directional words *forwards, back; right, left* on the phantasy [sic] product or imagined object just as well as in the primary situation

of actual perception. And the same holds for the hearer. The hearer understands them when he is similarly 'displaced' himself, that is, when his own present tactile body image is connected to a corresponding visual scene.

(2011, p. 153, italics in the original)

Deixis am phantasma therefore describes the use of deixis within discussion of an imagined scene, in which aspects of the scene are described from the perspective of a deictic centre (remembered or imagined) within that scene. The speaker's 'displace[ment]' from her/his actual deictic centre in the spatio-temporal context of utterance to the deictic centre within the imagined scene is what has come to be called 'deictic projection' (Duchan, Bruder, and Hewitt, 1995). In saying that the "hearer understands them [local deictic words] when he is similarly 'displaced' himself", Bühler is explaining the most critical element of comprehension of deixis: the conceptual projection required of the reader or hearer to the speaker's projected, imagined deictic centre in order to understand, make sense of, and resolve the deictic words.

Deictic projection has been regarded by some as derivative of deixis proper (cf. Levinson, 1983, p. 64) in that it appears to annul the subjective and particularly speaker-anchored aspects of deictic reference. However, deictic projection is still deictic in that it involves subjective anchoring to an origo using a deictic system of relations. Lyons originally coined the term 'deictic projection' to refer specifically to a speaker's ability to "project himself into the spatiotemporal location of the addressee" in circumstances where the deictic context is not shared by speaker and hearer (1977, pp. 578–579). The term has been used more widely, however, to encompass several possible forms of what Bühler (1982) described as "transition" or "translation" of deictic orientation. These forms include a speaker's conceptual projection to the locus of the addressee in circumstances in which the context of utterance is shared, as in *demonstratio ad oculos* (Bühler, 1982, p. 14; see also Lyons, 1977, p. 677). The speaker's conceptual projection to the addressee's deictic centre, and vice versa, is inherent within the canonical situation-of-utterance, as even in these circumstances—the speaker and hearer sharing the same space (and time)—they cannot entirely share a deictic perspective. For example, they will each have different referential values for 'I', and slightly different values for 'here'. The substantial difference in deictic projection between *deixis ad oculos* and *deixis am phantasma* is that in the latter the deictic centre to which each may project is not only outside of their local spatio-temporal context but also at a different ontological plane.

The creation of a specifically fictional referential context, and projection to deictic centres within it, constitutes a particular kind of *deixis am phantasma*, which Ehlich (1983) terms *deixis im vorstellungsraum* (deixis in the realm of invention, as opposed to, for example, memory).

This creates a space which, in addition to being outside of the spatio-temporal context of the speaker and hearer, is also of a different ontological status. Here

> the narrator leads the hearer into the realm of [. . .] constructive imagination and treats him to the same deictic words [. . .] so that he may see and hear what can be seen and heard there [. . .]. Not with the external eye, ear, and so on, but with what is usually called the "mind's" eye or ear [. . .].
>
> (Bühler, 2011, p. 141)

For Ehlich, *deixis in der sprechsituation* (deixis in the speech situation) describes the case in which the centre of orientation is present in the canonical situation-of-utterance but the object being referred to may or may not be. In the case of *deixis im vorstellungsraum* (deixis in invention), neither the centre of orientation nor the object being referred to are part of the canonical situation-of-utterance (Ehlich, 1979; Rauh, 1983, pp. 29, 54–55).

One identifying feature of *deixis im vorstellungsraum* is that the author, the 'actual' speaker, is backgrounded: the narrator constitutes the primary participatory speaker—the primary deictic centre of the narration—who then creates and projects into the secondary deictic centres of characters within the imaginative realm of the story. As Rauh writes,

> the narrator [. . .] *counts as* the encoder of the utterances assigned to him [and] may himself establish new centers of orientation by introducing new characters and the latter then count as the encoders of the utterances assigned to them. The indexical meanings of deictic expressions have to be interpreted accordingly.
>
> (1983, p. 47)

The kind of *deixis im vorstellungsraum* described does not preclude a speaker being a narrator and telling a story in which she is in an imagined scenario, but the version of her that is within that imagined storyworld is a fictive version: she is projecting into a narratorial deictic centre which is imagined. *Deixis im vorstellungsraum* gives us one dimension of deixis in literature, then: the conceptual. In literary discourse, the deictic centre, the elements referred to, and the deictic relations between the centre and elements are conceptual, specifically, based on imaginative invention.

A second feature of deixis in literature relates to what Ehlich (1983, p. 89) calls *deixis im textraum* (deixis in the realm of the text). Ehlich uses this term to refer to a particular use of discourse deixis. Along with the conceptual space of the storyworld, deixis in written literature, and discourse deixis especially, involves the 'space' of the material written text. The deictic centres in question here are that of the writer in the act of producing the text and that of the reader in the act of processing the text and her corresponding sequential conceptual act of imaginatively realising the text. The elements deictically referred to are units of text. Rauh describes this kind of deictic centre as

> a center of orientation [. . .] which corresponds [. . .] to his momentary situation within the course of a text, considered either temporal or local and with respect to which either temporal or local domains of the textual context are determined. [. . .] Establishing a center of orientation in discourse is possible because the encoding of discourse is a continuous process along which at any point the encoder may stop and establish a center of orientation. Since a continuous piece of discourse may be looked upon as having either temporal or (in writing) local extension, the fixing of temporal or local points of orientation is respectively possible. [. . .] If a continuous piece of discourse is treated as having local extension, practically all local deictic expressions can be used. In this context their symbolic meanings are unchanged and only their indexical meanings are different, their referents not being extra-linguistic local areas but segments of discourse.
>
> (1983, pp. 48–49)

Rauh seems to focus on the centre of orientation of "the encoder"—the writer—within the temporal and local "extensions" of the textual discourse. Levinson does the same in stating that "the discourse centre is the point which the speaker is currently at in the production of his utterance" (Levinson, 1983, p. 64). However, the same principle and "extensions" apply to the centre of orientation of the reader in processing the discourse.

Deixis in literature can thereby involve deictic centres and deictic referents which are conceptual—in the imagined storyworld—and also deictic centres and deictic referents which are textual. Literary fiction involves the construction, manipulation, and variable foregrounding of the reader's deictic centre in the textual dimension and the (projected) conceptual dimensions, each with person, spatial, and temporal relations. Metafiction thematises this construction, manipulation, and foregrounding in both the textual and conceptual dimensions.

A third feature of written literary discourse is that the discourse participants are situated in a split discourse context, in the sense that the context of creation and the context of reception are different (Semino, 1997, p. 5). As mentioned previously, this is true to some extent even in the case of the canonical situation-of-utterance, in that the discourse participants have a different 'I' and a slightly different 'here'. Written communication tends to be created in one place and time, by one or more participants, and read at a different place and time, by anything from one participant to billions of participants. This split discourse context can be considered with respect to the real inscribing author and the reader, but also with respect to the enunciating narrator and the reader, who are 'split' in terms of relative ontological reality. The situation is complicated yet further in the case of the pseudo-authorial narrators common in metafiction, as will be explored next.

2.5 Discourse Deixis in Written Literature

The prior section discussed the conceptual and textual dimensions of deixis in written literature. Discourse deixis in written literature can be used to construct, manipulate, and foreground the reader's deictic centre in relation to three different cases of discourse across the textual and conceptual dimensions:

1. the physical text (e.g. a portion of discourse, the sequential arrangement, and the reader's movement through it, etc.)
2. the propositional content of a preceding, immediate, or subsequent portion of discourse (which overlaps cases 1 and 3)
3. the act and process of creation of the storyworld, which can be further broken down into

   a) the act and process of composition,
   b) the act and process of narration, and
   c) the act and process of readerly imaginative conceptualisation

The following paragraphs work through these cases, drawing on examples from metafiction to illustrate each case.

References to the physical text can include references to specific sections of the text and/or to particular points in the text-continuum. One example of this is 'in the last chapter' in which the deictic 'last' combines with the non-deictic 'chapter' to create a deictic expression, in the same manner as 'last week', etc., as discussed in section 2.3. Similar examples include 'this page', 'these lines', 'the next scene', and so on. Furthermore, in Christie's exclamation "Just think, it may have been caused through those misshapes I had on page 67!" in *Christie Malry's Own Double-Entry*, (Johnson, 2001 [1973], p. 180), "page 67" implicitly means 'page 67 of this book' (see Chapter 4, section 4.2 for a detailed discussion of this quote). In order to make sense of the reference the reader must relate it to her current locus in the sequential progression of the material text, that is, which book she is currently reading, which chapter, which page, etc. This locus could be described as the reader's textual deictic centre. As Levinson asserts, this kind of deixis "has to do with the encoding of reference to portions of the unfolding discourse in which the utterance (which includes the text referring expression) is located" (1983, p. 62). Since, as

Levinson notes, "discourse unfolds in time", its segments can be referred to in terms of the temporal flow of that unfolding (usually presuming a continuous progression and pace of reading). Pronouns functioning as demonstrative person or spatial deixis (e.g. 'this') can also function as discourse deixis, encoding the relative proximity of discourse portions deictically referred to, as in the use of 'this' in "You've read me this far, then? Even this far?" (Barth, 1988 [1968], p. 127). These kinds of discourse deictic referents can also include a directional element, that is, to a preceding or forthcoming portion of discourse (Levinson, 1983, p. 85; Rauh, 1983, p. 49).

Chapter titles can be included as deictic, by the same extension outlined in section 2.3, regarding firstly definite referring expressions, and then proper names. A chapter title fundamentally means '*This* chapter is titled' (i.e. 'the segment of text which immediately follows this heading is titled') and so entails a deictic value. Stockwell includes chapter titles within his inventory of deixis as "explicit 'signposting'" (2002, p. 46). Further deictic values can be entailed in the nature of the wording of the title. As Genette notes,

> a good many internal titles make sense only to an addressee who is already involved in reading the text, for these internal titles presume familiarity with everything that has preceded. For example, the title of the thirty-seventh chapter of *Les Trois Mousquetaires* is 'Milady's Secret', and this name, or nickname, obviously sends the reader back to a previous encounter with the character who bears it.
>
> (1997, p. 294)

Chapter titles are therefore deictically referential and anchored within the textual sequence in several implicit and explicit ways.

Discourse deictic references to particular points within a text are not entirely disconnected from the ways deixis works in the canonical situation-of-utterance. Discourse deictic reference to the physical text which is visible at that point in the reader's processing (i.e. within the immediate open two-page spread) is arguably a form of *demonstratio ad oculos*. Furthermore, if (assuming the text is analog) the reader has the physical text in front of her and a discourse deictic reference points to a section a few chapters earlier, for example, or a few pages later, the reader has the option of physically turning the pages to that point. To do so takes the reader away from the page at which the reference is made (the immediate textual context of utterance). This could be equated to an act of processing spatial deixis in the canonical situation-of-utterance in which the thing referred to is in the room next door to the participants—arguably proximal within the context of utterance (on a scale of proximal—medial—distal, cf. Fludernik, 1991, p. 216), but not actually visible unless some physical shift is made.

The relationship between cases 1 and 2—discourse deictic reference to the physical text (e.g. a portion of discourse, the sequential arrangement, and the reader's movement through it, etc.), and discourse deictic reference to the propositional content of a preceding, immediate, or subsequent portion of discourse—is complex, and remains an area of theoretical disagreement. The second case is illustrated by examples such as "The slopes are gentle that meet where he lies, they flatten out under him, it is not a meeting, it is not a pit, *that* didn't take long, soon we'll have him perched on an eminence", from Beckett's *The Unnamable* (1979 [1953], p. 330, my italics). This quote is rich in metafictional discourse deixis of different kinds, and will be returned to later in this section, but the use of "that", specifically, exemplifies the case in point: "that" refers to the contradiction or reversal entailed in the four prior phrases. The pronoun therefore refers to the propositional content of the immediately preceding text. For some, but not others, this counts as deixis, and for some, but not others, this counts as anaphora. It is arguably both deixis and anaphora. Given the continually contentious nature of the relationship between deixis and anaphora, though, this position needs to be briefly clarified and justified.

Levinson includes anaphora as one of several subtypes of discourse deixis, alongside connectives. Some connectives such as 'anyway', 'so', etc.—particularly when in the utterance-initial position—can serve deictically to signal the relation of the current utterance to the surrounding co-text. Bühler acknowledges the deictic quality of anaphora, whereby demonstrative pronouns function deictically to "refer back to things just treated in discourse [and] forward to things immediately to be treated" (Bühler, 1982, p. 20). Anaphora bears a complex relation to discourse deixis. Levinson argues that "anaphora [. . .] is so closely linked to deixis that it is not always separable" (Levinson, 2004, p. 103), though he proposes a possible distinction: "where a pronoun refers to a linguistic expression (or chunk of discourse) itself, it is discourse-deictic; where a pronoun refers to the same entity as a prior linguistic expression refers to, it is anaphoric" (Levinson, 1983, p. 86). In practice, though, these two functions of a pronoun can be simultaneous and difficult to distinguish, as Levinson observes of his example "*I've been living in San Francisco for five years and I love it here* (where 'here' is both anaphoric and deictic)" (2004, p. 103, italics in the original). For Levinson, then, "here" in this example refers back to the textual unit "San Francisco", and is therefore discourse deictic, and also refers to the same entity which "San Francisco" refers to, and is therefore anaphoric. "Here" is also, in this usage, spatial deixis, arguably both independently and anaphorically via its antecedent. For both Ehlich (1979, 1982) and Rauh (1983), anaphora does not describe a relationship of deictic reference as such, but rather "a coreferential relationship between a deictic expression [e.g. 'she'] and a lexical antecedent [e.g. 'the woman']" (Rauh, 1983, p. 54).

What Levinson, Ehlich, and Rauh describe as the anaphoric and non-deictic quality here, others see as a deictic quality, chiefly through consideration of the significance of sequentiality. As Levinson elsewhere notes,

> Lyons points out that if one thinks of anaphora as reference to entities already established in the domain of discourse, then the ways in which they are referred to in anaphoric reference commonly make use of the order in which they were introduced by the discourse itself. [Therefore] there are good arguments for considering that anaphora ultimately rests on deictic notions.
>
> (1983, p. 87; see also Lyons, 1977, pp. 670–671)

Levinson adds, in his more recent work,

> A distinction is often made between textual deixis and general anaphora along the following lines. Whereas textual deixis refers to portions of the text itself (as in *See the discussion above* or *The pewit sounds like this: pee-r-weet*), anaphoric expressions refer outside the discourse to other entities by connecting to a prior referring expression (anaphora) or a later one (cataphora, as in *In front of him, Pilate saw a beaten man*). Insofar as the distinction between anaphoric and cataphoric expressions is conventionalized, such expressions have a clear conventional deictic component, since reference is relative to the point in the discourse.
>
> (2004, p. 119, italics in the original)

In this view, anaphora and cataphora are discourse deictic in that the referential value is related to the particular juncture in the text at which the reference is made. For example, in 'Steve retreated into his shed. He needed some peace and quiet', the referential value of 'he' can only be resolved as the same referent of 'Steve' through consideration of where in the text the pronoun 'he' occurs in relation to where in the text the antecedent 'Steve' occurs. Examples such as this illustrate Levinson's description: "such signals are deictic because they have the distinctive relativity of reference, being anchored to the discourse location of the current utterance" (1983, p. 85). Anaphora and cataphora can thus be considered deictic in the sense that the meaning (and the possibility of resolving the meaning) of the anaphoric or cataphoric referent depends on the reader's position with respect to the linear discourse. Incidentally, in a footnote to his discussion on the chapter title example from *Les Trois Mousquetaires*, 'Milady's Secret', Genette states "it has an anaphoric, or reminding, value: this woman who is already familiar to you", and adds that a title which "introduces a name as yet unfamiliar" would "take on a cataphoric value, that is, the name would serve as an advance notice" (1997, p. 294). Though the theoretical debates have focused on anaphora, endophora which is neither anaphora or indeed cataphora, but rather refers to the immediate discourse, as in the example from Barth cited earlier, "You've read me *this* far, then? Even *this* far?" (p. 127, my italics), is likewise deictic.

Beyond this stance, though, residual debates about discourse deixis and anaphora rest partially on where theorists sit on the issue of whether the referent must be a unit of text or can be the propositional content of the unit of text, and, underlying this, whether reference is considered from a cognitive view, a pragmatic view, or otherwise. Levinson's own examples seem to expose these complexities. To recap, he states that

> Whereas textual deixis refers to portions of the text itself (as in *See the discussion above* or *The pewit sounds like this: pee-r-weet*), anaphoric expressions refer outside the discourse to other entities by connecting to a prior referring expression (anaphora) or a later one (cataphora, as in *In front of him, Pilate saw a beaten man*).
>
> (2004, p. 119, italics in the original)

Levinson seems to be suggesting that in "The pewit sounds like this: pee-r-weet", "this" refers to the textual unit "pee-r-weet". However, it seems to refer to the sound created when one pronounces "pee-r-weet", rather than referring to the unit of text representing those sounds. Also, compare 'the discussion above' and 'the paragraphs above': the latter refers to a unit of text, whereas the former arguably refers to a prior section of text by reference to a summary of its propositional content (which the author evaluated as being 'a discussion'). Incidentally, both phrases require the reader to infer how far 'above' (i.e. how far back in the text) the section referred to may be, relative to the reader's current position, and also require the reader to infer the bounds (the beginning and end) of the section being referred to (both phrases entailing the presupposition that this should be sufficiently obvious).

This brings us to the point that anaphora does not always have an explicit antecedent nominal expression, and also brings us back to the related issue of 'unit of text' vs. 'propositional content' as a potential referent of discourse deixis. For some, an explicit antecedent nominal expression is in fact the determining 'qualifier' for anaphora, but for others (e.g. Hankamer and Sag, 1977), the referent must merely be decipherable from the co-text and context combined, as in the case of "A large dog approaches A and B. A says to B: I hope it's friendly" (Brown and Yule, 1983, p. 215). As Brown and Yule point out, a reader may draw from her understanding of a range of elements to interpret the referent of a pronoun in discourse (1983, pp. 215–221). This range of elements increases in cases of informal discourse where pronoun use can be a little more 'loose', examples of which include 'There's a car going up the road and he comes to a crossroads' and 'Even an apprentice can make over 150 pounds a week and they don't get much tax taken from that' (examples adapted from Brown and Yule, 1983, p. 217). The notion of an explicit textual antecedent is therefore a little messier than it might seem. Brown and Yule also include not just explicit or implicit antecedents within the discourse context (i.e. not necessarily just co-text, as in the case of the dog), but also predicate expressions. Levinson (1983, p. 87) discusses the following example from Lyons (1977, p. 668): "[Speaker] A: I've never seen him. [Speaker] B: That's a lie". Here 'That' refers to the propositional content of the preceding sentence. Lyons calls this "impure textual deixis" (1977, p. 670), but textual deixis, nonetheless.

A cognitive viewpoint sheds a different light on these issues. Traditional accounts of discourse deixis are clouded by what Emmott calls the "referent in the text" understanding of reference (with implications for anaphora) (1997, p. 199). Rather than a referent in the text, cognitivists argue that what we are fundamentally dealing with is—if not always the 'propositional content' as such, even when there is a direct nominal antecedent—certainly always the reader's conceptual construct of the referent. Emmott (1997) proposes that in the process of reading a reader constructs mental representations of characters and scenes. These mental representations are contained in 'conceptual frames', as cued by the text, which she then attends to and develops or disattends, as directed by textual cues. Anaphoric references thus do not simply refer backwards along a linear text but rather to elements within the reader's previously constructed, and perhaps since neglected, conceptual frames, taking her conscious attention back away from newer, more recently constructed frames, to focus on and develop anew a preceding frame once more. This view more properly connects the 'text' as both a linear material sequence of words and as a dynamic mental construct in the mind of the reader.

This view allows us to add a cognitive layer to explanations of anaphora. For example, in the case of the anaphora within the two sentences 'Steve's gone out. He didn't say when he'd be back', the pronoun 'he' does not refer to the antecedent nominal expression 'Steve' as a unit of text itself. Rather, the pronominal expression 'he' refers to the person Steve, or, more accurately, a mental representation of Steve (varying from reader to reader), via the nominal expression 'Steve'. It is that 'via' which creates the discourse deictic quality. This use of the pronoun 'he' is deictic in its own right, as a third-person pronoun, signalling a person deictic relationship, just as 'here' in Levinson's example ("I've been living in San Francisco for five years and I love it here", 2004, p. 103) is spatially deictic. The anaphoric relationship in the he/Steve example, though, is specifically discourse deictic in that the reader's ability to comprehend the referential value of 'he' depends on her locus in the linear progress of the text relative to the pronoun and nominal expression.

So far, this section has identified and described the following as discourse deictic: textual 'signposting' such as chapter titles; references to preceding, current, and subsequent units of text (the first case), such as in Barth's "You've read me this far, then? Even this far?" (p. 127); and references to the propositional content of preceding, current, and subsequent units of text (the second case), such as in one of the most well-known quotes from Fowles: "although all I have described in the last two chapters happened, it did not happen quite in the way you may have been led to believe" (1996 [1969], p. 327, discussed in Chapter 5). These kinds of discourse deictic references feature in all kinds of discourse, often primarily for the purposes of signposting and cohesion. In the context of fiction, and in particular metafiction, however, these kinds of discourse deictic references can be exploited to disrupt the reader's immersion in the story, and draw her attention to the act of processing the material text, thereby highlighting the fictionality and constructedness of the story-world, etc. They do so specifically via requiring her to register the context of the utterance, including her deictic centre within the discourse situation, in order to resolve the meaning of the referent. The use of these kinds of discourse deictic references in the service of metanarration, metalepsis, and disnarration will be explored in detail in the following chapters.

The third case of discourse deixis, though, is more predominantly and primarily metafictional in its functions and effects. This case moves away from the textual dimension further towards the conceptual dimension of discourse deixis. The first and second cases described earlier tend to use personal pronouns, demonstratives, and spatial and temporal terms to refer to the material text or its propositional content. In these cases the spatial and temporal relations in question are those between the reader's point of progress through the material text and the referent (physical or propositional), measured spatially (e.g., 'a few pages back') or temporally (e.g., 'that didn't take long'), while the person relations (use of 'he', 'she', 'it', etc.) function in the service of endophora. The third case uses the same deictic language, but does so differently. In this case the deictic language is used to construct, manipulate, and foreground the reader's deictic centre in relation to the spatial and temporal contexts (and span) of the author's (or pseudo-authorial narratorial's) act and process of composing the fiction, the narrator's act and process of narrating, and the reader's act and process of imaginatively conceptualising what she is reading (cf. Duchan, Bruder, and Hewitt, 1995; Green, 1992; Semino, 1997). Person deixis is used in this case to convey deictic relationships between the discourse participants, which in the context of literary fiction are the author(s), narrator(s), character(s), and readers (and potentially also an editor, a translator, etc.).

Discourse deixis which relates to the act and process of composition includes examples such as "I've put down all I have to say, or rather I will have done in another twenty-two pages [. . .] Surely no reader will wish me to invent anything further", said by Johnson's pseudo-authorial narrator in *Christie Malry's Own Double-Entry* (p. 165). Here we have a prototypically metafictional pseudo-authorial narrator. The real author—the actual creator and originary discourse participant—is backgrounded. The textual construct of the pseudo-authorial narrator takes the first-person pronoun overtly—four times in fact—as the primary speaker-participant, while at the same time claiming compositional capacities. The temporality of the compositional process is foregrounded in the tensed verbs in "I've put down [. . .] or rather I will have done", albeit deictically anchored spatially, measured by the physical materiality of the text, 22 pages from the end. The use of "will" in "surely no reader will wish me to invent anything further" implies a deictic simultaneity between the reader's act of engaging with and processing the fiction and the pseudo-authorial narrator's act of creating it. That is, this deixis creates the illusory impression that the reader's 'now' at this juncture in the act of reading a text is the same as the pseudo-authorial narrator's 'now' at that point in his ongoing creation of the fiction, i.e. before its completion. This impression of the simultaneity of (pseudo-)authorial composition and readerly processing evokes the kind of discursive immediacy typical of the canonical situation-of-utterance, whilst at the same time highlighting the ontological impossibility of this immediacy (foregrounded by the references to writing and reading). This is just one example of the effects common to composition-related discourse deixis.

Discourse deixis relating to composition does not always come from a pseudo-authorial narrator. For example, in the same novel the protagonist Christie at one point states "there are too many exclamation marks in this novel already" (p. 166). Only the latter part of the sentence is discourse deictic, in the proximal demonstrative "this novel", and in the temporal "already" (implicitly meaning by this juncture in the progression of the novel). However, as with the previous example, the discourse deixis is intertwined with other non-deictic references related to the act of composition—here to the use of punctuation. Exclamation marks are graphological, part of the typed material discourse of the novel: he does not say "too many exclamations", but rather specifically comments on the graphological signalling of those exclamations. A character suggesting awareness of the material discourse and ongoing composition of the novel within which that same character has been invented is, again, (although differently) ontologically impossible, as will be discussed in Chapter 4. The discourse deixis here works with the other discourse-oriented references to draw attention to the fictionality of characters and the storyworld within which they exist, the materiality of the text, and the conventional ontological distinctions between the different levels of fiction (e.g. the authoring, the narrating, and the narrated), etc. The constructedness of realities, and the "semipermeable membranes" of the "ontological boundaries" between them (McHale, 1987, p. 34), are core thematic concerns of metafiction, which discourse deixis of this kind is regularly exploited to express.

Discourse deixis which relates to the act and process of narration can be hard to distinguish from that which relates to composition, particularly when narrators are donning pseudo-authorial guises. The following quote, from *The Life and Opinions of Tristram Shandy, Gentleman*, could be viewed as either:

> I am now beginning to get fairly into my work; and by the help of a vegetable diet [. . .] I make no doubt but I shall be able to go on with my uncle Toby's story, and my own, in a tolerable straight line.
> (Sterne (2003) [1757–1759], p. 425)

Here the temporally deictic 'now' foregrounds the deictic centre of the pseudo-authorial narrator specifically in relation to the act of composition and/or in the act of narration. Again, the "I", as pseudo-author, is foregrounded, and the authorship of the "work" is claimed with the deictic possessive "my". The distinction between composition and narration is clouded by the portrayal of the stories as purportedly biographical and autobiographical ("my uncle Toby's story, and my own"). While the narrator implicitly denies creative invention per se, the novel metafictionally thematises the choices made in selecting, arranging, and mediating a version of reality, and uses discourse deixis to do so.

Comments on the process of narration can also include comments on the conventions of that process. Take, for example, one of the quotes included in the epigraphs for this chapter:

> How the hell did you manage to pass from the level of the present to the level of the past? From outside to inside this very personal recitation? This doesn't make sense! Normally such transfers are not permitted. They go against the logic of traditional narrative techniques!
> (Federman, 1976, Chapter xvii [np])

(For a detailed analysis of this quote see Macrae, 2010.) In this extract, the narrator-protagonist is protesting against the intrusion of a new narrator in the storyworld, sent by a group of fictionalised readers who are dissatisfied with his narration. This is an example of metalepsis (introduced in Chapter 1 and discussed in much more detail in Chapter 4). This quote involves general and non-deictic references to aspects of the discourse situation, for example "the logic of traditional narrative techniques" whereby "such transfers are not permitted" (i.e. metaleptic transfers). These non-deictic references are combined with discourse deixis, such as the second-person address from a diegetic character to a fictional participant who was previously extradiegetic but is apparently now diegetic (hence direct address being possible). The realms described as "the level of the present" and "the level of the past", though referred to using definite referring expressions, are implicitly the levels of the present and past of this particular narrative. This becomes less implicit and more explicit through their syntactic parallelism with "from outside to inside this [. . .] recitation" in the next sentence. The latter is most explicitly discourse deictic, using spatial deixis to locate and foreground the narrator-protagonist's deictic centre within the storyworld, the extrafictional level being "outside" specifically relative to his position. Together the non-deictic and discourse deictic metafictional references foreground the conventional boundaries—the semipermeable membranes—between narrative levels and the conventional discourse relationships (or lack thereof) across them.

Lastly, there is discourse deixis which relates to the act and process of readerly imaginative conceptualisation. This type of discourse deixis is involved in the brief quote from Beckett's *The Unnamable*, mentioned earlier: "The slopes are gentle that meet where he lies, they flatten out under him, it is not a meeting, it is not a pit, that didn't take long, soon we'll have him perched on an eminence" (p. 330). This is discourse deictic in the anaphoric sense, whilst also relating to the processes of composition, narration, and readerly imaginative conceptualisation, and so it serves as a good example of how many discourse deictic references can function in several different ways at the same time. The deictic first-person plural pronoun "we" includes the reader, and attributes some of the seemingly collaborative creative agency to her. She is at least complicit in, if not co-responsible for, the dynamic realisation of the storyworld (in particular, here, the negation and reversal of the "pit" and the "meeting slopes"). The backward-looking "that didn't take long" and forward-looking "soon" temporally situate the pseudo-authorial narrator and reader, seemingly simultaneously, relative to the chronological progression of the co-creative act. The narration reverses the description of the storyworld. This foregrounds the paradoxes within the relationship between the ongoing text and the act of conceptualisation. The progressing text may negate a detail, but that detail cannot be 'un-imagined': the imaginative conceptualisation is irreversible and ongoing (as is discussed in Chapter 5). The discourse deixis here works to highlight the reader's constructive agency in bringing the storyworld into being (cf. Ingarden, 1973).

In metafiction, the reader's deictic centre, in the act of processing the text and conceptualising the storyworld, is often foregrounded relative to material, spatial, and temporal dimensions of these acts, examples of which have been described earlier. The interpersonal dimension is often inherent within this metafictional foregrounding, and is usually involved through the use of person deixis employed within discourse deixis. The reader can be referred to and/or addressed with definite referring expressions, as in the first quote in this chapter's epigraphs: "*Note to Reader before proceeding further*: Before proceeding further, the Reader is respectfully advised to refer to the Synopsis or Summary of the Argument on Page 60" (O'Brien, 1939, p. 103). This quote comes from Flann O'Brien's metafictional novel *At Swim-two-birds*. The first words prior to the colon function as cataphoric textual signposting (effectively, 'the immediately following words are a note to the reader'), involving implicit temporal and spatial deixis in "before proceeding further" (i.e. further than this point in the your reading of the text). The words "the Synopsis or Summary of the Argument on Page 60" involve an anaphoric deictic reference to the propositional content of a previous section, and reference to the physical text. Just as "Page 60" here is implicitly 'page 60 of *this book*', so too "the Reader" is 'the reader of *this book*'. The definite referring expression functions as both impersonal reference and indirect address, at once somewhat alienating and anonymising but also engaging; specifically, engaging the reader in a thereby foregrounded communicative act, the written textual nature of the communicative discourse albeit simultaneously foregrounded.

More often, metafiction involves and locates the reader through more personal reference, and/or implicitly direct address, such as 'Dear reader' or 'You'. As mentioned earlier, the quote from Beckett uses the first-person plural pronoun 'we' to deictically align the pseudo-authorial narrator and reader. A quote from Barth's *The Floating Opera* offers an example of second-person address:

> come along with me, reader, and don't fear for your weak heart; I've one myself, and know the value of inserting first a toe, then a foot, next a leg, very slowly your hips and stomach, and finally your whole self into my story, and taking a good long time to do it. This is, after all, a pleasure-dip I'm inviting you to, not a baptism.
>
> (1968 [1956], p. 3)

The scales of personalisation and implicit directness involved in these kinds of reader address are explored in discussions of metanarration in Chapter 3 and metaleptic address in Chapter 4, along with their variable effects of illusory intimacy, immersion, and/or alienation. At the heart of their functioning, though, is their foregrounding of the position of the reader as a discourse participant, the 'you' of the pseudo-authorial narrator's 'I' in the discursive relationship.

We can talk about the reader's deictic centre in several ways, then: her 'actual' deictic centre in the spatio-temporal context in which she is reading the fiction, her 'textual' deictic centre moving through the physical material text, and her 'conceptually projected' deictic centre moving through the imaginative conceptualisation of the content of the physical material text. The reader 'projects' her deictic centre in processing and resolving deictic cues anchored to the deictic centres of other, fictional discourse participants. These include, for example, a pseudo-authorial narrator's 'I' within narration, and characters' deictic centres, such as

Federman's protagonist's, positioned 'inside', relative to the 'outside' of the storyworld, etc. Both the actual and textual deictic centres are ontologically 'real', whereas the conceptual deictic centre is an imaginatively constructed locus. Arguably, the reader may be projecting to the imagined position of the narratee in engaging with direct address such as 'dear reader' and 'you' (as discussed in Chapter 4, section 4.3; for more on which see Macrae, 2012), but the effect of second-person address in foregrounding the reader's deictic centre and processual act is the same irrespective of this issue. Cognitive theory of deixis is making progress in discerning these conceptual operations (cf. Duchan, Bruder, and Hewitt, 1995; McIntyre, 2006; Stockwell, 2002, 2009). It is hoped that the account presented in this book can strengthen, enrich, and further clarify the background for some of that work while stopping short of directly engaging with those ongoing cognitive poetic debates.

A broader view of discourse deixis than that which is presented here can be found in Green (1995), Stockwell (2002), and Macrae (2010). In Stockwell, for example, discourse deixis includes "word-choice, syntax and register" which serve to "anchor [the text] in a literary tradition, which inevitably is located in relation to other literary works" (2002, p. 45). Stockwell argues that "epigrams, paragraphing, and other graphology all encode textual deixis, by drawing attention to the evidence for an authorial arrangement", while "generic or proverbial sentences draw attention to themselves as textual constructs", and "external presentational factors (such as the book cover)" and "any register selections that index a literary convention (such as a fourteen-line sonnet, a cast list at the head of a play [text], or the dedication of a novel, for example)" also "have a deictic dimension" (2002, pp. 54–55). For Green, discourse deixis includes what he calls "syntactic deixis", which is the label he gives to grammatical forms such as interrogatives and imperatives that signal the communicative participation of the addressee (1995, p. 22). The chief difference between the account of discourse deixis presented in this chapter and that which is presented in the likes of Green (1995) and Stockwell (2002) is that they do not seem to wholly align with the criteria outlined earlier: i) deictic reference is anchored to a perceptual origo, and in turn, ii) interpretation of deictic terms depends upon the addressee relating the deictic terms to one or more dimensions of the context of the utterance (e.g. spatial, temporal, person (i.e. participant relations)). As part of its creation of metafictional effects, discourse deixis as defined in the present account does, though, as stated, often interact and co-occur with the kinds of language and textual features Stockwell describes.

The three cases of discourse deixis delineated in this section are discourse deictic reference to the physical text (e.g. a portion of discourse, the sequential arrangement, and the reader's movement through it, etc.); discourse deictic reference to the propositional content of a preceding, immediate, or subsequent portion of discourse; and discourse deictic reference to the act and process of creation of the storyworld. As has been seen, they engage with and foreground the reader's deictic centres in different ways. Likewise, they can be employed across different types of metafictionality. As we turn from focusing on developing a coherent account of discourse deixis to more concentratedly focusing on how discourse deixis is used in metafiction, a clearer delineation of these types of metafictionality is useful. The preceding discussion can be roughly mapped onto the following categorisation (adapted from Macrae, 2010):

- the metatextual (related to the material, physical text and its sequentiality, etc.)
- the metacompositional (related to the writing process and imaginative invention of the story)
- the metadiegetic (related to the storyworld, its ontological status and its creation)
- the metanarrative (related to the process of narration)
- the metadiscursive (related to the discourse context, the discursive relationship between the reader and pseudo-authorial narrator, etc.)

Chapter 3 expands on these types and illustrates how discourse deixis is used across them in the service of metanarration, specifically, while Chapters 4 and 5 demonstrate, respectively, how discourse deixis is used to create the effects of metalepsis and disnarration.

2.6 Conclusion

This chapter has provided an overview of deixis in general and has outlined a definition of the characteristics of deixis. On the basis of this definition, the chapter has worked through some of the theoretical sticking points involved in deictic theory of discourse deixis, focusing in particular on the context of written literature, to offer a systematic and detailed account of what discourse deixis is and how it works. This account serves as a platform for the three central chapters of this book which illustrate how discourse deixis works in metafiction.

References

Barth, J. (1968) [1956]. *The Floating Opera*. London: Secker & Warburg.

Barth, J. (1988) [1968]. *Lost in the Funhouse: Fiction for Print, Tape, Live Voice*. New York: Doubleday.

Beckett, S. (1979) [1959/3]. "The Unnamable". In *The Beckett Trilogy*. London: Pan Books. 293–418.

Benveniste, E. (1971) [1966]. *Problems in General Linguistics*. Trans. M. E. Meek. Coral Gables: University of Miami Press.

Brown, G. and Yule, G. (1983). *Discourse Analysis*. Cambridge: Cambridge University Press.

Bühler, K. (1934). *Sprachtheorie: Die Darstellungfunktion der Sprache*. Jena: Gustav Fischer.

Bühler, K. (1982). "The deictic field of language and deictic worlds". In *Speech, Place and Action: Studies in Deixis and Related Topics*. Eds. R. J. Jarvella and W. Klein. Chichester: John Wiley. 9–30.

Bühler, K. (2011). *Theory of Language: The Representational Function of Language*. Trans. D. E. Goodwin. Amsterdam and Philadelphia: John Benjamins.

Burks, A. (1948). "Icon, index and symbol". *Philosophical and Phenomeno-Logical Research* 9. 673–689.

Duchan, J. F., Bruder, G. A. and Hewitt, L. E. (Eds.). (1995). *Deixis in Narrative: A Cognitive Scientific Perspective*. Hillsdale, NJ: Lawrence Erlbaum Associates.

Ehlich, K. (1979). *Verwendungender Deixis beim Sprachlichen Handeln: Linguisticisch-philosophische Untersuchungen zum Hebräischen Deictischen System*. Frankfurt am Main: Peter Lang.

Ehlich, K. (1982). "Anaphora and deixis: Same, similar, or different?" In *Speech, Place and Action: Studies in Deixis and Related Topics*. Eds. R. J. Jarvella and W. Klein. Chichester: John Wiley. 315–338.

Ehlich, K. (1983). "Deixis und anapher". In *Essays on Deixis*. Ed. G. Rauh. Tubingen: Gunter Narr Verlag. 79–98.

Emmott, C. (1997). *Narrative Comprehension: A Discourse Perspective*. Oxford: Clarendon Press.

Federman, R. (1976). *Take It or Leave It: An Exaggerated Second-Hand Tale to Be Read Aloud Either Standing or Sitting*. New York: Fiction Collective.

Fillmore, C. (1982). "Towards a descriptive framework for spatial deixis". In *Speech, Place and Action: Studies in Deixis and Related Topics*. Eds. R. Jarvella and W. Klein. Chichester: John Wiley. 31–59.

Fludernik, M. (1991). "Shifters and deixis: Some reflections on Jakobson, Jespersen, and reference". *Semiotica* 86.3–4. 193–230.

Fowler, R. (1986). *Linguistic Criticism*. Oxford: Oxford University Press.

Fowles, J. (1996) [1969]. *The French Lieutenant's Woman*. London: Vintage.

Frawley, W. (1992). *Linguistic Semantics*. Hillsdale, NJ: Lawrence Erlbaum Associates.

Genette, G. (1997). *Paratexts. Thresholds of Interpretation*. Trans. J. E. Lewin. Cambridge: Cambridge University Press.

Green, K. (1992). "Deixis and the poetic persona". *Language and Literature* 1.2. 121–134.

Green, K. (1995). "Deixis: A revaluation of concepts and categories". In *New Essays in Deixis: Discourse, Narrative, Literature*. Ed. K. Green. Amsterdam: Rodopi. 11–25.

Hankamer, J. and Sag, I. (1977). "Syntactically versus pragmatically controlled anaphora". In *Studies in Language Variation*. Eds. R. W. Fasold and R. W. Shuy. Washington, DC: Georgetown University Press. 120–135.

Hanks, W. F. (1990). *Referential Practice: Language and Lived Space Among the Maya*. Chicago, IL: University of Chicago Press.

Hanks, W. F. (2009). "Fieldwork on deixis". *Journal of Pragmatics* 41.1. 10–24.

Herman, D. (2001). "Spatial reference in narrative domains". *Text* 21.4. 515–541.

Herman, D. (2002). *Story Logic: Problems and Possibilities of Narrative*. Lincoln, NE: University of Nebraska Press.

Ingarden, R. (1973). *The Literary Work of Art: An Investigation on the Borderlines of Ontology, Logic and Theory of Literature*. Trans. G. Grabowics. Evanston, IL: Northwestern University Press.

Jakobson, R. (1960). "Closing statement: Linguistics and poetics". In *Style in Language*. Ed. T. A. Seboek. Cambridge, MA: MIT Press. 350–377.

Johnson, B. S. (2001) [1973]. *Christie Malry's Own Double-Entry*. London: Picador.

Jungbluth, K. and Da Milano, F. (2015). *Manual of Deixis in Romance Languages*. Berlin: De Gruyter.

Landau, B. and Jackendoff, R. (1993). "'What' and 'where' in spatial language and cognition". *Behavioural and Brain Sciences* 16. 217–265.

Langacker, R. W. (2008). *Cognitive Grammar: A Basic Introduction*. Oxford: Oxford University Press.

Levinson, S. C. (1983). *Pragmatics*. Cambridge: Cambridge University Press.

Levinson, S. C. (2004). "Deixis". In *The Handbook of Pragmatics*. Ed. L. Horn. Oxford: Blackwell. 97–121.

Lyons, J. (1977). *Semantics. Vols 1 and 2*. Cambridge: Cambridge University Press.

Macrae, A. (2010). "Enhancing the critical apparatus for understanding metanarration: Discourse deixis refined". *Journal of Literary Semantics* 39.2. 119–142.

Macrae, A. (2012). "Readerly deictic shifting to and through *I* and *You*: An updated hypothesis". In *Texts and Minds: Papers in Cognitive Poetics and Rhetoric*. Ed. A. Kwiatkowska. Frankfurt am Main: Peter Lang. 41–56.

Macrae, A. (forthcoming). "Social deixis in fiction". In *Stylistic Manipulation of the Reader in Contemporary Literature*. Ed. S. Sorlin. London: Bloomsbury.

McHale, B. (1987). *Postmodernist Fiction*. London: Routledge.

McIntyre, D. (2006). *Point of View in Plays*. Amsterdam: John Benjamins.

O'Brien, F. (1939). *At Swim-two-birds*. New York: Plume.

Peirce, C. S. (1955). *Philosophical Writings of Peirce*. Ed. J. Buchler. New York: Dover.

Rauh, G. (1983a). "Aspects of deixis". In *Essays on Deixis*. Ed. G. Rauh. Tubingen: Gunter Narr Verlag. 9–60.

Rauh, G. (Ed.). (1983b). *Essays on Deixis*. Tubingen: Gunter Narr Verlag.

Ryan, M-L. (2001). *Narrative as Virtual Reality: Immersion and Interactivity in Literature and Electronic Media*. Baltimore, MD: Johns Hopkins University Press.

Semino, E. (1997). *Language and World Creation in Poems and Other Texts*. London: Longman.

Sterne, L. (2003) [1759–1767]. *The Life and Opinions of Tristram Shandy, Gentleman*. London: Penguin Books.

Stockwell, P. (2002). *Cognitive Poetics: An Introduction*. London: Routledge.

Talmy, L. (2000). *Toward a Cognitive Semantics. Vols 1 and 2*. Cambridge, MA: MIT Press.

Thorne, J. P. (1972). "On the notion of definite". *Foundations of Language* 8.4. 562–268.

3   Discourse Deixis in
       Metanarration

Some worlds are made of atoms but yours is made of tiny marks marching in neat lines, like armies of insects, across pages and pages and pages of white paper.

(Gray, 1981, p. 485)

These people aren't real. I'm making them up as they go along, any section that threatens to flesh them out, or make them 'walk off the page', will be excised. They should, rather, walk into the page, and break up, disappear.

(Sorrentino, 1971, p. 27)

Metanarration, as introduced in Chapter 1, is commentary within fictional discourse on an aspect of the "composition, constitution and/ or communication" of that narrative (Macrae, 2010, p. 119). Because of the breadth of aspects of fictional narrative discourse that metanarration can focus upon, and because metanarration often occurs within or alongside other metafictional techniques such as metalepsis and disnarration, metanarration can be quite difficult to distinguish. Discussions of metanarration have often been subsumed within more general discussions of metafictionality (Nünning, 2005, p. 11). The most significant contributions to narratological understanding of metanarration in fiction are the studies by Fludernik (2003a), Genette (1980), Nünning (2005), Prince (1995 [1982]), and Wolf (2009). Much of this work is oriented towards the creation of typologies based on different sets of priorities or principles of categorisation. However, even within these valuable contributions, there is an absence of close analysis of *how* metanarration works (as noted by Fludernik, 2003a, pp. 30–31), and in particular a lack of attention to the formal linguistic features of metanarration. Both Fludernik (2003a, p. 23) and Nünning (2005, p. 42) perceive deictic elements within the constitution of metanarration, but neither develop these observations. In this chapter, section 3.1 outlines the prior insights presented by these scholars, and draws on

Fludernik (2003a), Nünning (2005), and Wolf (2009) in particular to create a framework into which discourse deictic theory can be added to facilitate a linguistic investigation of metanarration (adapting and developing Macrae, 2010). This framework breaks metanarration down into types following the categories of metafictionality which were first introduced at the end of Chapter 2: the metatextual, the metacompositional, the metadiegetic, the metanarrative, and the metadiscursive. Sections 3.2, 3.3, 3.4, 3.5, and 3.6 explore each in turn, analysing a selection of examples of metanarration dominated by each type taken from Barth, Brophy, Coover, Fowles, Johnson, and Katz, and drawing out the workings of discourse deixis within them.

3.1 Defining Metanarration

In *A Dictionary of Narratology*, Prince defines metanarration as narration

> about narrative; describing narrative. A narrative having (a) narrative as (one of) its topic(s) is (a) metanarrative. More specifically, a narrative referring to itself and to those elements by which it is constituted and communicated, a narrative discussing itself, a self-reflexive narrative, is metanarrative. Even more specifically, the passages or units in a narrative that refer explicitly to the codes or subcodes in terms of which the narrative signifies are metanarrative and constitute metanarrative signs.
>
> (1987, pp. 50–51)

The codes or subcodes Prince is referring to here are clarified, in his later work, as the linguistic, proairetic, hermeneutic, and socio-cultural codes which frame narrative and in relation to which readers infer meaning (1995 [1982]). Prince is here drawing on and adapting Barthes's codes as outlined in *S/Z* (1973), which are in turn a reconsideration of Jakobson's functions (Jakobson, 1960). Though Prince's discussion of examples of metanarration prove these codes difficult to delineate in practice, his basic definition of metanarration is a useful starting point.

Genette's model of metanarration also draws on a reworking of Jakobson's functions. Genette proposes five "extranarrative functions", that is, functions which go beyond the act of telling to reflect on that act (1980, pp. 255–259). Genette restricts all but one of these five functions to expression by the narrator. The "narrative function" relates to the narrator's act of telling the story (p. 255). The "directing function" is performed through narratorial references to the internal structure of the text (p. 255). The "function of communication" relates to the narrative communication from narrator to narratee (and correlates most closely to Jakobson's phatic and conative functions) (pp. 255–256). The "testimonial function" is enacted through the narrator's expression of attitude (intellectual, affective, etc.) towards her/himself and towards the story she/he is telling (echoing Jakobson's emotive function) (p. 256). Lastly, and relatedly, the "ideological function" is the narrator's voicing of an ideological stance towards the story (pp. 256–257). This last function is the only one which Genette feels can be performed by a character as well as by a narrator.

Nünning (2005) offers a slightly different appropriation of Jakobson's functions, drawing a parallel between metanarration which focuses on the speaker and Jakobson's expressive function, a parallel between metanarration which focuses on the channel of communication and Jakobson's phatic function, and another parallel between metanarration which focuses on the reader and Jakobson's appellative function (pp. 30–31). All three foci and functions are subsumed under Nünning's concept of discourse-oriented metanarration, which he contrasts with story-oriented metanarration. However, this is just one of 18 contrasting sets (predominantly pairs) which comprise his comprehensive suite of types of metanarration.

Nünning's 18 types of metanarration are organised into four categories, the first of which is dedicated to forms of metanarration. Within this category, Nünning starts by distinguishing metanarration according to the narrative level at which the metanarration is expressed (e.g. a character voicing a metanarrative comment from within the diegesis vs. a third-person narrator doing so from the extradiegesis). Nünning includes a "paratextual level" for metanarrative comments within chapter titles and the like, which, even in the context of novels with pseudo-authorial narrators, he attributes specifically to "a fictive editor" (p. 23). Continuing his categorising of forms, he also considers whether the metanarration is internal to one narrative level or is metaleptic, whether the metanarration is explicit or implicit, and whether it is metaphoric or non-metaphoric (pp. 35–36). Nünning includes explicit address of the reader as an example of implicit metanarration in cases in which it "render[s] obvious the process of narration [. . .] in an indirect way" (p. 24).

Within Nünning's second category, "structural types", he distinguishes types according to the "qualitative and quantitative relationship" between the "metanarrative and non-metanarrative parts of the text" and the degree to which and manner in which the metanarration is integrated into the text as a whole. Within this category he distinguishes between "marginal" and "central" metanarration; "punctual" and "extensive" metanarration; "integrated" and "isolated" metanarration; the relative contextual plausibility or relevance of the metanarration (that is, relevance to and/or connection with recent or immediately following plot events); and whether or not the metanarration constitutes a substantial digression from the narration (closely related to the punctual vs. extensive type) (pp. 36–37). Nünning extends this last type to include "metadigressive metanarration", in which the digressive quality of the metanarration becomes the subject of the metanarration (offering an illustrative example from *Tristram Shandy*) (p. 28).

Nünning's third category is the largest. This category follows Genette's system in differentiating types according to the focus of the metanarration, though Nünning's "object[s] of metanarrative comments" are slightly more abstract than Genette's (p. 37). Nünning distinguishes metanarrative comments according to their scope, in terms of the breadth and depth of the comment's discussion of narrative, and also in terms of whether they relate to "the author's own narrative practice, other authors' peculiarities, or storytelling in general" (p. 37). He also delineates metanarrative comments according to whether they refer to the story or the discourse (this being the type mentioned earlier) and identifies discourse-oriented metanarration as focusing on the speaker, the channel of communication, or the reader. He differentiates further types according to whether or not they characterise the narrative as "belonging to a genre or text type", whether they are positive or negative about the narrator's "narrative competence", and whether the metanarrative comment expresses a critical assessment of conventional narrative forms or is "non-critical" (pp. 37–38).

Nünning bases his fourth and final category on a differentiation of the potential effects of metanarrative commentary. His first type within this set contrasts metanarrative comments which "evoke the impression of a speaking voice" and a "schema of an oral communication situation" with metanarrative reference to the narration as "written communication", including reference to the material aspects of writing or of written texts (p. 33). His second type within this category compares metanarrative comments which encourage the reader to empathise with characters and those which distance readers from the storyworld. Lastly, he compares the relative illusion-affirming or illusion-disturbing (i.e. antimimetic) nature of the metanarration (p. 39).

Nünning's fourth category is explicitly focused on effects, while his second is focused on the relationship between the instance of metanarration and its co-text. Within his first category, two of the types relate to the ontological position from which the metanarration is voiced (cf. Wolf's story- vs. discourse-transmitted metafiction, 1993, pp. 234–239), while the other two types both essentially relate to the relative explicit or implicit quality of the metanarration. The first and second categories therefore seem to describe (potentially co-occurring) features of metanarration rather than distinct types as such (cf. Wolf, 2009, pp. 36–37, n. 42). The third category, distinguishing metanarration according to the particular aspect of the narrative discourse that it focuses upon, seems to offer the strongest potential for drawing clear distinctions between types as a basis for analysis.

Fludernik (2003a) builds on an earlier version of Nünning's typology and also early work by Wolf, and presents a model which delineates the relationships between metafiction, metanarration, and metalepsis. Within her model, she identifies four different types of metanarrative comments. "Metacompositional" metanarrative comments "touch on" the "plot level" of the fiction (p. 27). These are comments "relating to plot construction, or the temporal relation between story and discourse" and what Fludernik calls "the problem of representation". Fludernik also includes chapter titles and prefaces within this type if they involve metanarrative comment (p. 30), though these are only considered implicitly metanarrative as Fludernik feels they are issued by the author rather than a narrator or editor, and for Fludernik only narratorial comments can be metanarrative (p. 22).

Fludernik's further three types of metanarrative comment all "touch on" the "discourse and narration levels" (p. 27). Fludernik defines as "metadiscursive" any comments which involve "references to the articulative level of the discourse". She explicitly paraphrases such references as "the narrational text-deixis" (p. 30). She includes within this type expressions which refer to "the writing process and the textual ordering" (p. 24). The "meta-aesthetic" type is described as narratorial comments on "generic peculiarities, the reader's response to the text, production-related issues, politeness and authorial intention" (pp. 29–30). Finally, Fludernik's "metanarrational" metanarrative comments are "statements addressing the narrational process and its participants", those which refer to "the utterances and disquisitions of the narrator, to the role of the narratee", and "to the narrational process" (pp. 29–30).

Fludernik's terminology is helpfully specific, though there seem to be some areas of ambiguity. For example, "production-related issues" are considered "meta-aesthetic", and yet references to "the writing process", which seem to be related, are "metadiscursive". Fludernik and Nünning both work with a distinction between the level of the story and the level of narration/discourse, but their identification and distribution of strategies in relation to these levels is different. Additionally, characters' comments on the narrative process cannot be accommodated by Fludernik's model due to her assertion that all metanarrative comments are voiced by the narrator, even if the metanarrative comment "touch[es] on" the "plot level" (to touch on does not mean to originate from, after all). For Fludernik, metanarrative strategies "exclude those outside narratorial language" (p. 28).

Wolf (2009) presents a model of metareference, labelled as such and with sufficient scope in order to accommodate metafiction and its equivalents in non-textual and non-literary media. This work is a development of his earlier work on metafiction specifically (1993), which informs the typologies by Fludernik (2003a) and Nünning (2005). Though the focus of Wolf's later model is much broader than metanarration, its criteria are in many ways applicable to metanarration specifically.

Wolf proposes four pairs of forms. The first pair is metareference which discusses the work within which that metareference is expressed and metareference which is more general, for example "parodies" and "general reflections on the beginnings and endings of novels" (p. 39). He terms these types "intracompositional/direct" and "extracompositional/indirect" (p. 37), respectively, and suggests that the latter is "usually perceived as a 'weaker' form of metareference" (p. 39). The second pairing is "explicit vs. implicit metareference" (p. 37). Explicit metareference involves clear and direct reference to aspects of narration. As examples, Wolf suggests use of phrases such as " 'reader', 'pen', 'beginning' or 'good book' " which he describes as "metareferential phrases" (p. 40). Implicit reference involves "covert devices" such as "deviating" typography which foregrounds and "impl[ies] a comment on, and an awareness of, the medial conventions" (p. 40). His third pairing is the only one which "uses the *content* of the metareflection as its criterion of differentiation" (p. 41, italics in the original), as in Genette's model, much of Fludernik's model, and Nünning's third category. In this pairing Wolf contrasts metareference which refers to the "shaping" or "formation" of the work and metareference which refers to the work's relative fictionality or truthfulness (p. 41). Wolf's final pairing differentiates between metareference which exposes the artificial, constructed nature of the work and disrupts any illusion of mimesis, and metareference which does not disrupt this illusion or related immersion (p. 43), thereby, like Nünning's fourth category, focusing on effects.

In discussing use of the words "reader" and "pen" as examples of explicit metareference within his second pairing, Wolf is referring to their use within a passage he quotes from George Eliot:

> With a single drop of ink for a mirror, the Egyptian sorcerer undertakes to reveal to any chance comer far-reaching visions of the past. This is what I undertake to do for you, reader. With this drop of ink at the end of my pen, I will show you the roomy workshop of Mr Jonathan Burge.
>
> *(Adam Bede, 2008 [1858], p. 1)*

The first sentence of this quote is an example of Nünning's metaphoric and implicit types of metanarration, and Wolf's extracompositional/indirect, general type, albeit an example which relates to the presentation of something as truthful (a mirror reflecting the real past) rather than a fictional creation. The passage becomes intracompositionally and explicitly metanarrative in the next two sentences, but not simply through use of the words "reader" and "pen", as Wolf suggests. Rather, the phrase "you, reader" involves the person deictic "you", which has a discourse deictic function in foregrounding the reader's deictic centre as addressee (and, indirectly, the deictic centre of the narrator in their pseudo-authorial role, the "I" from whose perspective the reader is "you"). The deictic "you" in the phrase "you, reader" also clarifies the referential value of "reader" as a deictic term of address, directed at that "you", and refers to the reader's discursive role *as* reader. This additionally foregrounds the writtenness of the communication (as per Nünning's fourth category), which is further foregrounded in other ways. The deictic "my" in the phrase "my pen" gives this phrase discourse deictic value and further foregrounds the narrator's deictic centre and pseudo-authorial role (along with the two other first-person pronouns across the two sentences).

Added to this, the narrator refers to "this drop of ink". The demonstrative pronoun "this" conventionally (though not always) suggests the referent is proximal and recognisable to the addressee. The most logical inference is that "this drop of ink" refers to the ink in the form of the visible words on the page that it has been supposedly used to create. This foregrounds the narrator's authorial guise, the creative process, and the constructedness of the work (an aspect of Nünning's third category, Fludernik's metacompositional type, and Wolf's third pairing). This also backgrounds the real printing production process, potentially heightening a sense of one-to-one, intimate communication. It is specifically "with this drop of ink" that the pseudo-authorial narrator "undertakes" to "reveal" the "past" and "show" the reader the workshop, which foregrounds the medium and constructedness of the fiction while nonetheless presenting it as the historically real past, hence Wolf's categorisation of this quote as not disrupting the mimetic illusion (p. 38). It is the discourse deixis in these phrases which takes the nouns "reader" and "pen" beyond references associated with fiction in general to reference to the reader of this fiction and to the creation of this fiction, specifically, and which makes the passage as a whole explicit and intracompositional metanarration.

This quote reveals three important points. Firstly, it confirms that, as Wolf points out, several types of metanarration can occur within one instance of metanarration (2009, p. 38). The quotes explored in the rest of this chapter are categorised by type according to which aspect dominates their metanarrativity, but with the caveat that other kinds of metanarrativity are often involved.

Secondly, this quote is illustrative of a pattern in which general, extracompositional, indirect metanarration can be followed by intracompositional, direct metanarration, the latter serving to make clearer the relevance of the general metanarration to the current text. An analogous pattern occurs with implicit and explicit metanarration. Fludernik includes within her typology of metafiction a category of "non-narrational self-reflexivity" which "consists of *mise-en-abyme* (a story within the story, with themes which echo those of the embedding narrative), visual paratextual elements such as illustrations or typographic arrangements echoing the tale", etc. (2003a, p. 29). Notably, Fludernik excludes this category from metanarration, potentially as it need not be narrative, but potentially because of its implicit rather than explicit metanarrative value: she points out that it corresponds to Wolf's "implicit" type within his second pairing (with which Nünning's implicit and metaphoric types, within his first category, both overlap). For Wolf, implicit metanarration includes, for example, the reduction of one chapter to one short sentence in *Tristram Shandy*, and typographic deviance (2009, p. 40). Katz's *The Exagggerations of Peter Prince* (2017 [1968]) contains diagrams, images of posters, and overlapping and criss-crossing text, though much less radical kinds of typographic deviance can have similar effects. Worthington discusses the use of italics in 'Lost in the Funhouse', for example, which also contains a short general metanarrative discussion of the semiotic value of italics. Worthington argues that the implicit metanarrative meaning lies in the fact that the

> digression from the story to a discussion of the use and meaning of italics calls attention simultaneously to the fact that the book is a piece of printed material and to the fact that the narrative itself is also a construction where certain words are emphasized, certain parts considered more noteworthy than others.
>
> (2001, p. 125)

Wolf proposes that implicit metanarration chiefly draws attention to aspects of the discourse, such as its medium, predominantly having a solely indirect "foregrounding" function (2009, p. 40). Stonehill's typology of metafictional techniques includes many elements which fall into this implicit, foregrounding category, including "the intentionally unconvincing rendering of a character and action" and "grotesque or comical [character] names", both of which are arguably manifest in "the Shrike" (the protagonist's girlfriend) in Johnson's *Christie Malry's Own Double-Entry* (2001 [1973]). Stonehill also includes "use of polysemous language, including puns, anagrams, and palindromes", which feature throughout Brophy's *In Transit* (2002 [1969]), and other "incongruities of style" (Stonehill, 1988, pp. 30–31), such as Johnson's occasional inclusion of rare and/or archaic words (e.g. "trituration", "helminthoid", and "eirenicon" on page 42 alone). Intertextuality could be added to this list, of which there are many examples in Fowles (chiefly in his epigraphs) and Brophy (in more covert forms). Wolf argues that, as a consequence of the implicit quality of this kind of metanarration, "markers are requisite in order to ensure a metareferential reception"—that is, to ensure that the reader infers metareferential meaning—and Wolf includes within these markers "the supplementary employment of explicit metareference in framing paratexts or in the vicinity of implicit elements" (pp. 40–41). This pattern of explicit markers nearby implicit metanarration, to signal its metanarrative quality, parallels the pattern we see in Eliot of direct, intracompositional metanarration nearby indirect, general metanarration, to signal its direct relevance.

Thirdly, the quote from Eliot demonstrates the significance of discourse deixis within metanarration, and the discussion of this quote reveals some of the ways in which close attention to discourse deixis within metanarrative extracts can help to explain precisely how those lines are functioning as metanarrative. To recap, discourse deixis, as outlined in the previous chapter, co-opts person, spatial, and temporal deixis in its service to refer to the discourse participants in the context of their roles (as pseudo-authorial narrators, readers, etc.), to demarcate the boundaries of the ontological levels within the fiction (the storyworld, the extradiegesis), to refer to the moment in which the pseudo-authorial narrator is purportedly creating the fiction, and so on. Discourse deixis can refer to the physical text; to the propositional content of a preceding, immediate (i.e. current), or subsequent portion of discourse; and to the act and process of creation of the storyworld. All of these kinds of discourse deictic reference can engage with and foreground the reader's deictic centre relative to material, conceptual, and spatio-temporal dimensions. That is, discourse deixis can draw on the reader's textual deictic centre in moving through the physical text-continuum, her conceptual projected deictic centre moving through the imaginative conceptualisation of the text, and her actual deictic centre within the real spatio-temporal context in which she is reading the fiction. Discourse deixis can appeal to and foreground the deictic centres of pseudo-authorial narrators and characters relative to analogous dimensions: for example, their loci within the text-continuum, their position within the conceptualised worlds, a pseudo-authorial narrator's spatio-temporal context within which she/he is (presented as) creating the fiction, etc. Each of these dimensions is prevalent in metanarration. The discussion of the quote from Eliot illustrates the role of discourse deixis in explicit markers of metanarrativity, and also demonstrates the ways that discourse deixis helps general, implicit metanarration "acquire a clearly metafictional emphasis" (Fludernik, 2003a, p. 26) and gain text-specific (intracompositional) metanarrative value. Discourse deixis is heavily involved in the workings of explicit metanarration, and yet discourse deixis is very rarely included in discussion of the technique. Two exceptions are Fludernik's mention of "text-deixis", referred to earlier, and Nünning's brief point that foregrounding the "temporal and local deictic situatedness of the act of narration" can work to thematise the act of narration (2005, p. 42).

The rest of this chapter explores discourse deixis in some examples of metanarration from Barth, Brophy, Coover, Fowles, Johnson, and Katz. The examples selected for discussion are indicative of the kinds of metanarration that appear in this mini corpus, but the discussion itself is in no way comprehensive—nor could it be, given the ubiquity of metanarration throughout some of these texts. The typology offered in this chapter appropriates, and occasionally slightly reorients, some of the precise terminology introduced by Nünning and Fludernik, while chiefly adopting the organising principle underlying Genette's and Fludernik's models, Nünning's third category, and Wolf's third pairing: types of metanarration are distinguished according to the dominant focus or object of the metanarrative comment. Several categories in the typology are closely related, and many examples of metanarration involve multiple metanarrative features and foci. The categories nonetheless offer a useful heuristic through which to investigate the different functions and forms of metanarration. They are drawn along the same lines as the types of metafictionality outlined in Chapter 2, but narrowed to focus on metanarrative elements. These categories are the metatextual, the metacompositional, the metadiegetic, the metanarrative, and the metadiscursive.

3.2 Metatextual Metanarration

Metatextual metanarration is narration which focuses predominantly on the textual medium of the narrative. It involves references to the sequential, material, physical text, and to the textual nature of the communication (the writtenness of the narration). For example, this might include references to print, ink, typing, pages, the book form, etc. Metatextual metanarration often highlights the relationship between the sequential, printed text-continuum and the development of the plot and characterisation, via the reader's progress through the text and her consequent text-directed, dynamic conceptual realisation of the storyworld. One example of metatextual metanarration, from *Christie Malry's Own Double-Entry*, is the narrator's comment "Headlam paused to provide a paragraph break for resting the reader's eye in what might otherwise have been a daunting mass of type" (Johnson, 2001 [1973], p. 100). Headlam, a storyworld character, is presented as being aware of the reader (and thereby implicitly conscious of the written nature of the discourse and of the discourse context) and also aware of the way in which the narration is being graphologically arranged on the page. The reference to "the reader" here is logically a reference to the reader of this fiction. He is 'paus[ing]', in his speech to the protagonist, aware that this speech is being relayed to the reader in printed "type". His pause is therefore implicitly anchored both to his temporal locus within the chronology of the storyworld and also to his and the reader's textual deictic centres relative to the text-continuum.

A character's consciousness of the discourse context and the physical form of the text is a form of metaleptic awareness, discussed in Chapter 4. Similar metaleptic awareness is involved in a more well-known example from Barth, in which discourse deixis plays a much more overt role. The metaleptic implications of this quote and the paragraphs in which it occurs are addressed in Chapter 4, section 4.3, but the inherent metatextual metanarration involved warrants discussion here. Towards the end of the tale 'Life-Story', a paragraph opens with "The reader! You, dogged, uninsultable, print-oriented bastard, it's you I'm addressing, who else, from inside this monstrous fiction. You've read me this far, then? Even this far?" (1998 [1968], p. 127). These four sentences have been discussed by a range of critics with regards to their metafictional effects (e.g. McHale, 1992, p. 94; Phelan, 1989, p. 108), in particular with reference to their postmodern foregrounding of the reading context (Ruthrof, 1981, p. 30) and their engagement and/or alienation of the reader (Hutcheon, 1984 [1980], p. 151; Kacandes, 2001, p. 184; McHale, 1987, p. 225). Analysis of the discourse deixis within the lines adds to this scholarship by elucidating how some of these effects are achieved.

For example, discourse deixis is used to insistently foreground the deictic centre of the reader in their role as reader—that is, as the addressee of the fictional speaker, and in their act of processing the text and conceptually realising the storyworld. The initial reference to "the reader" is firmly clarified as direct address with the immediately subsequent deictic second-person pronoun "you". The comma immediately after "you" signals its independent function as a term of address. The speaker then explicitly states "it's you I'm addressing". The reader is also addressed as a "print-oriented bastard", foregrounding the physical textuality of the discourse. The speaker refers to his position, speaking "from inside this [. . .] fiction" (as discussed further in Chapter 4, section 4.3). The speaker also uses the spatial deictic "this far" signalling his deictic centre relative to the ongoing textual sequence of the printed material (again signalling a metaleptic awareness of the physical text). The use of "this far" in the context of direct address to the reader and the manner of its repetition ("this far, then? Even this far?") work to suggest that the speaker and reader share that deictic centre within the progress of the text. For the reader, however, this locus (as always) has two dimensions: the progressing linear, printed textual sequence, and her progressing dynamic conceptual realisation of the storyworld. The speaker's use of the first-person pronoun in "you've read me this far" implies that he identifies with the text (in that to read the text this far is to read the speaker this far). This suggests an awareness that his existence is dependent on the text and the reader's engagement with that text. The lines are confronting, suggesting that the heretofore ontologically separate realm of the reader has been and can be breached, leaving the reader no longer anonymous and exposed as an unfeeling consumer of print.

The two examples from Johnson and Barth are both instances of characters commenting on aspects of the sequential, printed representation of the narrative discourse and the reader's relationship to this text-continuum. A brief example from Brophy's *In Transit* (2002 [1969]) captures a narrator referring to the print medium of the narration in an altogether different fashion, though still likewise attending to the nature of the reader's consumption of the text. Late in the novel, the following metanarration occurs:

> In logic, the vital passage should come somewhere not too long after the start. [. . .] This is admittedly not the wholesale exegesis we are seeking, but is it a clue? Or is it merely a further appearance on the part of the unacknowledged, unsung, unstrung heroine of our story, Miss Print?

(p. 144)

The first sentence is similar to general, extracompositional metanarration, but refers not to narrative but instead to the conventional discourse structure of logical argumentation. It does, nonetheless, imply a comparison with the structure of the current text, drawing attention to the fact that the juncture in the text at which this comment is being made is a long way from the novel's start. It is with the words "This [. . .] exegesis" that discourse deixis serves to draw the implicit metanarration of the preceding sentence into an overall explicit metanarrative effect. The referent of the demonstrative "this" in "this [. . .] exegesis" anaphorically refers to the section of narrative which precedes the metanarrative interruption. The exegesis being sought is an explanation regarding a male character in an embedded story which might in turn reveal the gender identity of the protagonist of the central story. Poignantly, the narrator's use of the deictic first-person plural "we" presents the narrator and reader as together in this search, situating them at a shared locus within the processing of the text and the realisation of "our story". This backgrounds the narrator's general guise in this novel as pseudo-authorial narrator—as creator of this story. The narrator goes on to hypothesise that the potential clue in the prior passage may merely be further print, or perhaps a misprint: which of these it is the narrator's intention to communicate is deliberately obscured by the potentially punning reference to "Miss Print". Given that "Miss Print" is presented as the "heroine of our story", one could assume that the title "Miss" signals the female gender (rather than serving to construct a pun on 'misprint'). The reference to "merely a further appearance" of print foregrounds the sequential, physical textual basis of the discourse. However, the ambiguity surrounding the gender of the novel's protagonist could arguably be due to an original misprint, and so misprint could conceivably be regarded as at the heart of the novel, the pun thereby intended.

The metanarrative foregrounding of the physical textuality of the narration is more radical in the next few sentences. The narrator soon concludes that the potential clue "cannot be a reference to our mysterious 'He'ro" (p. 144). In a highly unusual move, the narrator continues with "All the same, that's quite a revelatory slip you're shewing down there,

Miss Print" (p. 145), directly addressing the print (i.e. the type), using "Miss Print" as a term of address along with the person deictic "you". With the next sentence, the narrator shifts focus from the print itself to the printer, referred to in the third person: "On second thoughts we exonerate the printer and assume the translator was a touch fatigued at this point" (p. 145).

Brophy is particularly playful and persistent in her metanarrative fore-grounding of the textuality of the narrative. Like Johnson and Katz, she involves italics, diagrams, columns (see Chapter 5), and other kinds of graphological deviance in the narration as an implicit and indirect means of foregrounding the medium and the craftedness of the discourse. Katz, more than Brophy, adds to his implicit graphological deviance instances of explicit discourse deictic reference to the physical form of the book as part of metanarrative comments made by both the characters and the pseudo-authorial narrator. As indicated in the previous examples, such metatextual observations can involve an assertion of metaleptic aware-ness on the part of the character or narrator expressing the metanarra-tion. Further examples of this kind of metanarration are touched upon in relation to metalepsis in Chapter 4.

3.3 Metacompositional Metanarration

While metatextual metanarration focuses on the textual medium, the physical form, of the narrative, metacompositional metanarration focuses on the act of composition of that narrative, the "shaping" and "formation" (Wolf, 2009, p. 41), the imaginative invention of the story, and the creative writing process. This type of metanarration exposes the craftedness, and hence the artifice, of the fictional discourse. When voiced by a pseudo-authorial narrator, depending on its nature, meta-compositional metanarration can also function to affirm the impression of the narrator as creator. In the context of postmodern metafiction, this illusion can provide an avenue for an interrogation of the concept of the author-god, and an exploration of the relationship between this author and his creation.

Johnson's narrator appears to begin a little hesitantly when metanar-ratively discussing his compositional choices and describes his narration as an "attempt". His first comment of this kind is "For the following pas-sage it seems to me necessary to attempt transcursion into Christie's mind; an illusion of transcursion, that is, of course, since you know only too well in whose mind it all really takes place" (p. 23). His second is "I shall now attempt a little dialogue between Christie and the Office Supervisor, as if it had happened" (p. 39). In the first comment the narrator explic-itly foregrounds his deictic centre in relation to the text-continuum—specifically, in relation to "the following passage". In the second, the deictic 'now' in "I shall now attempt" may be alluding to his deictic centre within the temporal chronology of the creative process, or it may be metaphorically referring to his textual deictic centre at the immediate juncture in the text-continuum. In both comments he exposes the fictionality of the storyworld; in the first by referring explicitly to the "illusion" of internal focalisation, and in the second through the implicit negation entailed in "as if it had happened" (see Chapter 5, section 5.4). The first comment goes further, directly addressing the reader as "you" and foregrounding her awareness of the conventional illusions underlying fictional mimesis. That said, the narrator does not make clear whether he feels that "it"—presumably the story—takes place in his mind, or the reader's (and given that "mind" here is singular, the implication is that it is not both). The two comments overtly destroy the illusion of mimesis in relation to the storyworld, but do so through the affirmation, in contrast, of the illusion of the narrator as author.

The narrator's further metacompositional metanarrative comments tend to assert authorial control. For example, he states "the observant will be aware that I have avoided a claret-burgundy comparison here [. . .] and use of the cliché *crème de la crème* was also rejected for its punning awkwardness" (p. 65). Later, while presenting some background for Christie's character, he interrupts himself to announce "I'm going to pack this in soon: both everything and nothing in a person's past and background may be significant" (p. 81). Later still, he reports

> [Christie] had contrived a method of throwing these switches by remote control [. . .] in an unusual way which I am not going to bother to invent on this occasion. But I will go so far as to tell you that it involved a shovel.
>
> (p. 101)

Again, the pseudo-authorial narrator's locus within the text-continuum is deictically foregrounded, with the spatial "here", the temporal "soon", and "on this occasion". He refers to choices he has "avoided", "rejected", will soon cease, or will not "bother to invent". He offers explanations for some of his compositional choices, but pointedly not others. The first and last examples make reference to the reader—the first covertly, describing what the "observant" reader would notice, and the last overtly, using second-person address in announcing what he is willing to "tell you". Each of these comments refers to the pseudo-authorial narrator's choices regarding what to include and exclude in the composition and (latterly) "invent[ion]" of the discourse. Even when the pseudo-authorial narrator occasionally confesses that he has been influenced in some of his choices, as when he states "I am told one has to put incidents like that in; for the suspense, you know" (p. 107) and refers to the judgements of "my editor Collins" (p. 80), he is still presented as the one choosing to act on that direction.

Despite the impression given by these metacompositional comments, though, the narrator does not seem to have full control over the narrative composition. One metanarrative comment implies that the narrative is not wholly under his command. About a third of the way into the story, the narrator states "nothing happens by accident in this novel. Or almost nothing" (p. 57). The first assertion is offered to explain the relationship between parts of the plot, and suggests that all of the events in "this novel" are deliberate and planned, implicitly by him. The discourse deictic reference to "this" discourse as a "novel" and the proclamation regarding the controlled orchestration of the plot foreground the fictionality of the text and imply conventional authorial control. The second sentence humorously and ironically undermines this implication, however, which in turn undermines the conventional relationship between creator and created. To suggest that some things do happen "by accident" in the novel is to imply that the author is not in complete control, radically challenging the ontological relationship between the author and text, and indirectly endowing the storyworld with conditions akin to reality.

The ontological status of the storyworld and its relation to authorial control is the primary theme of the opening of Chapter 13 of Fowles's *The French Lieutenant's Woman* (1996 [1969]). Though Nünning uses the chapter as a whole as an example of "non-integrated" metanarration (2005, p. 26), there is precedence for the disruption of the mimetic illusion it presents as recently as the final paragraph of the preceding chapter. The narrator intrudes with an overt first-person assertion of authorial control over a character, stating "I will not make [Sarah] teeter on the window-sill, or sway forward, and then collapse sobbing" (p. 96). This metanarrative comment is touched upon in an extensive discussion of the metafictional disnarration within this chapter's close in Chapter 5, section 5.4.

The opening of Chapter 13 deeply damages the suspension of disbelief through a series of metacompositional manoeuvres. The preceding chapter has ended with two seemingly rhetorical questions: "Who is Sarah? Out of what shadows does she come?" (p. 96). Chapter 13 then begins with

> I do not know. This story I am telling is all imagination. These characters I create never existed outside my own mind. If I have pretended until now to know my characters' minds and innermost thoughts, it is because I am writing in [. . .] a convention universally accepted at the time of my story: that the novelist stands next to God. [. . .] But I live in the age of Alain Robbe-Grillet and Roland Barthes; if this is a novel, it cannot be a novel in the modern sense of the word.
>
> (p. 97)

One of the dominating effects of this paragraph is to subvert the mimetic illusion and conventions of historical realism which have dominated the narrative up until now (albeit not without regular metafictional under-tones). Like Johnson's narrator's claim that his story takes place wholly in the mind, the second sentence here, "This story I am telling is all imagi-nation", could initially be interpreted as referring to the author's or the reader's imagination. However, the third sentence, "These characters I create never existed outside my own mind", seems designed not only to negate any prior historical realism and demote the portrayed ontology of the characters to the imaginary, but also to specifically locate their exist-ence as internal to the narrator's imagination (implicitly denying readerly conceptualisation any relevance or significance to the text's realisation).

A second effect of this paragraph is to expose the conventions of (stere-otypical) Victorian realist novels, and in particular the mimetic certainty and the security of unquestionable authorial agency that the genre often presented. A by-product of the manner in which the narrator demolishes any impression of the historical reality of the characters, though, is the strengthening of the illusion of his own reality and authorial status, not least by illusorily deictically situating himself at a locus at the extrafic-tional level. In stating "I live in the age of Alain Robbe-Grillet and Roland Barthes" the narrator is portrayed as a living person, rather than a textual entity, located specifically in the postmodern era on the same ontological plane as the reader. Various discourse deictic metacompositional expres-sions, e.g. "This story I am telling", "These characters I create", "I am writing", and "my story" portray the narrator as the real author of the text. The deictic "now" within his words "If I have pretended until now to know my characters' minds" evokes the narrator's temporal locus within the process of supposedly writing the novel, or metaphorically refers to the immediate juncture within the text-continuum, or potentially aligns the two positions. Holmes (1995 [1981], p. 211) is but one critic among many others noted by Hutcheon (1978, pp. 82–83) who slips into attrib-uting the words of the narrator here to Fowles directly, manifesting the persuasive effect of the various deictic means by which the narrator por-trays his authorial compositional role and extrafictional location.

The potential paradox within this paragraph lies in the first four words, the implications of which become the theme of three subsequent pages of metanarration, discussion of which is continued in section 3.6. Given the context, the narrator's claim not to know who Sarah is could reasonably be interpreted as merely part of his foregrounding of the fact that Sarah is a character, not a historically real person who existed prior to or "outside" of his authorial act, and that the role of the fictional author cannot be to "know" and report, in the manner of a biographer or historian, but rather can only be to "invent". However, within the next few paragraphs of Chapter 13, he reveals that the basis of his denial of knowledge of Sarah is rather because "in the age of Alain Robbe-Grillet and Roland Barthes", characters must have free will. Again, then, meta-compositional metanarration is being used to subvert the conventional ontological conditions of the storyworld and to play with illusions of authorial control.

As Nünning suggests (in relation to his third category), metanarrative comments can offer positive or negative assessments of the pseudo-authorial narrator's competence (2005, pp. 37–38). Katz's narrator offers several self-critical examples in relation to his compositional prowess. Having described the conditions under which he is writing—by fluorescent light, in a library with a "plinking" air-conditioning unit (2017 [1968], p. 75)—the narrator says

> I want you to imagine the difficulties involved [. . .] holding the various threads of this narrative together [. . .]. In this environment any surprise is possible, and as much as I try to avoid chaos, chaos too often waits for me at the end of a story line [. . .]. Despite these gloomy predictions I'm going to try to demonstrate that I'm a novelist in good faith. At this point I'm going to attempt to tie in one of the ends that was left quite loose some pages back. I'm doing it because I know you need some sense of continuity [. . .] and getting this done now will save me having to tuck in this strand with all the others at the final denouement.
>
> (pp. 75–76)

As with all of the examples in this section, the paragraph is presented as direct address to the reader. Like the metanarrative comments from Johnson, this extract involves use of the second-person pronoun 'you'. That said, the first-person pronoun features with much greater frequency than the second-person pronoun, as the narrator persistently asserts his authorial role in constructing "this narrative". As in the first few examples from Johnson, the pseudo-authorial narrator portrays his compositional acts as things he will "try" or "attempt" to perform, and, also like Johnson's narrator, he suggests that he does not always fully control the story line, as he is subject not to accident but to "surprise" and "chaos". He refers to "this point" in the story, signalling his current textual deictic centre in relation to the text-continuum. He also anaphorically refers to a loose end abandoned "some pages back", which further foregrounds the sequential physical text. Additionally, he reaffirms the illusion he has spent the previous page creating, portraying the realm of the extradiegesis in a manner analogous to describing the storyworld, in referring to "this environment"—the library in which he is purportedly composing the story. Again, the corollary of the flaunting of the act of composition and artificiality of the fiction is a strengthening of the illusion of the narrator as author.

Two further paragraphs complicate this construction of pseudo-authorial agency, however, and subvert conventional conceptualisations of the ontological relationship between author and text. The narrator introduces, and then metanarratively assesses, a paragraph supposedly having been written by the New York poet Peter Schjeldahl: "Wow. Isn't that amazing? Not only does this paragraph turn out to be about Peter Prince, but it almost gets the job done, and in a manner far more breathtaking than the author's own small capabilities" (p. 199). The anaphoric deictic demonstrative references "that", "this paragraph", and "it" refer back the previous unit of text under assessment, foregrounding the narrator's and reader's deictic centres with respect to the ongoing text-continuum. The narrator also makes a third-person reference to himself as "the author", in a negative comparison of creative "capabilities". A few sentences later, ruminating on the need to "write the paragraph that would get Peter Prince to Cairo", he mentions another New York writer, saying "Maybe Ted Berrigan will do it. [. . .] I have a suspicion he has already written part of this novel, but I won't tell you which part. It could be the next paragraph" (p. 199). These few lines involve an assertion of authorial control: the narrator uses first-person reference, foregrounding his role as pseudo-author, within a reference to his oversight of the novel and within a refusal to "tell" the reader, addressed as "you", some information. At the same time, however, this pseudo-authorial narrator is asserting that part of the novel may have been written by someone else, and that he suspects this but cannot be certain (as, logically, an author would be). Moreover, with "it could be the next paragraph" the reader is left questioning the authorial attribution of not only any one section of the preceding text, but in particular the immediately following text. Nonetheless, however, paradoxically, the pseudo-authorial narrator's claims regarding the intrusion of other authors ultimately chiefly affirm the illusion of his own (albeit apparently co-)authorial status.

The predominant theme expressed through all of these examples is authorial control: the assertion of it, lack of it, and relinquishing of it. The extradiegetic narrators persistently intrude into third-person narratives with first-person reference to their authorial roles and second-person reference to the reader. Discourse deixis is used to refer to segments of texts, to the novels' storylines and characters, and to other agencies and influences purportedly shaping the fictional composition, including accident and chaos, editors and other writers, and literary epochs. These metacompositional metanarrative extracts are pithy expressions of stereotypical postmodern anxieties about the role of the author-god, self-determination, and ontological stability.

3.4 Metadiegetic Metanarration

Metadiegetic metanarration is metanarration which refers to the construction and representation of the storyworld, specifically; to the construction and representation of the plot and/or the characters; and to the ontological status of the storyworld. For example, metanarration of this type might refer to the setting *as* a setting, characters *as* characters, the storyworld's parameters, the plot structure, and so on.

True to form, Katz is particularly experimental and ostentatious in his use of metadiegetic metanarration. In one instance, the character Philip Farrel is asked to a meeting by the President of a company, to whom Philip Farrel confirms, when asked about Peter Prince, "we're both characters, so to speak, in the same novel" (p. 224). A character's discourse deictic reference to himself as a "character" existing "in" a "novel" is highly ontologically paradoxical. Philip Farrel then discovers that this company is trying to arrange product placement within the novel—they want Philip Farrel to ask Peter Prince, the protagonist, to promote their product. Philip Farrel, who usually exists at a narrative level ontologically higher than that of Peter Prince, insists he cannot actually communicate with the protagonist (implicitly because this would be metaleptically impossible, though, as discussed in Chapter 4, such metalepsis is prevalent in the novel). The narrator reports Philip Farrel's reaction to the President's insistence that he can influence the protagonist:

> "Nonsense. The book is almost over. I understand my function in it and it's not to talk to Peter Prince. I know what I do by now [. . .]". Philip Farrel smoothed his sideburns. He could tell that things weren't going as he'd expected them to. He wasn't sure, flipping quickly back through the pages, that they ever did.
>
> (pp. 225–226)

Here Philip Farrel makes an explicit discourse deictic reference to "the book" of which he is part, and in asserting that it is almost over, situates his current juncture relative to the progressing arc of the story, the end point of which he seems to be aware of. His temporal deictic "now" in "I know what I do by now" similarly situates his deictic locus relative to the progress of the story, or potentially to the progress of the text-continuum, or both. In making further explicit discourse deictic reference to "my function in" the novel he manifests a higher-order awareness of his role, an awareness which runs contrary to his status as a character. Most paradoxically, having been overtly situated within the storyworld and at a juncture in the text-continuum, in the final sentence Philip Farrel is portrayed as able to check "back through the pages" of the novel, to compare his understanding of and expectations about the plot with how "things" had actually been "going". The discourse deictic reference to the pages of the book foregrounds the textual medium of the discourse and its physical book form, of which Philip Farrell should logically not be aware, and with which he certainly should not be able to interact.

This instance is but one of many ontologically confusing moments of deviant metaleptic awareness manifest in Katz, several of which are discussed in detail in Chapter 4. Here, a character seems to have an awareness of the storyworld as a storyworld, an awareness of the fictional discourse containing that storyworld, and an awareness of its form as a book. A different example of metanarrative commentary upon the storyworld occurs a little later in Katz's novel. Peter Prince is being interrogated and has been forced to read a "story" about his troubled childhood friendship with a boy called Stoop. The story, as discussed further in Chapter 5, section 5.5, is presented as a scene originally written by the pseudo-authorial narrator, as part of Peter Prince's personal history, but one the narrator decided not to include (and he is presented as being surprised that the interrogator has found and introduced it). This story therefore has the same ontological status, in certain respects, as the interrogation scene in which Peter Prince and his interrogator are discussing it *as* a story. The interrogator asks Peter Prince " 'Did you like the story? [. . .] You have to admit, then, that you were cruel to him' ". Peter Prince replies

> God you're simple minded. Even the author of that piece demonstrates that the attitude there was more complicated than mere cruelty. There were exigencies [. . .]. It's there, right there in the story, as inept as the damned thing is, with an author who never bothers to really get to know his characters. [. . .] It's there in the text, in the story [. . .]. And it doesn't take literary analysis. This is no subtle author. It's all right there, on the surface, where he leaves it.
>
> (p. 284)

Despite recognising this story as a biographical portrayal of his past, Peter Prince discusses it as "that piece", a "story" with "characters" and an "author", potentially subject to "literary analysis". He seems to both recognise the story as his history and ontologically distance himself from it. In commenting on the implicit explanation for his behaviour, he repeatedly locates it with the distal deictic "there" (repeated six times), "in the text", "in the story". He explicitly metanarratively critiques the construction of the story—his history—as "inept", lacking subtlety and depth. Peter Prince's discussion of this biographical rendering as fiction, in metadiegetic terms, somehow reaffirms his relative 'reality' by contrast, whilst undermining the storytelling competency of the pseudo-authorial narrator.

Coover is more conventionally metafictionally playful in his use of metadiegetic metanarrative commentary. Schmitz argues that "the narrator is relentlessly manifest" in Coover's fiction (1974, p. 210). This is overtly the case in his story 'The Magic Poker', in which the narrator makes frequent metanarrative comments reporting his construction of the storyworld (Schofield, 2006, p. 222). The story opens with the words

> I wander the island, inventing it. I make a sun for it, and trees [. . .] and cause the water to lap the pebbles of its abandoned shores. [. . .] I deposit shadows and dampness, spin webs, and scatter ruins. [. . .] I impose a hot midday silence, a profound and heavy stillness. But anything can happen.
>
> (2011 [1969], p. 7)

The story starts with a foregrounding of the pseudo-authorial narrator's creative role. A pattern repeats across several sentences: the narrator voices a first-person self-reference and flaunts his creative acts in "inventing" and constructing the storyworld, with phrases such as "I make [. . .] and cause", "I deposit [. . .] and scatter", and "I impose". The paragraph begins with a paradox, however, and ends with another. The narrator cannot both "wander" the island and "invent" it. The former presents the island as already actualised and as real as the narrator, while the second presents it as a fiction, and he, by contrast, as its implicitly real author. A metaphorical reading of "wander" would be reasonable, e.g. "I wander, in my imagination" but for the last sentence of the paragraph. The narrator's control over the storyworld he has created is implicitly undermined. The contrary implications of the connective "but" in "But anything can happen" suggests that narrative events can somehow counter and override his creative impositions, as does the suggestion, recalling the example from Johnson, that things might simply "happen", that is, without his direction.

The narrative then immediately continues in a more historically realist style:

> This small and secretive bay, here just below what was once the care-taker's cabin [. . .] probably once possessed its own system of docks. [. . .] Schools of silver fish [. . .] fog the bottom [of the bay], and dragonflies dart and hover over its placid surface.
>
> (p. 7)

The demonstrative deictic "this" and spatially proximal "here" in this paragraph's first sentence portray the scene as though the bay is close and visible to both the narrator and reader. The island is presented as having a historical past. The verbs are no longer verbs related to invention, anchored to the narrator: his agency is absent—the dragonflies appear to dart and hover of their own volition. The metanarrative commentary seems to have been left behind as the story settles into a more realist mode.

However, on the next page this structure is repeated. Another paragraph of metanarrative commentary on the construction of the story-world begins with "I arrange the guest cabin. I rot the porch and tatter the screen" (p. 8). A second sequence of sentences comprised of narratorial first-person references and dynamic verbal processes ensues. This sequence ends, though, with "Really, there's nothing to it. In fact, it's a pleasure", the narrator explicitly commenting on the ease and pleasure of "it", his storyworld construction. The next paragraph begins "Once, earlier in this age, a family with great wealth purchased this entire island, here up on the border". Again, then, the narrator employs proximal deictics ("this" and "here") and portrays the island as having a history, contrary to the impression suggested by the preceding depiction of his crafting of the island.

A paragraph a few pages later significantly complicates the ontological arrangement yet further. The narrator interrupts the narrative to say

> But where is the caretaker's son? I don't know. He was here [. . .] when Karen's sister entered. Yet, though she catalogues the room's disrepair, there is no mention of the caretaker's son. This is awkward. Didn't I invent him myself [. . .]? I don't know. [. . .] To tell the truth, I sometimes wonder if it was not he who invented me.
>
> (p. 13)

The narrator's question about the caretaker's son, followed by "I don't know", echoes Fowles's narrator's response to his own question about his character Sarah. Whereas Fowles's narrator goes on to proclaim that he invented his characters, however, Coover's narrator, having already proclaimed he has done this, goes on to question it. The narrator's asserted act of "invent[ion]" of the storyworld is subverted: the narrator now, ontologically impossibly, suggests that one of the storyworld characters may have invented him.

These examples illustrate the ways in which discourse deixis can be exploited to contribute to metanarrative exposure and ontological problematisation of the construction of the storyworld, of characters, and of plot. As has been shown, metadiegetic metanarration is an apt tool for the expression of postmodern metafictional subversions of ontological certainties and authorial power.

3.5 Metanarrative Metanarration

Metanarrative metanarration, the most cumbersomely named category, is metanarration about the narrative, specifically. The version presented here is slightly narrower than Fludernik's "metanarrational" type, in that it does not include metanarration which focuses on the roles of the discourse participants, for example the narrator, the reader, etc., in the narrative (2003a, pp. 29–30): in the current typology this is included instead in the final type, metadiscursive metanarration, described in section 3.6. Metanarrative metanarration as outlined here might refer to, for example, the structure or organisation of the narrative, narrative techniques and conventions, and the narrator's act of telling.

Coover's short story 'Klee Dead' involves metanarrative intrusions of equivalent frequency to those in 'The Magic Poker', but instead of focusing on the construction of the storyworld, the focus is on the narrator's act of telling. The narrator is highly self-conscious, concerned about the timing and order of his revelations, his motives for introducing characters, and his adherence to narrative conventions.

The story begins with

> Klee, Wilber Klee, dies. Is dead, rather. I know I know: too soon. It should come [. . .] at the end: and thus, gentle lector, Wilber Klee is gathered to his fathers. But what's to be done? He's already gone.
>
> (pp. 85–86)

The narrator's hesitations, self-corrections, and clarifications are present from the start. Also present is his overt consciousness of the reader and her expectations, in that "I know I know" is a defensive response to a hypothetical complaint by the reader. What the narrator "know[s]" is that "it", the death, the climax of the story, "should come [. . .] at the end" according to conventional narrative trajectories. The narrator then offers wording appropriate to that conventional close in a style parodying stereotypical Victorian literary formalities, including formalities of direct address of the reader as "gentle lector".

A little further into the story, ruminating on his introduction into the narrative of a minor character, the son of Millie, the narrator says

> To tell the truth, I wish I hadn't brought him up in the first place. Please forget I mentioned him, if you can. What's more I'm not entirely sure why I told you about Millie. [. . .] Perhaps it was merely to demonstrate, before facing up to Klee, that I could tell a story without bringing the hero to some lurid sensational end.
>
> (pp. 87–88)

Again the narrator directly addresses the reader, here with the second-person pronoun "you". The narrator explicitly questions his own rationale in introducing characters and telling the reader certain things, and suggests it may be to prove his capacity to "tell a story" that does not simply abide by popular "sensational[ist]" codes, thus his capacity to *resist* narrative conventions. Some of the verbal processes anchored to his narrating "I" foreground acts of "tell[ing]", "mention[ing]" and "demonstrat[ing]".

That said, these processes tend to be qualified by epistemic and boulo-maic modality (e.g. "I'm not entirely sure why" and "I wish", respec-tively), these qualifications simultaneously foregrounding the narrator's regrets and uncertainties about those acts of telling.

The narrator's metanarrative address of the reader and concerns about her preferences and (potential) queries are more pronounced in a section a few paragraphs later, in which the narrator reports

> As for Wilber Klee, I've not much more to say about him either, you'll be glad to know, just this: that he jumped from a high place and is now dead. I think you can take my word for it. [. . .] Need I tell you from *what* high place? Your questions, friend, are foolish, disease of the western mind.
>
> (p. 88, italics in the original)

The metanarration here mimics a verbal exchange and starts to create the impression that the narrator can hear the reader (i.e. that she and he are somehow in the canonical situation-of-utterance). The narrator moves from presupposition about what "you'll be glad to know" to an appar-ent defence against mistrust on the reader's part regarding his telling (i.e. "I think you can take my word for it"). He then voices a question, appar-ently on behalf of the reader, and attacks the reader for the nature of that question, it being seemingly based on a "western" voyeuristic need for detail. The narrator's defensive claims and his presumption and derision of questions could reasonably be read as grounded in the narrator's met-anarrative anxieties and his projection of them onto the reader. However, his voicing of such a specific question on the reader's behalf could suggest the possibility that the narrator may be reacting to a fictional "gentle lec-tor" whose responses he can perceive.

This impression and the related ambiguity is soon perpetuated with the comment "Who was Klee, you ask? I do not know, I do not care" (p. 88). Again, the narrator directly addresses the reader with "you" and presumes to voice a question on her behalf. The parallel with Fowles's narrator's question "Who is Sarah" and his answer "I do know now" is even more direct in this case than in 'The Magic Poker'. However, in the context of 'Klee Dead', this lack of knowledge is not presented as a result of Klee being a character: the opposite, in fact. With metanarrative com-ments such as "And already I may have pushed too far, perhaps that's not his name at all, I may have made it up, very likely in fact" (p. 89), the narrator differentiates between his potentially inadequate and erroneous-ous telling, with possible but only accidental fictional fabrications, and a purported underlying reality. His telling remains in focus: this is not a pseudo-authorial narrator, inventing the story, but a supremely self-conscious narrator portrayed as reporting a story badly, that story thereby presented as fact rather than fiction.

When the narrative finally crawls to a halt, with no discernible arc and no central event beyond Klee's prematurely announced death, the narrator says "I'm sorry. What can I say? Even I had expected more. You are right to be angry. Here, take these tickets" (p. 93), and he is presented as offering the reader tickets to the touring circus. These are the same tickets which, he reported in the first paragraph of the tale, he had used to try to bribe the city clerk to delay registering Klee's death, implicitly to allow for a more effective narrative. The narrator indirectly acknowledges the failure of his narrative, and again directly addresses the reader and appears to make assumptions about her response. The words "Here, take these tickets" confuse the situation, however. The demonstrative deictic "these" suggests that the tickets are near to both the narrator and the reader, and the use of "here" in this manner conventionally accompanies a physical gesture offering and/or presenting something. The spatial deictics combined with the direct address therefore suggest more clearly and powerfully than before that the reader and narrator are together in a shared space. Nonetheless, the reader has been addressed as "gentle lector", which foregrounds the written nature of the communication. The narrator's closing words can be most easily resolved as a playful, partly paradoxical illusion of intimacy—a mimesis of a certain kind of storytelling in the context of a catastrophic collapse of actual narrative.

While Coover's story presents a particularly postmodern collapse of narrative structure and logic, Johnson's *Christie Malry's Own Double-Entry* is more conventional in many ways, not least in the fact that the hero dies at the end rather than at the beginning. The metanarrative metanarration in the chapter titles could be regarded as parodic of more traditional narrative styles, though some are more metafictionally playful than others. As discussed in Chapter 2, chapter titles have a discourse deictic function in the sense of implicitly meaning "*This* chapter, i.e. the immediately following section of text, is titled" (cf. Genette, 1997, p. 294; Stockwell, 2002, p. 46). Fludernik (2003a, p. 30) and Nünning (2005, p. 23) both discuss chapter titles as potential vehicles for metanarration. Indeed, Nünning offers Johnson's chapter titles in this novel as an example of metanarration at the "paratextual level" of "a fictive editor" (2005, p. 23), though given the narrator's overtly asserted pseudo-authorial guise, there is no reason to attribute the chapter titles to an editor rather than the pseudo-authorial narrator. Several of Johnson's chapter titles involve metanarrative description of the contents of the chapter, for example "Chapter II. Here is Christie's Great Idea!" (p. 21) and "Chapter IV. In which a Goat Is Succoured" (p. 31)—with the additionally discourse deictic "here" and "in which"—and "Chapter VI. Christie Described, and the Shrike Created" (p. 49). Some chapter titles make implicit reference to the preferences of readers, for example "Chapter XI. Christie Begins in Earnest; and (Something to please all Model Railway

Enthusiasts) an Account of the Little Vermifuge" (p. 91) and "Chapter XVII. The No Doubt Welcome Return of the Shrike" (p. 135), while other chapter titles take this further to imagine readers preferring the inclusion or ignoring of certain chapters, as discussed in Chapter 5, section 5.5. The most explicitly metanarrative and discourse deictic chapter titles are "Chapter IX. A Promise Fulfilled, and Christie's Younger Life; a Failed Chapter" (p. 77) and "Chapter XX. Not the Longest Chapter in this Novel" (p. 159).

Johnson's narrator also offers intermittent metanarrative asides within the chapters. On page 16, for example, at the end of a chapter about Christie, the narrator states "A simple man, as I have too often said", which seems a fair evaluation, given that "Christie Malry was a simple person" is the first sentence of the book, and, after a paragraph of evidence, "I did tell you Christie was a simple person" is the fourth sentence, too (p. 11). The narrator also mentions Christie's school days and adds "(of which I shall probably not tell you much)" (p. 13). Within the first few pages, then, the narrator makes several references to himself and his narrative act of "tell[ing]". In addition, narrative progression, and the reader's preference for it, is explicitly foregrounded in two comments: "You begin to perceive a progression: Christie had begun in earnest!" (p. 107) and "That would be a logical progression of the kind that very much appeals to the vast majority of readers" (p. 139). The first is a metanarrative comment by the narrator directly addressed to the reader, designated with the deictic pronoun "you". The second is a comment by Christie to the Shrike, in which he nonetheless refers to both the narrative arc and the reader, revealing a metaleptic awareness which is further discussed in Chapter 4.

The narrative progression that is explicitly foregrounded in Johnson by the metanarrative chapter titles and the two incidental comments is exactly the kind of narrative progression that is absent in Coover's 'Klee Dead', where the metanarrative comments instead thematise that absence. Frustrated narrative progression is also thematised in Barth's 'Lost in the Funhouse'. In 'The Magic Poker', as described in section 3.4, there is a pattern of a metadiegetic metanarrational paragraph followed by non-metanarrational, conventionally mimetic paragraph. In 'Lost in the Funhouse' there is a pattern of a shift from extracompositional, indirect metanarrative metanarration to intracompositional, direct metanarrative metanarration, or vice versa. For example, on the sixth page of the story, the narrator interrupts the tale with a significant passage of metanarration, parts of which were introduced in Chapter 1 as an example of discourse deixis in metafiction. The narrator points out that "The function of the *beginning* of a story is to introduce the principal characters, establish their initial relationships, set the scene [. . .] and initiate the first complication [. . .] of the 'rising action'" (p. 77, italics in the original). As explained in Chapter 1, this is wholly extracompositional, general, non-deictic metanarration. However, the paragraph continues directly with

> Actually, if one imagines a story called 'The Funhouse', or 'Lost in the Funhouse', the details of the drive to Ocean City don't seem especially relevant. The *beginning* should recount the events between Ambrose's first sight of the funhouse early in the afternoon and his entering it with Magda and Peter in the evening.
>
> (p. 77, italics in the original)

Though presented as a hypothesis about what might be appropriate if such a story should exist, the title and proper names function as discourse deictic references to the current story and its characters.

The intracompositional, direct quality of the metanarrative metanarration is intensified towards the end of this paragraph, when the narrator states "So far there's been no real dialogue, very little sensory detail, and nothing in the way of a *theme*. And a long time has gone by already without anything happening [. . .]. We haven't even reached Ocean City yet" (italics in the original). As mentioned in Chapter 1, with "So far", the narrator makes an implicit discourse deictic reference to the development of the storyworld from the beginning of the tale up until the current juncture in the discourse—his current deictic centre relative to this progression. The temporal dimension of this span is foregrounded with "a long time has gone by already", implicitly between the start of this story and the current point. The reader is implicitly located with the narrator at this juncture, through his use of the first-person plural "we" in "We haven't even reached Ocean City yet", though this deictic locus could be relative to the characters' physical journey within the storyworld, the sequential progression of the textual discourse, or the more general conceptual development of the diegesis and plot. All of the metanarrative description in the comment is framed in the negative, explicitly commenting on what has not been included in the narrative thus far.

The opposite shift occurs on the following page, moving from intracompositional to extracompositional metanarrative comment: "at this rate our protagonist will remain in the funhouse forever. Narrative ordinarily consists of alternating dramatization and summarization" (p. 78). It is the first-person plural pronoun in "our protagonist", uniting the narrator and reader in their relation to Ambrose, which does the work of creating the intracompositional meaning-value of the first statement. A series of independent intracompositional metanarrative comments are then interspersed through the next few pages, including "we should be much further along than we are; [. . .] not much of this preliminary rambling seems relevant" (p. 79) and "There's no point in going further; [. . .] they haven't even come to the funhouse yet" (p. 83). Both comments again foreground the narrator's and reader's shared deictic locus relative to the progression of the story.

In the story's most deviant metafictional flourish the pattern reverses again, moving from extracompositional to intracompositional metanarration, on page 95, at which point the narrator describes the "action of conventional dramatic narrative" via diagrams of Freytag's Triangle and a rumination on the dangers of "forsak[ing]" this convention. This time the paragraph continues with another stretch of narration of the story before it returns to the metanarrative comment regarding Freytag's Triangle and connects it to the current narrative. Towards the paragraph's close, the narrator states "A long time ago we should have passed the apex of Freitag's [sic] Triangle and made brief work of the *dénouement*" (italics in the original) (p. 96), again uniting the narrator and reader and referring to a temporal juncture in their shared history, "a long time ago", relative to their joint current locus within the progression of the story.

Whereas in the preceding examples the narrator has taken responsibility for the narrative progression and voiced metanarrative comments in the first person, the narrator of 'Lost in the Funhouse' overtly resists doing so, and instead situates himself with the reader as subject to the author's mishandling of the narrative. The following, penultimate section of this chapter examines metanarration which addresses, among other things, the roles of author, narrator, and reader, and the relationships between them.

3.6 Metadiscursive Metanarration

Metadiscursive metanarration is metanarration which focuses on the narrative discourse, the discursive participants involved—the author, reader, narrator, and characters—and the discursive relationships between them, and between them and the narrative text. In most of the examples discussed in this chapter, the real author has been backgrounded, and the narrator, usually designated with the deictic first-person pronoun 'I', together with the reader, usually designated as 'you', have been foregrounded.

The narrator is the textually manifest entity through which the narrative is voiced. Several theorists have argued that the figure of the narrator is not fundamental to narrative (Banfield, 1982; Chatman, 1978, pp. 151–159; Fludernik, 1996; Hamburger, 1973), and/or that the anthropomorphising notion of a singular, human-like, psychologically consistent narrator is too simplistic (Fludernik, 1996, p. 287, 2003, pp. 33–34; Richardson, 2006, p. 86, pp. 135–136; Ryan, 2001, p. 152). However, narration is necessarily anchored to a perspectival locus in relation to the storyworld, and that locus is conventionally attributed human-like properties (hence the very notion of a narratorial 'voice'). The position of the narrator in relation to the storyworld determines the perspective through which the storyworld is conveyed.

The narrator has often been discussed as a corollary of, and even a potential obstacle to, the mimetic portrayal of the story, possibly in part due to the dominance of realist models of literature in shaping conceptions of literary conventions. Even within some branches of cognitive narratology, the communicative function of the narrator within the reader's processing operations remains neglected (cf. Duchan, Bruder, and Hewitt, 1995; Herman, 2002). The relative presence of the narrator within a narrative is addressed by Genette through the Platonic contrast between the mimetic and the diegetic, "mimesis being defined by a maximum of information and a minimum of the informer, diegesis by the opposite relationship" (Genette, 1980, p. 166). (Note 'diegesis' is here translated from the French *diegesis*, meaning "telling, recounting, as opposed to showing, enacting", rather than *diégèse* from which the identically translated 'diegesis' and adjective 'diegetic' are derived to connote "the (fictional) world in which the situations and events narrated occur", Prince, 2003, p. 20). According to Genette's understanding, a narrative in which the narrator constantly asserts her/himself as a presence performing the function of telling is 'diegetic'. A narrative in which the narrator is minimally present or entirely 'absent' (the act of telling not mentioned, and the teller making no self-reference) is more purely 'mimetic' (Genette, 1980, p. 167). Bal similarly writes of narratorial 'visibility' as either "perceptible (p) or non-perceptible (np) as a specifically mentioned agent in the text" (1985, p. 125).

Nünning (2005) posits an overt, personalised narrator and foregrounded act of narrating as constitutive of a "mimesis of telling" (2005, p. 43). In doing so he re-conceives fictive mimesis as potentially encompassing not only mimetic presentation of the story but also mimetic presentation of the communicative nature of narratorial discourse: the illusion that the participants in the narrative discourse are portrayed as ontologically equal, and also, sometimes, the illusion of the implicitly direct and immediate communication from the narrator to the reader. Metafiction confronts, exploits, investigates, and undermines these illusions: explicit reference to the narrator as the textual telling agent is a prototypical feature of metafictional self-reflexive investigation.

In the context of metanarration, however, as many of the examples discussed earlier show, the narrator is often portrayed not simply as a teller, but as a pseudo-author. This allows the narrator to become a vehicle for further metafictional thematisation of the postmodern concerns with master-narratives and governing author-gods, as discussed in Chapter 1.

Related to these concerns, a further theme of postmodern metafiction, also discussed in Chapter 1, is the subjective constructedness of 'reality'. The epistemic and ontological crises that exposed the mediated fictionality of History likewise propelled an awareness of the same discursive construction of everyday experience. Recognition of the influence of the perceiving mind on the resultant conceptualisation of reality increasingly seeped into Anglo-American intellectual thought via translations of the work of Husserl and Heidegger. Within the same critical wave, literary-theoretical reflections, epitomised in Barthes (1977 [1967]) but present elsewhere around him, drew attention to the ways in which the realisation of the content of narrative discourse is dependent on the reader. Through this lens, the text is a heteronomous construct, dynamically imaginatively evolving through the active engagement of the reader. It is only through the act of reading that the characters and storyworld gain meaning (Iser, 1978). Some of the metafictional works discussed in this chapter variably foreground the author's role and responsibility for the creation of the storyworld, some variably foreground the reader's role, and some do both.

One of Coover's stories—that which precedes 'Klee Dead'—arguably offers an example of an implicit, metaphorical form of metadiscursive metanarration. Gordon describes 'In a Train Station' as "one of Coover's most enigmatic pieces" (1983, p. 106). The story involves a protagonist, Alfred, buying a train ticket at 09:27 and waiting on a train station platform, talking to the Stationmaster. It slowly becomes apparent that the conversation is seemingly pre-scripted, as the Stationmaster implicitly urges the reluctant Alfred to say the correct words of his lines. An intruder arrives, drunkenly saying "The su'jeck f' my dishcoursh is" (p. 83), and "our fazher whish art 'n heaven [. . .] *is eating hish own goddamn chil'ren!*", adding, to Alfred, "So *help* me!" (p. 84, italics in the original). Alfred is pressured by the Stationmaster to murder him, but, weeping, Alfred fails, and so the Stationmaster intervenes and decapitates the intruder. The Stationmaster, apparently dissatisfied with Alfred's performance, turns the station clock back to 09:26, and the story, it seems, is about to begin again. The intruder's speech seems to make reference to either a Heideggerian breakdown of the distinction between subject and discourse (Heidegger, 2001 [1962]), or to the narratological concepts of the Russian Formalist notions of the 'fabula' and 'sjuzhet', reformulated as "histoire" and "discours" by Todorov (1966), and then later, after the Coover's publication, as "story" and "discourse" by Chatman (1978). This is the only element which could arguably be considered implicit metanarration. In the context of the story as a whole, and its context in a highly postmodern metafictional collection, this character's metanarrative references to the "dishcoursh", his statement about a god eating his own children, and the killing of this character can potentially be interpreted as a metaphorical reference to the increased sense of a breakdown of the distinction between the subject and discourse, and/or to the undermining of the author-god prevalent in 1960s literary theory and its impact on fiction. The cyclical narrative is predominantly metanarrative by implicit sinister metadiscursive allegory. The metanarrativity of this story remains merely implicit, however, partially through the absence of any discourse deixis which could serve to explicate its intracompositional metanarrative relevance—that is, to anchor its metanarrative implications within and in relation to this storyworld and story, hence, perhaps, the story remaining 'enigmatic'.

A much less enigmatic rumination on the relationship between the author-god, the reader, and the realisation of the text is presented in Johnson's *Christie Malry's Own Double-Entry*, in which the narrator writes

> An attempt should be made to characterise Christie's appearance. I do so with diffidence, in the knowledge that such physical descriptions are rarely of value in a novel. It is one of the limitations; and there are so many others. Many readers, I should not be surprised to learn if appropriate evidence were capable of being researched, do not read such descriptions at all, but skip to the next dialogue or more readily assimilable section. Again, I have often read and heard said, many readers apparently prefer to imagine the characters for themselves. That is what draws them to the novel, that it stimulates their imagination! Imagining my characters, indeed! Investing them with characteristics quite unknown to me, or even at variance with such description as I have given! [. . .] What writer can compete with the reader's imagination!
>
> (p. 51)

The use of the word "characterise", in the first sentence, as opposed to, for example, 'describe', is poignant, as is the absence of agency for that characterisation in this line. The next few words overtly clarify the pseudo-authorial narrator's adoption of agency for the characterisation, but he also explicitly pronounces his reservations. In what follows, the narrator voices general metanarrative comments specifically about the ways in which readers engage with and treat novels and the liberties readers take in how far they usually accept or ignore the direction of authors when imagining characters. James proposes that Johnson's allegation against the reader regarding readers' habits of skipping descriptions is an illustration of Johnson's consistent experimentation with the physical form of the book, of which many of his narrators, across his works, express metanarrative awareness. James points out that "Johnson was insistent on the rationale behind his exploitation of what he called 'the technological fact of the bound book' (*Aren't You Rather Young to be Writing Your Memoirs*, p. 25)", and that Johnson was "all too mindful that the novel's graphic inventions remained susceptible to" the whims of the reader (James, 2007, p. 34, citing Johnson, 1973), this being "one of the limitations" of the novel of which the narrator here speaks. The second allegation against readers—that they presume to override narratorial description in imaginatively constructing characters—is more explicitly deictically anchored to this novel and to the narrator's descriptive choices: he refers to "my characters", to "characteristics quite unknown to me", and to "such descriptions as I have given", the discourse deictics of which give the metanarration explicitly intracompositional meaning.

The narrator talks of "many readers" in general here, then shifts to a representative notion of "the reader" in his final line, in which he seemingly voices a resignation, not quite Barthesian but with similar implications: "What writer can compete with the reader's imagination!" In the next paragraph, though, the narrator addresses the reader directly with the second-person pronoun "you" within an apparent compromise regarding creative agency. He says

> Christie is therefore an average shape, height, weight, build and colour. Make him what you will: probably in the image of yourself. You are allowed complete freedom in the matter of warts and moles, particularly; as long as he has at least one of either.
>
> (p. 51)

The narrator seems to permit the reader "complete freedom" in "mak[ing]" Christie, though this is somewhat paradoxically contained with some (humorously first vague, and then indelicate) specifications.

Notably, the narrator suggests that the reader will probably "make" Christie "in the image of" herself. This could be suggestive of the sense of identification readers can feel with characters. However, given Christie's name and the implicit intertextual echo of Genesis 1:26 which describes man being made in the image of God, an analogy may be being drawn between the reader and the figure of an author-god. The reader may thereby be being implicitly endowed with creative omnipotence and responsibility for her creations (or that omnipotence and responsibility may at least ultimately be being recognised).

Fowles's Chapter 13, the beginning of which is explored in section 3.3, also explicitly discusses the topics of authorial control and the author-god in relation to both the pseudo-authorial narrator and the reader. The significant difference, though, between the assertions of Johnson's narrator and those of Fowles's narrator, is that Fowles's narrator allows the reader no implicit or explicit co-creative responsibility for the conceptual realisation of the discourse (though this is not the case elsewhere in the novel, as discussed in Chapters 4 and 5). He writes

> The novelist is still a god, since he creates [. . .]; what has changed is that we are no longer the gods of the Victorian image, omniscient and decreeing; but in the new theological image, with freedom our first principle, not authority.
>
> I have disgracefully broken the illusion? No. My characters still exist, and in a reality no less, or no more, real than the one I have just

broken. Fiction is woven into all [. . .]; and I would have you share my own sense that I do not fully control these creatures of my mind, any more than you control [. . .] your children, colleagues, friends, or even yourself.

But this is preposterous? A character is either 'real' or 'imaginary'? If you think that, *hypocrite lecteur*, I can only smile. You do not even think of your own past as quite real; you dress it up, you [. . .] censor it, tinker with it . . . fictionalize it [. . .]—your book, your romanced autobiography.

(p. 99, italics in the original)

The narrator here explicitly refers to himself as among contemporary authors, using the deictic first-person plural "we" and the possessive "our" in relation to current writers and principles of writing. He then continues to use the first-person pronoun to position himself as the author throughout the passage: he refers to the characters of the novel as "my characters" and as "these creatures of my mind", and also refers to the previously constructed storyworld "reality" as "one I have just broken".

The metanarration here is presented as direct communication from narrator to reader, constructing exactly the kind of "mimesis of telling" described by Nünning. The narrator even creates the illusion of discursive immediacy. He directly addresses the reader with the discourse deictic pronoun "you", with increasing frequency as the paragraphs continue, and opens each paragraph with questions apparently voiced on the reader's behalf, suggesting he is able to at least perceive her responses to his narration. At the same time, though, he also addresses the reader as "*hypocrite lecteur*" (as briefly discussed in Chapter 4, section 4.3), foregrounding the written nature of the communication and so, logically, the split discourse context of that communication.

While foregrounding his own authorial agency over the fiction, the narrator makes two quite radical claims: he reasserts that he does not fully control his characters, in that they have free will (Onega, 1989, p. 79), and he proposes that all versions of any "reality", including the reader's "own past", are fictions. What begins as a general comment about the relationship between fiction and reality—"Fiction is woven into all"—is made specific to the reader's reality. The narrator describes the reader's process of creating, distorting, and "fictionaliz[ing]" her reality, and parallels his characters with her friends, her family, and even herself. It is not the storyworld reality which the reader is presented as conceptually creating, as in Johnson, but rather her own reality. The chapter has turned from the narrator ruminating on his authorial control relative to what he refers to as "my book's reality" (p. 97) to thematising the reader's authorial role in creating what he refers to as "your book, your romanced autobiography", the two "book[s]" set on an ontological par.

The last example under discussion here comes from Barth's 'Life-Story', occurring a little further beyond the character's metatextual metanarration described in section 3.2. The metadiscursive metanarration in this example also draws attention to the textual medium of the discourse and the linear text-continuum, in particular, but it does so as part of a comment on the relationship between the reader, the textual discourse, and the central character. The impression of a 'mimesis of telling' is both constructed and complicated, but more so here than in Fowles. Though direct narratorial address of the reader abounds, potentially suggesting a shared communicative context, the metanarration centres upon the deictic locus of the narrator, reader, and character with respect to progress through the linear text and the ongoing conceptual realisation of the story, foregrounding the written narration of that communication. The narrator writes

> his life is in your hands! He writes and reads himself; don't you think he knows who gives his creatures their lives and deaths? Do they exist except as he or others read their words? Age except we turn their pages? And can he die until you have no more of him?
>
> (p. 127)

The central theme here is the heteronomous nature of the text. Characters are portrayed as existing only as far as readers "read their words" and "turn their pages". Whereas the significance of the reader's engagement with the text in realising the storyworld is neglected in Fowles's Chapter 13, here is it critical.

The story continues, on the next page, with the following:

> But as he longs to die and can't without your help you force him on, force him on. Will you deny you've read this sentence? This? To get away with murder doesn't appeal to you, is that it? As if your hands weren't inky with other dyings! [. . .] Come on. He dares you.
>
> (p. 128)

The reader is directly addressed and positioned as both the tortuous force behind the character's ongoing existence and the agent of other characters' deaths. The reader's physical interaction with the material text is foregrounded through the metatextual discourse deictic references to "your hands" being "inky" from "turn[ing] their pages". The discourse deictic reference to "this sentence? This?" echoes the discourse deixis in the example from earlier in this story, "You've read me this far, then? Even this far?" (p. 127, discussed earlier), signalling the narrator's and reader's shared textual deictic centre relative to progress through the text-continuum. The last sentence, "He dares you", meanwhile, echoes a line from an earlier tale in Barth's collection, 'Autobiography: A Self-Recorded Fiction' (discussed in Chapter 4, section 4.3), in which a character, addressing her/his father, begs and dares him, with "I dare you!", to *"put an end to this* [. . .] *Now! Now!"*, just as she/he has begged the reader to do likewise, should the reader have *"the means to my end"* (p. 38, italics in the original). In this example, the author is backgrounded, and it is the reader and her active engagement with the text upon which the functioning of the narrative discourse wholly depends.

The examples in this section overlap in many ways, but they create quite different metafictional propositions about the roles of the author and reader in the narrative discourse and its conceptualisation. Johnson's narrator's partial and slightly put out, compromising description of Christie overtly acknowledges and cedes some control to the reader's co-creative role in realising the narrative discourse. Fowles's narrator cedes his own control over his characters' behaviour as part of an explicit literary-theoretical comment on the new kind of author-god, while excluding the reader from that process and portraying her own world as a self-constructed fiction, undermining her ontological security. Barth's narrator is the only one of the three not to assert a pseudo-authorial role, backgrounding the author entirely and instead wholly conferring responsibility for the "lives and deaths" of the characters onto the reader and her conceptual engagement. The metanarrational implications of the three extracts rely to a greater or lesser extent on discourse deictic references to the relative positions of the narrator and reader in relation to each other, in relation to progress through text-continuums, and in relation to evolving conceptual worlds.

3.7 Conclusion

This chapter has drawn out the roles that discourse deixis can play in the workings of metanarration. It has reviewed previous studies of metanarration and distilled the various models into five types—the metatextual, the metacompositional, the metadiegetic, the metanarrative, and the metadiscursive—based on what, precisely, within and in relation to fictional narration, is the object of the metanarrational discussion. These types directly parallel the range of foci of metafiction more broadly. The dividing lines between these types, in the case of metanarration, are sometimes thinly drawn: the discussions of examples here reveal the ways in which, as Wolf points out, various types of metanarration can co-occur (2009, p. 38). Nonetheless, the typology provides a useful structure through which to examine the significance of discourse deixis to this metafictional technique.

The close analysis of examples of metanarration across Barth, Brophy, Coover, Fowles, Johnson, and Katz has illustrated both the prevalence of different kinds of discourse deixis within metanarration and the critical contribution it makes to metanarrational meaning. Analysis of discourse deixis has also been shown to be useful in helping to account for the differences between general, extracompositional, indirect metanarration and intracompositional, direct metanarration. The frequent role of discourse deixis in drawing the former into the latter has also been demonstrated. The study of discourse deixis in metanarration across the selected texts has added to the analytical means by which critics' interpretations of these texts can be partially accounted for and has facilitated further insights into the ways in which these texts communicate their metanarrational effects. Some of the examples discussed in this chapter have also revealed how often metanarration is intertwined with metalepsis. It is to the latter technique that the next chapter will now turn.

References

Bal, M. (1985). *Narratology: An Introduction to the Theory of Narrative.* Toronto: University of Toronto Press.

Banfield, A. (1982). *Unspeakable Sentences: Narration and Representation in the Language of Fiction.* Boston, MA: Routledge & Kegan Paul.

Barth, J. (1988) [1968]. *Lost in the Funhouse: Fiction for Print, Tape, Live Voice.* New York: Doubleday.

Barthes, R. (1977) [1967]. "The death of the author". In *Image/Music/Text.* Ed. S. Heath. New York: Hill and Wang. 142–148.

Barthes, R. (1973). *S/Z.* Paris: Éditions du Seuil.

Brophy, B. (2002) [1969]. *In Transit: An Heroi-Cyclic Novel.* Chicago, IL: Dalkey Archive Press.

Chatman, S. (1978). *Story and Discourse: Narrative Structure in Fiction and Film.* Ithaca, NY: Cornell University Press.

Coover, R. (2011) [1969]. *Pricksongs and Descants.* New York: New American Library.

Duchan, J. F., Bruder, G. A. and Hewitt, L. E. (Eds.). (1995). *Deixis in Narrative: A Cognitive Scientific Perspective.* Hillsdale, NJ: Lawrence Erlbaum Associates.

Eliot, G. (2008) [1858]. *Adam Bede.* Oxford: Oxford World's Classics.

Fludernik, M. (1996). *Towards a 'Natural' Narratology.* London: Routledge.

Fludernik, M. (2003). "Metanarrative and metafictional commentary: From metadiscursivity to metanarration and metafiction". *Poetica* 35.1–2. 1–39.

Fowles, J. (1996) [1969]. *The French Lieutenant's Woman.* London: Vintage.

Genette, G. (1980). *Narrative Discourse.* Trans. J. Lewin. Ithaca, NY: Cornell University Press.

Genette, G. (1997). *Paratexts. Thresholds of Interpretation.* Trans. J. E. Lewin. Cambridge: Cambridge University Press.

Gordon, L. (1983). *Robert Coover: The Universal Fictionmaking Process.* Carbondale, IL: South Illinois University Press.

Gray, A. (1981). *Lanark.* Edinburgh: Canongate.

Hamburger, K. (1973). *The Logic of Literature.* 2nd edn. Trans. M. J. Rose. Bloomington, IN: Indiana University Press.

Heidegger, M. (2001) [1962]. *Being and Time.* Trans. J. Macquarrie and E. Robinson. Oxford: Blackwell.

Herman, D. (2002). *Story Logic: Problems and Possibilities of Narrative*. Lincoln, NE: University of Nebraska Press.

Holmes, F. M. (1995) [1981]. "The novel, illusion, and reality: The paradox of omniscience in *The French Lieutenant's Woman*". In *Metafiction*. Ed. M. Currie. Harlow, Essex: Longman. 206–220.

Hutcheon, L. (1978). "The 'real world(s)' of fiction: *The French Lieutenant's Woman*". *English Studies in Canada* 4.1. 81–94.

Hutcheon, L. (1984) [1980]. *Narcissistic Narrative: The Metafictional Paradox*. Revised edn. London and New York: Methuen.

Iser, W. (1978). *The Act of Reading: A Theory of Aesthetic Response*. Baltimore, MD: Johns Hopkins University Press.

Jakobson, R. (1960). "Closing statement: Linguistics and poetics". In *Style in Language*. Ed. T. A. Seboek. Cambridge, MA: MIT Press. 350–377.

James, D. (2007). "The (w)hole affect: Creative reading and typographic immersion in *Albert Angelo*". In *Re-reading B. S. Johnson*. Eds. P. Tew and G. White. Houndmills, Basingstoke: Palgrave Macmillan. 27–37.

Johnson, B. S. (1973). *Aren't You Rather Young to Be Writing Your Memoirs?* London: Hutchinson.

Johnson, B. S. (2001) [1973]. *Christie Malry's Own Double-Entry*. London: Picador.

Kacandes, I. (2001). *Talk Fiction: Literature and the Talk Explosion*. Lincoln, NE: University of Nebraska Press.

Katz, S. (2017) [1968]. *The Exagggerations of Peter Prince*. Singapore: Verbivoracious Press.

Macrae, A. (2010). "Enhancing the critical apparatus for understanding metanarration: Discourse deixis refined". *Journal of Literary Semantics* 39.2. 119–142.

McHale, B. (1987). *Postmodernist Fiction*. London: Routledge.

McHale, B. (1992). *Constructing Postmodernism*. London: Routledge.

Nünning, A. (2005). "On metanarrative: Towards a definition, a typology and an outline of the functions of metanarrative commentary". In *The Dynamics of Narrative Form: Studies in Anglo-American Narratology*. Ed. J. Pier. Berlin: Walter de Gruyter. 11–57.

Onega, S. (1989). *Form and Meaning in the Novels of John Fowles*. Ann Arbor, MI: U.M.I. Research Press.

Phelan, J. (1989). *Reading Narrative: Form, Ethics, Ideology*. Columbus, OH: Ohio State University Press.

Prince, G. (1987). *A Dictionary of Narratology*. Revised edn. Lincoln, NE: University of Nebraska Press.

Prince, G. (1995) [1982]. "Metanarrative signs". In *Metafiction*. ed. M. Currie. London: Longman. 55–68.

Prince, G. (2003). *A Dictionary of Narratology*. Revised edn. Lincoln, NE: University of Nebraska Press.

Richardson, B. (2006). *Unnatural Voices: Extreme Narration in Modern and Contemporary Fiction*. Columbus, OH: Ohio State University Press.

Ruthrof, H. (1981). *The Reader's Construction of Narrative*. London: Routledge.

Ryan, M.-L. (2001). *Narrative as Virtual Reality: Immersion and Interactivity in Literature and Electronic Media*. Baltimore, MD: Johns Hopkins University Press.

Schmitz, N. (1974). "Robert Coover and the hazards of metafiction". *A Forum on Fiction* 7.3. 210–219.

Scofield, M. (2006). *The Cambridge Introduction to the American Short Story.* Cambridge: Cambridge University Press.

Sorrentino, G. (1971). *Imaginative Qualities of Actual Things.* New York: Pantheon Books.

Stockwell, P. (2002). *Cognitive Poetics: An Introduction.* London: Routledge.

Stonehill, B. (1988). *The Self-Conscious Novel: Artifice in Fiction from Joyce to Pynchon.* Philadelphia: University of Pennsylvania Press.

Todorov, T. (1966). "Les catégories du récit littérataire". *Communications* 8. 125–151.

Wolf, W. (1993). *Ästhetische Illusion und Illusiondurchbrechung in der Erzählkunst: Theorie und Geschichte mit Schwerpunkt auf Englischem Illusionsstörenden Erzählen.* Tübingen: Niemeyer.

Wolf, W. (2009). "Metareference across media: The concept, its transmedial potentials and problems, main forms and functions". In *Metareference Across Media: Theory and Case Studies.* Ed. W. Wolf. Amsterdam: Rodopi. 1–85.

Worthington, M. (2001). "Done with mirrors: Restoring the authority lost in John Barth's funhouse". *Twentieth Century Literature* 47.1. 114–136.

4 Discourse Deixis in Metalepsis

On the whole she did not think there would be any difficulty with Helena. Just then she heard the sound of a typewriter. It seemed to come through the wall on her left. It stopped, and was immediately followed by a voice remarking her own thoughts. It said: on the whole she did not think there would be any difficulty with Helena.

(Spark, 1957, p. 42)

Word by word, immersed in the sordid dilemma of the hero and heroine, letting himself go toward where the images came together and took on color and movement, he was witness to the final encounter in the mountain cabin.

(Cortázar, 1985 [1967], p. 64)

As discussed in Chapter 1, metalepsis, like metanarration, is not specific to postmodernist metafiction. Thoss (2015) and Kukkonen and Klimek (2011) demonstrate the wide-spread nature of metalepsis in popular fiction, for example, especially children's literature and fantasy, and also in film, particularly in the late twentieth century and early twenty-first century. Some definitions of metalepsis include within its remit techniques such as narratorial asides to the reader, which feature across many genres and periods. Genette (2004) goes so far as to argue that all literature involves metalepsis. A more conventional reckoning of metalepsis, though, narrows its scope to seemingly radical ontological shifts by characters and narrators across narrative levels. The most stereotypical type of metalepsis is a third-person narrator suddenly appearing within the fictional world of which she/he tells. In the context of postmodern metafiction, such shifts tend to serve to foreground the artifice of the fictional world, along with the illusory nature of any ontological boundary between the story and narration. Metalepsis can have yet more challenging implications, though, in undermining conceptualisations of 'reality' as privileged over and distinct from fictionally constructed worlds, and casting as precariousness any sense of a stable, secure, and self-determining subject.

This chapter analyses the contribution of discourse deixis to the construction of metalepsis and its effects. Section 4.1 provides an introduction to metalepsis, starting with the ontological structure of fiction, and the nature and effects of metaleptic violations of that ontological structure. This section also describes previous work on precisely how metaleptic effects are achieved and what contribution theory of discourse deixis can make to that work. Following this introductory section, sections 4.2, 4.3, and 4.4 explore three types of metalepsis in detail, incorporating and building on prior scholarship and analysing the role of discourse deixis in examples from Barth, Brophy, Coover, Fowles, Johnson, and Katz.

4.1 Defining Metalepsis

This section begins with the central concern of metalepsis: the ontological structure of fiction. As Hanebeck points out, the ontological structure of fiction (as it tends to be conceived in Western narratology) is based on a conventionalised system of representational logic (2017, p. 25) which "presupposes what Nietzsche has termed the 'construction of a pyramidal order [. . .] and clearly marked boundaries' " (p. 3, citing Nietzsche, 1999, p. 146). The diagram in Figure 4.1 is a depiction of the ontological levels of fiction: the level of the story, at which characters exist (the diegesis); the level of the narration, at which the narrator exists (the extradiegesis); and the level of reality, at which the author and reader exist (Genette, 1980, 1988). An additional 'hypodiegetic' level is possible, within the diegesis, when a character tells a (thereby 'embedded') story—and this

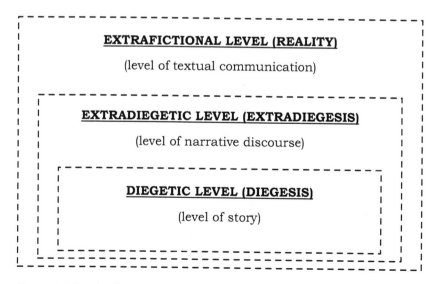

EXTRAFICTIONAL LEVEL (REALITY)

(level of textual communication)

EXTRADIEGETIC LEVEL (EXTRADIEGESIS)

(level of narrative discourse)

DIEGETIC LEVEL (DIEGESIS)

(level of story)

Figure 4.1 Levels of narrative

pattern can continue, for example with a hypo-hypodiegetic level, etc. Models of the ontological structure of fiction have conventionally prioritised Chatman's (1978) discourse/story distinction (i.e. distinguishing the story told from the discourse telling) or Genette's (1980) diegetic and extradiegetic levels, employing the concept of hierarchy of levels or concentrically embedded frames. Jahn and Nünning (1994) and Malina (2002) diagrammatically combine the two conceptualisations—the story/discourse distinction and the hierarchy or embedding—through versions of the model represented in Figure 4.1. This kind of diagram foregrounds two key aspects of the conventional conceptualisations of the structure of narrative fiction with which metafiction is concerned: an "ontological hierarchy" (Richardson, 1994, p. 319) that accepts reality as the 'highest' level, and a containment of the story within a mediating discourse. The Chinese box structure is adopted not to suggest encirclement as such, however, but to suggest an overlaying of realms. The extradiegetic level can therefore be regarded as underlying rather than encircling the diegetic level (see Young, 1987, p. 9).

The depicted model is only one way of conceptualising these relationships. Chatman (1978, p. 151) follows Booth (1961) in focusing on and depicting a model of the communicative relationships between narrative participants, backgrounding but nonetheless implicitly differentiating the ontological levels at which they exist (see also Stockwell, 2002, p. 42). Gavins (2007), Herman (1997), and Ryan (1991, 2001), conversely, focus on the distinguishable modal structures of the different worlds (and/or levels) involved and the relationships between those modal structures. Furthermore, even within the kind of model depicted here, the implicit ontological hierarchy suggested in discussions about these levels, with reality at the 'top', is debated, upheld in, for example, Dannenberg (2008), Duchan, Bruder, and Hewitt (1995), and McHale (1987), but reversed in Ryan (2006, pp. 204–218) and Ryan (2015). Additionally, some theorists have proposed much more complex versions of this diagram (e.g. Jahn and Nünning, 1994, p. 285). As Herman notes, classical models of narrative vary in the ways in which they "differentiate between, and differently rank, embedding and embedded diegetic levels of narration" (1997, p. 133). These caveats aside, Figure 4.1 roughly represents the ontological structure of conventional first-person past tense and third-person present tense or past tense narration, and offers a useful starting point for discussion of the crossing of ontological boundaries between levels which constitutes metalepsis.

Those which Genette terms the "diegetic level" (or "diegesis") and the "extradiegetic level" (or "extradiegesis") have been otherwise conceived as worlds (Gavins, 2007; Ryan, 1991; Werth, 1999), and relatedly as frames (Fillmore, 1985; Herman, 1997) and mental spaces (Fauconnier, 1994). As Hanebeck notes, the concept of levels suggests "a simple [hierarchical] structural relation" (p. 37), but "one cannot talk meaningfully about the transgression of [. . .] levels without the (implied) concept of a 'world' according to a realist paradigm that mirrors human sense-making capabilities", and so the structural concept of levels and the experiential concept of worlds are "intrinsically related" within narratology (p. 36; see also Wolf, 2009, pp. 51–52). The diegesis is conventionally mimetic of a real world, generally operating according to the principle of minimal departure. Herman's concept of a "storyworld" roughly corresponds to a mental model of the diegetic level, encompassing both "who did what to whom, when, where, why, and in what fashion" in "the world being told about" (2002, p. 5, p. 14) and that world itself—the surrounding context within which the characters and events are embedded (2002, p. 13). The terms 'storyworld' and 'diegesis' can be used interchangeably. As Fludernik observes, the act of narration rarely carries with it details of spatial or temporal relations (beyond the relation to the story narrated) (2003a, pp. 37–38). The realm of a third-person narrator, for example, is not conventionally fleshed out in Herman's sense, and so the extradiegesis, at which the narration takes place, is less world-like in its internal ontological structure. Thoss nonetheless argues that "the discursive dimension occupied by the narrator possesses certain world-like qualities" partially because "narrators are usually anthropomorphic" (2015, p. 35).

The extradiegesis and diegesis (and any further hypodiegesis, etc.) are equally fictional in that the narrator and characters are all fictional constructs (Ryan, 2006, pp. 204–205). Margolin (2007) goes so far as to include both "the spheres of narration and of the narrated" (p. 66), the extradiegesis and diegesis, respectively, within his notion of the storyworld, emphasising their shared ontology. The boundary, or "semipermeable membrane" (McHale, 1987, p. 34), that exists between them is illusory—a text-driven, conceptual construct. As Herman argues, the "normative expectations about the modal structure in the narrative universe" are "activated by textual cues included in the narrative discourse" (1997, p. 137; see also Young, 1987). Bridgeman (2007) states that "while readers do not, on the whole, try to map out hierarchical relations between narrative levels in the way narratologists do, they nevertheless have a sense that narratives can be divided into different temporal and spatial zones" (p. 52). The impression of ontological difference is constructed chiefly by the deictic person, spatial, and temporal distance between the narrator and characters—that is, in the case of most third-person narration, through the distal deixis employed by the narrator in referring to characters and/or focalising through characters' minds. This cognitively impossible mind-reading effect is expressed to some degree through narratorial partial projection to the character's deictic centre. It is primarily these deictic textual cues which create the illusion of the narrator having a different ontological status to that of the storyworld characters (and of a storyworld character having a different ontological status to that of any characters in a further fantasy she has or story she tells, for example). In the case of first-person past tense narration—that is, when a narrator tells a story in which she/he plays a part as a character, but narrates these experiences in the past tense—the first-person narrator, just like the third-person narrator, operates at the extradiegetic level, but focalises through a previous version of her/himself as a character within the diegesis. In this narrative mode the impression of an ontological division between the diegesis and extradiegesis is less pronounced than in the case of the third-person narrative mode, but the temporal distance nonetheless creates a distinction. In the rare narrative situations in which the narrator narrates the story from within the diegesis in the first-person present or future tense mode, this narrator operates as the primary narrator and there is no higher level extradiegetic narratorial position.

The narrator's relationship to the story and the stability of that relationship may not be consciously attended to by the reader, but that relationship is nonetheless an essential and significant aspect of the reader's processing of the narrative and her construction of the storyworld. As Genette states, "the narrator's relationship to the story is in principle invariable" (1980, p. 245). This convention of a consistent narratorial position and mode is demonstrated by the radically disruptive effect created by any sudden change in the narrator's ontological status and relationship to the story:

> the reader unfailingly takes [. . .] transition from one status to the other—when he perceives it—as an infraction of an implicit norm: for instance the (discreet) disappearance of the initial witness-narrator of [. . .] *Bovary*, or the (noisier) one of the narrator of *Lamiel*, who openly leaves the diegesis "in order to become a man of letters. Thus, O benevolent reader, farewell; you will hear nothing more from me" [Stendhal, 1948, p. 43]. An even more glaring violation is the shift in grammatical person to designate the same character: for instance, in *Autre étude de femme*, Bianchon moves all of a sudden from "I" to "he" [Balzac, n.d., pp. 75–77], as if he were unexpectedly abandoning the role of narrator; for instance, in *Jean Santeuil*, the hero moves inversely from "he" to "I" [Proust, 1971, p. 319].
>
> (Genette, 1980, pp. 245–246)

The various potential positions of the narrator in relation to the extradiegesis and the diegesis do not negate the functioning of the levels as ontologically distinct and hierarchically structured conceptual spaces. Nor does the possibility of narratorial metaleptic transgression from one level to another, as in Genette's examples, render the distinctions between levels obsolete. The effect is in fact the opposite, as Genette most clearly argues:

> [metaleptic] games, by the intensity of their effects, demonstrate the importance of the boundary they tax their ingenuity to overstep, in defiance of verisimilitude—a boundary that is precisely the narrating (or the performance) itself: a shifting but sacred frontier between two worlds, the world in which one tells, the world of which one tells.
>
> (1980, p. 236)

Rather than simply nullify the ontological distinction between the act of the narrating and the narrated, metalepsis both affirms the necessity of these conventional conceptual distinctions for the functioning of conventional verisimilitude and foregrounds their artificial and illusory status (a paradox explored by Hanebeck, 2017, p. 31). Indeed, McHale defines metalepsis as both "violations of ontological boundaries" (1987, p. 227) and "the foregrounding [. . .] of the ontological dimension of recursive embedding" (1987, p. 132).

Much of this thinking about the concept of metalepsis is summarised by Wolf (2005) in the form of three "typical" features of metalepsis: metalepsis involves "the existence of, or reference to, recognizable, logically distinct levels or possible (sub)worlds" which "usually differ ontologically from each other"; metalepsis involves "an actual transgression between, or a confusion and contamination of, the (sub)worlds [or levels] involved"; and this transgression is "paradoxical" with respect to the "conventional belief in the inviolability [. . .] of the (sub)worlds or levels involved" (2005, pp. 89–90).

One of the most comprehensive recent approaches to metalepsis is based on which particular boundary, within the ontological structure of fiction, is transgressed. Thoss's conception of metalepsis draws on Possible Worlds theory, cognitive narratology, and theory of intermediality. Thoss (2011) works with Wolf's definition of metalepsis as a "usually intentional paradoxical transgression of, or confusion between, (onto-) logically distinct (sub)worlds and/or levels that exist, or are referred to, within representations of possible worlds" (Wolf, 2005, p. 91). The kinds of transgressions which Thoss regards as metaleptic "involve entities from one world [or level] moving into or more generally interacting with an ontologically different world [or level]" (2015, p. 24).

Thoss's first type of metalepsis is metaleptic transgression between "a story world and another (imaginary) world" (2011, p. 190). The latter, he takes care to clarify, "need not actually be a story world in the sense of a narrated work. It may be any sort of imaginary world, for example one represented by a (non-narrative) painting" (2011, p. 192, n. 13; see also 2015, p. 25). Wolf likewise includes within his definition of metalepsis violations of "border(s) between represented worlds" (2013, p. 117). Thoss's second type of metalepsis is "feigned transgressions between a story world and reality" (2011, p. 194). Thoss points out that though metalepsis cannot really involve reality (2015, p. 29), there is no reason for fiction not to create the impression that this is possible, "or for readers not to go along with such a claim for as long as they are engaged in the game of make-believe" (2011, p. 198). The nature of the boundary between the fiction (including the extradiegesis and diegesis) and reality is the most problematic for accounts of metalepsis, as will be discussed further. Thoss uses the phrase "discourse-story metalepsis" to describe his third and final type of metaleptic transgression, and gives the example of an episode in which a character seems to be "no longer part of the narrated space of the story world but somehow part of the narrating space" (2011, p. 202).

Metaleptic boundary breaches can also be considered with respect to their directionality. Pier (2005, pp. 304–305), drawing on Nelles (1997) and Malina (2002, pp. 46–50), differentiates between "descending" and "ascending" metalepsis (see also Bell and Alber, 2012; Thoss, 2015, p. 26). Descending metalepsis, or "inward [. . .] intrametalepsis", in Nelles's terms (1997, p. 154), involves the movement of a narrator, narratee, or character downwards from the level at which they normally operate to a level presented as more fictional (e.g. from the extradiegesis to the diegesis). Ascending metalepsis, Nelles's "outward [. . .] extrametalepsis" (1997, p. 154), involves movement in the opposite direction.

A boundary-based typology of metalepsis is helpful, but there is a little ambiguity in work of Thoss and Wolf regarding the nature of metaleptic violations. Both include within their typologies not only the apparent transference of a character or narrator to a different narrative level, but also the more vague or general 'interaction across' narrative levels. This suggestion of the potential for different kinds of 'interaction' across levels opens up a further means of approaching and categorising types of metalepsis. That is, in addition to categorisation by the boundary crossed, metalepsis can be further defined by the nature of that boundary-crossing.

There are arguably three types of metaleptic transgression across narrative levels: metaleptic awareness, metaleptic communication, and metaleptic moves. Metaleptic awareness is an instance of, for example, a character demonstrating a conscious perception of being described by a narrator, or a character or narrator being aware of being controlled by authorial decisions, or being aware of the physical materiality of the book. Metaleptic communication is an instance of characters or narrators speaking from one narrative level to each other or to the reader at another narrative level. In such instances it is the act of communication which crosses the boundary. Both metaleptic awareness and metaleptic communication rely on characters and narrators not actually moving from one narrative level to another. It is only the third type of metalepsis—metaleptic moves—which involves the seeming transference of a narrator, character, or sometimes a representation of the reader from the narrative level at which they have thus far operated to a different narrative level, transgressing across the (albeit often illusory) ontological divide and manifesting 'physically' at a level at which that narrator, character, or reader does not 'belong'. Hanebeck and Thoss both point out that no instance of metalepsis is solely one type: any one instance may, in Hanebeck's words, "imply" or "rely on" several types (2017, p. 84; see also Thoss, 2015, p. 24). Metaleptic communication, for example, entails metaleptic awareness—as, for example, a character could not intentionally communicate with a narrator at a higher ontological level if she/he was not aware of that higher ontological level. Metaleptic awareness is probably the purest form of metalepsis, in that respect (i.e. least dependent upon other types). The roles of discourse deixis in these three types of metalepsis, across the different narrative boundaries, are explained and explored in detail in sections 4.2, 4.3, and 4.5, through analysis of their various manifestations in Barth, Brophy, Coover, Fowles, Johnson, and Katz.

Before moving on from this summary of the typology adopted in this chapter, three notable exclusions warrant explanation. The first is horizontal metalepsis, as proposed by Wagner (2002, p. 247). Horizontal metalepsis occurs in intertextual or "transfictional" forms (Pier, 2009, p. 199), in which characters or narrators from one fictional universe are represented as appearing in another (see also Bell and Alber, 2012, p. 168; Feyersinger, 2011; Ryan, 2015, p. 372). Thoss, too, argues that metalepsis can occur between worlds arranged in parallel (not just worlds arranged hierarchically), but notes problems with the concept, pointing out that "the distinction between parallel worlds is rarely as binary as that between a real embedding and a fictional embedded world" (2011, p. 192, n. 13). Thoss finds that Bareis's work on the explicit intertextuality of the phenomenon may offer "a workable criterion" (Thoss, 2015, p. 13, citing Bareis, 2008, p. 214). Nonetheless, Thoss sees horizontal metalepsis as an "extension" of the concept (p. 12). Hanebeck, however, regards horizontal metalepsis as beyond or apart from metalepsis proper, in that "transfictionality relies on the construction of various storyworlds", whereas metalepsis additionally "relies on the artefact-internal hierarchies established by representational logic" (2017, pp. 39–40). For these reasons (its less binary and non-hierarchical nature), Wagner's concept of horizontal metalepsis is not concordant with the approach to metalepsis taken in this chapter.

The second concept of metalepsis discounted by this study is Fludernik's "rhetorical or discourse metalepsis" (2003b). This is based on Genette's fourth type of metalepsis, a type which for him "play[s] on the double temporality of the story and the narrating" (1980, p. 235). Hanebeck terms this "figurative [. . .] rhetorical metalepsis" (2017, pp. 87–89) and Ryan terms it simply "rhetorical metalepsis" (2006, p. 218). By way of illustration, Genette cites an example from Balzac: "While the venerable churchman climbs the ramps of Angouleme, it is not useless to explain the network of interests into which he was going to set foot" (1980, p. 65). Genette discusses this example, saying it is "as if the narrating were contemporaneous with the story and had to fill up the latter's dead spaces" (p. 235). Fludernik explains how this can be considered metaleptic:

> It was only when I realized that the projected simultaneity metaphorically moves the narrator into the realm of the fictional world that I started to see where the boundary crossing might be located. In order to be able to talk while the cleric is climbing the stairs, the extradiegetic narrator would have to be located in the story, otherwise the 'while' cannot link the same kind of temporality.
>
> (Fludernik, 2003b, p. 387)

This kind of narrative phenomena can be regarded as metalepsis only if one conceives of the diegesis and extradiegesis as relating to each other in a certain way. It is specifically the 'while' which suggests the telling is occurring in the same (spatio-)temporal space as that in which the story is happening, rather than in/on some parallel, simultaneous (even if only sometimes so) ontological plane. This is different from narrative phenomena in which the narrator effectively 'freezes' the action in the story to offer metanarrative commentary or to narrate further storyworld details, such as background information or details of other scenes going on simultaneously elsewhere in the storyworld, which requires no ontological transgression. For these reasons and others, Cohn describes this as a "relatively inoffensive kind of discursive metalepsis" (2012, p. 106); Ryan finds it only "quasimetaleptic" (2006, p. 218); Pier describes it as "minimal metalepsis" (2009, p. 192); Wolf finds it to be not a "genuine" type of metalepsis (2005, p. 89); and Thoss (2015, p. 10), following Bell and Alber (2012, p. 167), finds it metaleptic only in a "metaphorical" sense. This concept of metalepsis, too, then, is outside of the understanding of metalepsis proposed in this chapter.

The final kind of metalepsis which is not covered in this chapter is that which Hanebeck terms ontological "recursive metalepsis": instances of metalepsis which "make the distinction between higher-order and lower-order domains [i.e. narrative levels] impossible" (2017, p. 100). Hanebeck here builds on accounts of metaleptic "strange loops", "tangled hierarchies", and "Mobius strips" developed by Kukkonen and Klimek (2011), Malina (2002, pp. 50–52), McHale (1987), and Wolf (2005, p. 90, 1993), and largely based on the ideas of Hofstadter (1979). Discussing the same phenomena, Ryan talks of an "interpenetration" or "contamination" of levels (2006, p. 207), Prince refers to "intrusion" and "mingling" (1987, p. 50), and Herman uses phrases such as "encroach on", "recontain", and "overlap with one another" (1997, p. 137). These kinds of metalepses present a more wholesale collapse of narrative levels—that is, a comprehensive dissolution of a boundary between narrative levels rather than a transgression across it. This too, then, is beyond the remit of this chapter's study.

In addition to delineating typologies of metalepsis, some theorists have attempted to provide an overview of the most common effects it creates and the themes to which these effects often contribute. One prominent note of debate in these attempts is whether or not metalepsis is inherently antimimetic. For Pier, antimimesis is the key and constant effect of metalepsis. He points out that "with metalepsis, it is the reader's belief, not disbelief, that is suspended, setting up a reading contract based not on verisimilitude, but on 'a shared knowledge of illusion'" (2009, p. 193, quoting Baron, 2005, p. 298). Pier argues that metalepsis always foregrounds this shared knowledge of illusion. Bell, conversely, argues that "metalepsis can be used to increase the reader's immersive experience of the text" (2016, p. 301). Wolf (2013), meanwhile, argues that metalepsis can be experienced as either alienating and unnatural or, contrarily, as enhancing a sense of immersion. He defines immersion as one "pole" of "aesthetic illusion" which

> consists predominantly of a feeling, of variable intensity, of being imaginatively and emotionally immersed in a represented world and of experiencing this world in a way similar (but not identical) to real life. This constitutive impression of immersion is, however, counterbalanced by a latent rational distance, which is a consequence of the culturally acquired awareness of the difference between representation and reality.
>
> (p. 144)

Wolf finds that various factors, including "epistemic, cultural, or generic contexts" along with "intracompositional filter factors", such as the relative frequency of (other) metareferential devices, can intersect with the effects of metalepsis to neutralise or enhance anti-immersive potential (p. 138).

Bell and Alber (2012) argue that readers presume metalepsis is meaningful, and that readers therefore form hypotheses about authors' intentions in using metalepsis and attempt to rationalise them within the context of the themes of the text in which they occur (p. 175–176; see also Hanebeck, 2017, pp. 108–110; Thoss, 2011, p. 200, p. 204, 2015, p. 40). They see a pattern in the kinds of thematic contexts in which metalepsis appears, and identify six common thematic uses: metalepsis as "a form of escapism", as "an exercise of control", as "highlighting the power [. . .] of fiction" (e.g. its power to shape reality), as suggestive of some kind of "mutual understanding" (e.g. a character and narrator having a mutual understanding of a particular state of affairs), as "a challenge to the creator", and/or as "a loss of control of the creation" (p. 176). In relation to the last two of this list, Thoss argues that "the conflict between creator and creation is actually one of the contexts metalepsis is most often found in", for the entertainment value of the spectacle, but also because of the relationship this conflict has with religious power structures, with escapism, and with postmodern self-reflexivity (2011, p. 198, see also 2015, pp. 43–44).

Each of these thematic uses seem to be essentially a matter of what McHale (1987) identifies as the epistemological and ontological crises central to much mid and late twentieth century fiction. From some postmodernist perspectives (as described in Hutcheon, 1988; McHale, 1987; Waugh, 1984), metalepsis primarily challenges the illusions promoted by realist fictional models of the nature of reality (e.g. that reality is fixed as opposed to intersubjectively constructed) and the easy distinction between reality and the imaginatively conceived. For Hanebeck (2017) and Klimek (2010), the most deeply disruptive effect of metalepsis is its ability to reflect a particularly postmodern "philosophical quandary" and "epistemological crisis" in its challenge to conventional logic and the resultant self-reflexive and irresolvable "openness" (Hanebeck, 2017, p. 7). Indeed, for Hanebeck the chief effect of metalepsis is that it encourages readers to "become aware of the (transgressed) representational logic on which the conception of narrative (understanding) usually relies" (2017, p. 111): it "throws into relief fundamental conditions of narrative sense-making" and the ideological and discursive basis of those conditions (p. 123; see also Wolf, 2005). As Malina points out, "during periods when the relationship between fiction and 'reality' is understood to be complex and unstable, the transgression of the narrative boundaries that mark degrees of fictionality proves a particularly strategic, and therefore conscious and pointed, tool" (2002, p. 6). Metalepsis within the context of postmodern literature can serve to highlight the permeable nature of these boundaries, appealing to them in order to subvert them and to challenge the conceptual paradigms upon which they are based.

The analyses of metalepsis in Barth, Brophy, Coover, Fowles, Johnson, and Katz that follow illustrate both the frequency of these epistemological and ontological thematic contexts, and the interesting array of further, text-specific effects metalepsis can have in relation to these themes. The radical and particularly postmodern effect which metalepses in these texts share, though, is summarised by Genette as follows: "The most troubling thing about metalepsis [. . .] lies in this unacceptable and insistent hypothesis, that the extradiegetic is perhaps always diegetic, and that the narrator and his narratees—you and I—perhaps belong to some narrative" (1980, p. 236).

So far this section has explored the ontological structure of fiction which metalepsis flouts, typologies of metalepsis, and common postmodern thematic uses of metalepsis. These areas have received significant critical attention. Within that attention, however, relatively little focus has been directed towards thinking about how metalepsis works—that is, what kinds of constructions of words can signal a metaleptic breach, and how. The final part of this section surveys the existent work on what linguistically constitutes metalepsis and what evokes recognition of metalepsis as such.

Two recently developed concepts which feature in the functioning of metalepsis are Bell and Alber's differentiation of 'transworld identity' and 'counterparthood' (2012), and Wolf's 'reception figures' (2013). Bell and Alber (2012) distinguish between metaleptic instances in which a literary entity moves levels, leaving and no longer existing in one as it enters another, thereby gaining 'transworld' status, and metaleptic instances in which a 'counterpart' of a character, narrator or the reader appears at a level different and in addition to the level at which the original version of that character, narrator, or reader exists. While Bell and Alber (2012) focus on the entities which are metaleptically moving, Wolf instead focuses on the characters around those entities. Wolf's "reception figures" are a trait of what he calls "immersion-hostile" kinds of metalepsis. They are characters or narrators who are presented as overtly reacting to instances of metalepsis within a story in such a way as to mark the metalepsis, "mirroring intended reader responses [. . .] as indicators of unnaturalness (or the absence of it)" (2013, p. 138). However, Wolf stops short of investigating in detail the nature of reception figures and their reactions—that is, he does not discuss examples of what reception figures are represented as thinking or saying in response to the metalepsis witnessed, which presumably creates the effect of both marking the metalepsis and marking them as reception figures. These concepts seem to be helpful in determining aspects of the ways in which metalepsis is actually constituted and signalled in texts, and so contribute to the analyses that follow.

Some other research on the functioning of metalepsis, meanwhile, begins to suggest the significance of deixis to its workings. Herman (1997) attempts to "sketch [. . .] a jointly formal and functional account of narrative metalepsis" within which he investigates the "textual markers" involved in metalepsis (p. 133). He finds lexical repetition to be one linguistic cue which helps to construct and distinguish frames. In examining lexical repetition, he notes both "patterns of markers of definiteness and indefiniteness" relating to the communication of given and new information, and "the outright repetition of lexical items" (p. 139 and p. 140 respectively). Another linguistic cue he identities is "register", finding that the different frames (or levels) of his sample story (O'Brien's *At Swim-two-birds*, 1939) have their own "characteristic subregister[s]"

(p. 144). Herman argues that the repetition of lexical items, with definite or indefinite reference, together with the mixing of subregisters at different levels, helps to construct the impression of metalepsis.

Herman's subregisters seem, however, to be a matter of voice rather than level: that is, they are more likely to be characteristic of particular narrator or character voices than of particular levels. That said, narrator and character voices tend to be located statically within one level, and this may be where the relevance to metalepsis lies, i.e. marking the penetration of a narrator's or character's voice from one level into another.

The use of definite or indefinite reference is intuitively a more logical and reliable marker of metalepsis. As discussed in Chapter 2, section 2.3, definite reference is deictic in that it signals that the referent can be found within the environment (e.g. the local spatial context or nearby co-text) and presupposes that the addressee has all the information she needs within that context in order to identify a specific referent. Within metalepsis, definite or indefinite reference to specific literary participants and objects within the fiction can potentially help to signal whether or not a literary participant or object has already been introduced and is expected to be recognisable to the literary participants, or is expected to be perceived as new, at the level at which it is being described.

Person deixis also appears in Kukkonen's work on metalepsis, in which she explicitly comments on the deictic quality of phrases such as "you" and "dear reader" in what she sees as metaleptic narratorial address to the reader (2011, p. 9, p. 16). McHale notes that this deictic value extends to uses of 'you' in second-person narration, in which the addressee is the character-protagonist, and also potentially in narratorial or character use of 'you' in self-address. He argues that in these cases the reader is not "directly implicated in the reference of the second-person pronoun" but that "nevertheless, even in these displaced forms *you* retains a connotation of the vocative, of direct appeal to the reader" (1987, p. 223, italics in the original). The deictic complexities and metaleptic potentialities of narratorial and character address of the reader are explored in section 4.3.

Beyond person deixis, two theorists broach the relevance of spatial and temporal contextualisation to metalepsis—contextualisation with which spatial and temporal deixis are inherently involved. Pier observes the fundamental relationship between metaleptic crossing of levels and narrative time and place (2005, p. 304). However, Pier does not address how these temporal and spatial contexts are established, or precisely how they relate to a hierarchy of levels, nor does he investigate how any crossing between them is manifest. Hanebeck seems to go further, attempting to distinguish different kinds of collapse between levels or worlds, and identifying temporal, spatial, holistic, and hierarchical dimensions (2017, p. 41), but does not discuss the role of deixis in demarcating temporal and spatial dimensions. These two theorists do, nonetheless, appreciate the significance of spatio-temporal contextualisation to metalepsis, which suggests the value of exploring spatial and temporal deixis in the workings of metalepsis.

This brief survey covers the small array of work thus far on what formally constitutes metalepsis—that is, on the stylistic devices through which readers recognise and interpret metalepsis. Within even the little research on the formal constitution and interpretation of metalepsis surveyed here, the relevance of deixis to metalepsis is manifest. As discussed in Chapter 3, discourse deixis is inherent to much of metanarration, and "metalepsis", writes Thoss, "cannot be divorced from metareference" (2015, p. 44; see also Wolf, 2009, pp. 52–56). Chapter 2 revealed some of the ways in which discourse deixis can be used to refer to literary participants; their roles or acts within the fiction, its construction, or realisation; the levels of narration; portions of physical text, etc. Reference to each of these elements is inherent in examples of metalepsis. To take just the last item on this list and just one example of metalepsis, a character's metaleptic awareness of the material book in which it features can be most directly communicated through that character making discourse deictic references to portions of the physical text (several examples of which are discussed below). The following three sections of this chapter explore the role and significance of discourse deixis in examples of metaleptic awareness, metaleptic communication, and metaleptic moves across Barth, Brophy, Coover, Fowles, Johnson, and Katz, to investigate the value of a theory of discourse deixis to an understanding of metalepsis.

4.2 Metaleptic Awareness

Thoss uses the term "metaleptic awareness" to describe an instance of a "protagonist's growing awareness that he is merely a character in a [. . .] book" (2011, p. 194). Hanebeck follows Nelles in terming metaleptic awareness "figurative [. . .] epistemological metalepsis" (cf. Nelles, 1997, pp. 154–155) and defines it as "a character's display of knowledge of superordinate diegetic universes in a paradoxical violation of representational logic" (Hanebeck, 2017, p. 85; cf. McHale, 1987, p. 123). Metaleptic awareness is not a particularly postmodern phenomenon. For example, Wolf discusses the " 'unnatural' awareness of the existence of spectators on the part of characters" in some medieval religious drama (2013, p. 131). It is, nonetheless, a more frequent phenomenon in postmodern metafiction.

Metaleptic awareness, though always 'upward', can involve awareness of various different aspects of superordinate levels. Within Thoss's description of his category of "storyworld-reality metalepsis", he includes instances of characters who "seemingly perceive reality from inside the storyworld" (2015, p. 28, p. 30). He also includes instances in which storyworld entities "perceive [. . .] their own medium, [and] the means of narration or representation that create them and their world" within his description of "storyworld-discourse metalepsis" (p. 31). As an example of the latter, Thoss describes an instance in which a character in a novel refers to "the previous chapters" (Rankin, 1997, p. 126), seemingly aware that he is in a novel, conscious of its physical materiality, and also "up-to-date on what happened in [those] previous chapters, despite the fact that he was not present in any of them" (Thoss, 2015, p. 66). In its "weakest form" this upward metaleptic awareness would involve characters who "simply know they are in a novel" (p. 34), but other (implicitly 'stronger') forms would involve awareness of the physical text (font, pages, etc.) (p. 35). Through analysis of examples of this kind of character metaleptic awareness in Johnson, Barth, and Katz, the nature of this kind of metaleptic awareness, and the role of discourse deixis within it, can be investigated.

There are several instances of Thoss's 'weakest' form of characters' metaleptic awareness of their discursive context and construction in Johnson and Katz. Johnson's protagonist, Christie, plus the two unnamed mothers in the book and a further minor character called Headlam all refer to the 'novel' within which they exist. Both Christie's mother and the mother of his girlfriend, the Shrike, use constructions which simultaneously affirm and disrupt the suspension of disbelief. Christie's mother says "My son: I have for the purposes of this novel been your mother for the past eighteen years and five months" (1973, p. 27), and later the Shrike's mother says "it was worth it, all those years of sacrifice, just to get my daughter placed in a respectable novel like this, you know" (p. 156). The references to the past made by the two mothers—"for the past eighteen years and five months" and "all those years of sacrifice"—construct the illusion of a real historical past for themselves and for the chronology of the world of the story, and yet with the phrases "for the purposes of this novel" and "in a respectable novel like this" these same figures acknowledge the fictionality of the discourse (and implicitly therefore of the storyworld and themselves). The phrase "this novel" has a metadiscursive function in deictically pointing to the fictional discourse context (with the demonstrative "this") from within that same discourse context. The Shrike's mother notably uses the spatial deictic "in", using a container metaphor for the unit of discourse which mirrors the conceptualisation of fiction's ontological hierarchy as concentrically contained levels whilst also suggesting awareness of the text as a complete and discrete unit of discourse. Their use of the word "novel" furthermore implies an ontologically impossible awareness of the story's end and its production in the form of a physical book. The effect is a humorously paradoxical reaffirmation of the novel's mimesis on the one hand, while flagrantly disrupting that illusion on the other.

Headlam's first reference to "this novel" works similarly to the uses by the two mothers. He tells Christie, "Parsons looks like being indisposed for the rest of this novel" (p. 95). The idea that Parsons can be indisposed creates an impression that he is real (and subject to real hindrances) rather than a textual construct, and yet the discourse deictic reference to "this novel" foregrounds the textually constructed nature of Parsons, of Headlam, and of the whole storyworld. Headlam's second use of the phrase comes when he says "I seem to be the comic relief in this novel", to which Christie responds "It needs it" (p. 103). Here both characters are offering some metanarrative evaluative commentary on the novel and how well it meets with expected conventions. In doing so, both are demonstrating an awareness of the novel as a whole, rather than just the scenes of which they are part, and an awareness of the novel as a novel. This awareness, on Christie's part, is manifest earlier in the text: when asked by his supervisor whether he was able to do something, Christie replies "There wasn't any more time. It's a short novel" (p. 40), the referent of the pronoun "it" being most easily resolvable as, again, "this novel". A similar kind of character metaleptic and metanarrative evaluative awareness occurs in Katz, in which a very minor character refers to "the way this bloody book is put together" (2017 [1968], p. 317). Characters exhibiting awareness of the novel in which they exist through discourse deictic reference to that novel is metaleptic in the sense that the discourse exists as a novel in the real world. This kind of metalepsis falls within what Ryan terms "rhetorical metalepsis"—instances in which literary participants at one narrative level discuss another narrative level (2006, pp. 206–207). Character metaleptic awareness is playfully paradoxical in various ways, not least in that the characters voicing these observations are affirmed as sentient personified beings at the same time as the very fictional and textual quality of the discourse through which they are comprised is foregrounded.

There are also examples, in Johnson, of Thoss's (implicitly) stronger form of characters' metaleptic awareness of their discursive context and construction—that is, examples in which a character demonstrates metaleptic awareness of the physical text (more explicitly so than simply referring to it as a 'novel'). Both examples occur towards the end of Johnson's text, during two instances of metaleptic moves in which the pseudo-authorial narrator joins Christie in the storyworld and the two converse (discussed further in section 4.4). At one point, Christie says to the pseudo-authorial narrator "there are too many exclamation marks in this novel already" (p. 166). A little later, he says "Just think, [the cancer] may have been caused through those misshapes I had on page 67!" (p. 180). Also, the Shrike, following a passage of metaphorical narratorial description of her, says to Christie "Enough of that metaphorical rubbish" (p. 138), swiftly followed by "how can we be said to be perfectly happy a few lines back, and now be complaining about the monotony of the diet?" (p. 139). As discussed in Chapter 2, "on page

67" implicitly means "on page 67 of this book". This reference therefore involves an anaphoric deictic reference relative to Christie's current textual deictic centre (on page 180 of the book). The deictic reference draws on the textual context and a relationship between two points in that text, overtly foregrounding both the textual nature of the discourse and Christie's ontologically impossible awareness of it. As with the previous comments by the mothers and in relation to Parsons, the sentence as a whole paradoxically affirms the reality of Christie (as a person liable to illness) at the same time as it draws attention to the textual nature of the discourse, whilst also flaunting his ontologically impossible awareness of the latter, which likewise undermines the realism.

The Shrike's metaleptic and metanarrative comments more simply and singularly work against the mimetic illusion. Here she uses anaphoric discourse deictic references to refer to the propositional content of a preceding paragraph (with "that [. . .] rubbish") and also that of a section "a few lines back". The latter phrase explicitly refers to the linear graphological sequence of the text, drawing a relationship between the Shrike's textual deictic centre within it, of which she must therefore be aware, and the prior lines. Such metaleptic comments are frequent across Johnson's text, as illustrated here, and also in his other novels (e.g. *House Mother Normal*, 1971). The Shrike is overall a more thinly drawn and explicitly functional character than some, however, hence the pseudo-authorial narrator's overtly reaching reliance on abstract and empty metaphors to describe her, on which she comments. Metaleptic and illusion-disrupting comments are perhaps more naturalisable and less radical in the context of the Shrike's character than other weaker character metaleptic awareness elsewhere in Johnson's already ubiquitously metafictional text.

Other interesting examples of character metaleptic awareness sit somewhere in between Thoss's stronger and weaker poles, and yet others perhaps go beyond his version of stronger metalepsis, being more extreme and more complicated in the kinds of metaleptic awareness they involve. For example, in Barth's 'Lost in the Funhouse', a character ends a paragraph of speech with the words "No character in a work of fiction can make a speech this long without interruption or acknowledgement from the other characters" (1988 [1968], p. 90). This includes, amongst other things, discourse deictic reference to "the other characters" *as characters*, and, those characters being "other" to the speaker, this thereby implies that the speaker, too, is a character and is aware of being so. Characters awareness of their status as character and of narrative conventions is manifest in another example from Barth, this time from 'Life-Story', in which we are told "Concluding these reflections he concluded these reflections that there was at this advancèd [sic] page still apparently no ground-situation suggested that his story was dramatically meaningless" (p. 126). The words "this advancèd [sic] page" foreground and signal the character's awareness of his textual deictic centre relative to the progress of the story, which, together with his reported conclusions regarding "his story", suggest his awareness of his status as a character.

Two further examples from Katz are differently radical and ontologically problematic. Linda Lawrence says to Philip Farrel

> "Of course if you're sick of the whole thing you can just walk out through Gottlieb's Exit on the next page, don't worry." [. . .] Philip Farrel waited till she left, and then turned around to gaze back through the pages he'd come.
>
> (p. 120)

A picture of "Gottlieb's Exit" (which looks like a line drawing of a double-door fire escape) covers the whole of the next page. Linda Lawrence is therefore portrayed as aware of the graphology of the discourse of the pages in which she exists as a character, and of her textual deictic centre within their linear sequence (the exit being on the page deictically "next" to and following the one on which her words, in this scene, are printed). Most radically, she implies that her co-character can leave the story of his own free will, through a depicted door in the text. For his part, Philip Farrel is described as having "come" "through" pages, with a deictic spatial directionality towards his current textual deictic centre, and, again radically, is able to both see, and see through, those pages, in "gaz[ing] back through" them.

A metaleptic gaze constitutes the second, later example, in which the pseudo-authorial narrator reports that Peter Prince "knew he was going to die, no doubt about it, and he tossed my way [. . .] an immense glare of hate" (p. 317). Here the protagonist is shown to be aware of the pseudo-authorial narrator and aware that his own fate is in that pseudo-authorial narrator's hands, and therefore aware that he himself is a fictional character. Furthermore, the apparent ontological possibility of Peter Prince directing a gaze at the pseudo-authorial narrator, together with the directional deixis of "he tossed my way", signals a spatial relationship between the two (the perspective anchored with the deictic centre of the pseudo-authorial narrator). A pseudo-authorial narrator and character cannot share the same ontological space, however, and so this seems akin to someone gazing skyward to (their perception of) a god. McHale describes this as a "gaze [. . .] direct[ed] beyond the footlights toward his author" (1987, p. 123). Whereas in the first example characters were able to see and gaze across the graphological constitution of the discourse, portrayed as metaleptically aware of the novel's physical form in reality, in this second example the character can metaleptically gaze across an ontological boundary from the diegesis upward to the equally conceptual extradiegesis at which his pseudo-authorial narrator exists.

Another pair of examples warrants attention for the further problems that they raise, both ontological and theoretical. Christie's mother and

Christie both refer to readers. His mother says to him "It was I who first told you the comic story of God, [. . .] which will no doubt be passed on to readers in due course" (p. 29). Later, within one of the metaleptic moves previously mentioned, the pseudo-authorial narrator says to Christie "Surely no reader will wish me to invent anything further", in relation to which Christie responds "If there is a reader [. . .]. Most people won't read it" (p. 165), 'it' logically meaning 'this novel'. In the second example, Christie and the pseudo-authorial narrator are within the storyworld and are both referring to readers of this novel. If the characters' references to readers of this novel are considered metaleptic, should the pseudo-authorial narrator's reference to readers not also be considered metaleptic? And, if a narrator's reference to readers is regarded as metaleptic when voiced from within the storyworld, what are the grounds for considering narratorial references to readers as not metaleptic when voiced from the extradiegesis?

Hanebeck, like Thoss, argues that metaleptic awareness is limited to characters because these are the only literary participants who are not logically aware of all other levels (unlike narrators and readers) (2017, p. 85). Logically, narrators (at least in the personified fashion in which we tend to conceive of them) are 'aware' of their readers as their addressees. This is perhaps even more naturally so in the case of pseudo-authorial narrators, given the frequent illusion of such narrators existing on the same ontological level as readers, and the prevalence of such narrators directly addressing readers in, for example, metanarrative commentary. However, an argument can be made that because narrators are textual constructs which exist conceptually at an ontological remove one level 'down' from reality, all narration entails a metaleptic awareness in its implicit or explicit address of a reader, unless, that is, that addressee is perceived to be to a narratee figure or role, equally textually constructed, within the ontological bounds of the fiction, and to which the reader conceptually metaleptically projects. This issue is debated further in section 4.3.

Awareness of readers aside, a narrator's awareness of the real-world conventions of narrative and/or the real world, post-production, physical form of the book would seem to be less contentiously metaleptic, even in the case of a pseudo-authorial narrator (who cannot be argued to be ontologically 'real'). Such awareness is part of many metanarrative comments. Chapter 13 of *The French Lieutenant's Woman*, for example, as mentioned in Chapter 3, opens with "This story I am telling is all imagination. These characters I create never existed outside my own mind", and the pseudo-authorial narrator goes on to refer to "the context of my book's reality" (1996 [1969], p. 97). Katz's narrator says, of Linda Lawrence and Philip Farrel, "they aren't per se characters in this book, but hired hands, like mercenary muses" (p. 140). Both narrators here refer to their characters *as characters*, and, from within it, refer to "my book" or "this book", evoking the whole, complete physical object (as opposed to 'this story' which is more suggestive of propositional content than physical form). Katz's narrator elsewhere demonstrates the same kind of awareness of the physical pages of the novel that Linda Lawrence and Philip Farrel exhibit in the previous example, albeit here a kind of meta-compositional awareness, as discussed in Chapter 3: he states "I'm going to try to demonstrate that I'm a novelist in good faith. [. . .] I'm going to attempt to tie in one of the ends that was left quite loose some pages back" (p. 75). Furthermore, what happens to Thoss and Hanebeck's distinction in the case of first-person narration, in which the pseudo-authorial narrator is the protagonist, as in Barth's 'Autobiography: A Self-Recorded Fiction', in which the narrator states "I hope I'm a fiction without real hope. [. . .] I see myself as a halt narrative: first person, tiresome" (p. 35)? Such metaleptic references seem hard to discount. Some of the questions they raise about the relationship between narration and metalepsis are explored in the next section.

Each of the examples of metaleptic awareness discussed here has depended on discourse deixis of some kind, such as a metatextual discourse deictic reference to the material physical text in relation to the textual deictic centre of a character, a metacompositional discourse deictic reference to the ongoing imaginative process of creation in relation to a pseudo-authorial narrator's juncture in that process, a metadiscursive discourse deictic reference to a character's ontological relationship to a pseudo-authorial narrator, etc. Discourse deixis is inherent to the signalling of the discursive roles, conceptual ontologies, and linear graphological textualities involved in metaleptic awareness. Discursive roles and conceptual ontologies play an even bigger part in the next type of metalepsis to which this chapter now turns: metaleptic communication.

4.3 Metaleptic Communication

Metaleptic communication involves the representation of narrators and characters as able to communicate across ontological boundaries. Specifically, metaleptic communication stereotypically involves a diegetic character addressing an extradiegetic narrator or addressing the reader, or an extradiegetic narrator addressing a diegetic character, or arguably, a diegetic character-narrator or extradiegetic narrator addressing the reader. Note metaleptic communication is not to be confused with Ryan's notion of 'rhetorical metalepsis', which in fact only describes metanarrative reflection within one diegetic level about another (e.g. discussion between two diegetic characters about the extradiegetic narrator), although this does entail metaleptic awareness, as mentioned previously (2006, pp. 206–207). The dyad of a narrator (character-narrator or extradiegetic) addressing a reader is the most theoretically problematic, and so will be given some additional attention below.

In the case of metaleptic communication, narrators and characters do not move levels—indeed the metaleptic quality of the communication relies on them staying at their different ontological levels. Instead, it is the communicative act which appears to cross the boundary. While metaleptic communication logically excludes metaleptic moves, it logically entails metaleptic awareness, in that narrators and characters must be aware of their addressees at other levels in order to intend to communicate with them.

Katz's *The Exagggerations of Peter Prince* involves metaleptic communication on the part of characters. In one example, the protagonist's metaleptic awareness is introduced by the narrator reporting

> [Peter Prince] mumbled to himself, "There ought to be some intensely relevant ending to this scene I've just been through, some symbolic final gesture", and he looked out at me as if to accuse me of enjoying what I just put him through.
>
> (p. 288)

Peter Prince's metaleptic awareness of the discourse is established through the discourse deictic references to "this scene" in combination with references to ideal endings and symbolic gestures which foreground his understanding both of storytelling conventions and of this scene as part of a story. His awareness of the pseudo-authorial narrator at the extradiegetic level is indicated by his "look[ing] at" the narrator, who is explicitly deictically positioned spatially "out" of the storyworld which Peter Prince is implicitly 'in'. Though Peter Prince is described as talking "to himself", he does nonetheless look "at" the pseudo-authorial narrator, seemingly directly. The pseudo-authorial narrator's use of "as if" could qualify what he infers as the meaning of Peter Prince's look, or could qualify what he may be presenting as an inferable extension of the meaning of what Peter Prince has said (i.e. the accusation), or could qualify his inference of Peter Prince's intended act of communication. The combination of Peter Prince's words and look, though, suggest that Peter Prince at least feels that the pseudo-authorial narrator is observing and can hear him, and so although he's presented as talking to himself, the narrator may be his intended indirect addressee.

The ontological confusion and impossibility entailed in this exchange is flaunted in the foregrounding of the pseudo-authorial narrator's agency, in his self-referencing assertion that "I just put him through" what Peter Prince refers to as "this scene I've just been through". This in turn highlights the discourse as fictional and implies that Peter Prince is subjected to the narrator's whims. Peter Prince's metanarrative comments in combination with his look in the direction of the narrator indicates that Peter Prince is aware of the narrator's control, and yet such a comment and look would go against conventional schema of what a pseudo-authorial narrator would deem desirable, suggesting perhaps at least some (impossible) independence and agency on the part of the protagonist.

A few lines later, the metaleptic communication becomes less ambiguous—that is, less indirect, implicit, and qualified. After Peter Prince has received a disappointing letter, the narrator states: "He rattled the letter above his head toward me. 'What good. What good have you ever done me?' he whistled" (p. 289). Here it is the preceding potential metaleptic communication, plus Peter Prince's gesture "toward" the pseudo-authorial narrator, together with the lack of any other potential proximal addressee, which suggest that Peter Prince's speech is directly addressed to the pseudo-authorial narrator—that is, that the referent of the deictic "you", and thereby the addressee of the unit of speech as a whole, is the pseudo-authorial narrator.

In these quotes, the narrator is portrayed as spatially "out" of the storyworld, and then "above" the protagonist, explicitly foregrounding the conceptual ontological hierarchical structure of fiction. In the second example from Katz, about 20 pages later, the real textual structure of the discourse is foregrounded, too. In this example, there seems to be an actual exchange between character and narrator, though it's not wholly clear that the character can 'hear' the narrator:

"You're sure going to fail," Peter Prince says, turning my way again [. . .]. "Who me?" I say, and let out a little cosmic laugh, and gaze deep into the long pages of this sequence. [. . .] Peter Prince [. . .] is grinning out at me through the haze of type.

(p. 318)

In this example, the spatial deictics of outward and inward directionality reaffirm the impression, constructed in the first example from Katz here, of the storyworld as some kind of contained space which the characters are 'inside', with the narrator positioned 'outside'. The narrator's description of his laugh as "cosmic" associates him with a mysterious, higher-order realm. With the reaction "who me?", the pseudo-authorial narrator is either expressing uncertainty about whether or not he is being addressed by his character, or is adopting the pretence of some kind of naïve innocence and lack of agency or responsibility with regard to the fiction and its relative 'success'. The description of the narrator's gaze "into the long pages of this sequence" and the character's grin "out through the haze of type" seem to involve discourse deictic references to the physical graphological sequence. However, the language here is not oriented around the textual deictic centres of the speakers in the same manner as references to 'the next page' or 'the last chapter' might be (i.e. relative to the textual sequence): rather, it is the speakers' ontological positions and relations which are being expressed through the impression of a boundary between them made up of a fog-like tissue of pages.

The physical and conceptual dimensions are portrayed as playfully and surreally blurred.

Metaleptic communication also occurs in Barth's short stories. Appel argues that "the components of 'Title' sustain a miraculous discussion amongst themselves, sometimes addressing the author" (Appel, 1980, p. 180). As an example, Appel offers the sentence "Once upon a time you were satisfied with incidental felicities and niceties of technique" (Barth, 1988 [1968], p. 107). It is seemingly the metaleptic quality of the communication which Appel perceives as "miraculous". However, due to the lack of line breaks between different speakers or quote marks to distinguish speech, it is not clear what is speech and what is thought, who speaks any particular sentences, and who the addressees are in any instance. The key markers of speech are proximal lines on shared topics which could be turns and responses, and the use of "you" within sentences. For example, the story seems to open with first-person narration, and so on the first page, prior to any dialogue between characters, the words "I'm as sick of this as you are" (p. 105) seem to be spoken by the narrator. The addressee, though, is ambiguous: it could be the reader, or it could be a character who is mentioned soon afterwards. Confusing the situation further, a few pages into the story the narrator is referred to in the third person and with phrases such as "the self-styled narrator of this so-called story" (p. 109). Some of the sentences in this story can reasonably be inferred to be metaleptic communication, and the most probable nature of that communication is character-narrator upward metaleptic communication to the reader. Overall, however, the effect is predominantly that of metaleptic collapse.

Character-narrator upward metaleptic communication with the reader is also present in Barth's 'Autobiography: A Self-Recorded Fiction', mentioned previously. The story opens with "You who listen give me life in a manner of speaking. I won't hold you responsible" (p. 35). Very soon the character-narrator says "Whether anyone follows me I can't tell. Are you there?" At this opening juncture the addressee seems to be the reader, addressed directly by the character-narrator with the second-person pronoun "you". The act of reading seems to be metaphorically transposed to listening, the extra spaces in the first line creating textual pauses of sorts to exaggerate this sense. Furthermore, this act of reading is portrayed as bringing the speaker into life. The address seems to split as the story continues, however. The character-narrator refers to her/his father in the third person (e.g. "Dad's infatuation passed") but also uses the second-person pronoun to address him directly, as in "*Father, have mercy, I dare you*" (p. 38, italics in the original) and "Here I am Dad: Your creature! Your caricature!" (p. 37). The latter is character-narrator-to-character address, and so storyworld-internal and not metaleptic. One section is more ambiguous, however, with regard to the addressee: "*if anyone hears me speaking from here inside like a sunk mariner, and has the means to my end, I pray him do us both a kindness*" (p. 38, italics in the original). The same conceptualisation of container that appeared in Katz is evoked here, in the character-narrator's foregrounding of her/his position with the spatial deixis "here inside", the hearer implicitly 'outside'. Given the suggestions on the opening page that the act of listening (or reading) brings the character-narrator into being, and that the character-narrator is not confident that anyone is "there", the addressee here is implicitly the same addressee of the opening lines—the reader—albeit addressed here indirectly and referred to in the third person as "him". However, the gendering of that addressee as male and the fact that a father is (partly) responsible for the creation of his child, and therefore possibly also has a kind of means to that child's end, allows for the interpretation of the section as addressed to the father and therefore not metaleptic address. One conceivable overall implication of the ambiguity is that an analogy is being drawn between the reader and father as creators.

This implication is also a central theme in 'Life-Story', which in turn also temporarily frustrates identification of the communicative participants. While in 'Title' the speaker and addressee identities are both difficult to discern, and in 'Autobiography: A Self-Recorded Fiction' the address shifts between being directed towards the reader and towards the father, in 'Life-Story' it is solely the speaker identity which is in places confused. The addressee in these instances, though, is consistently the reader. The story is written in the third person and does not use speech marks to differentiate speech. The most famous lines from this collection appear towards the end of this story. In addition to the metanarrative implications of these lines, as discussed in Chapter 3, section 3.2, critics have also noted the metaleptic transgressions they involve (Goffman, 1974, p. 383).

A paragraph begins "The reader! You, dogged, uninsultable, print-oriented bastard, it's you I'm addressing, who else, from inside this monstrous fiction. You've read me this far, then? Even this far?" (p. 127). The paragraph continues in this manner, riddled with the second-person pronoun. Initially, this outburst seems to be voiced by the extradiegetic narrator who thereby, it seems, locates himself spatially "inside this [. . .] fiction", as per Peter Prince in Katz, and as per the character-narrators of 'Title' and 'Autobiography: A Self-Recorded Fiction'. However, whereas in the prior examples a vertical relationship was implied (with words such as "above" and "sunk"), markers of vertical directionality are absent here. The word "inside" could therefore be reasonably read as being used relative to the unit of discourse (e.g. the story) rather than to the bounded ontological space of the storyworld, given that "this [. . .] fiction" could refer to both. Either way, the discourse deictic reference to "inside this [. . .] fiction" foregrounds the speaker's metaleptic awareness of the discourse context and his own fictional ontological status (Thoss's weaker form of metaleptic awareness), and also implies that the reader, the "you", is positioned "outside". As discussed in Chapter 3, section 3.2, the lines also foreground the speaker's and reader's purportedly shared deictic centre with respect to progress through the text-continuum (the speaker's awareness of the printed, physical text here constituting Thoss's stronger form of metaleptic awareness). The paradoxical implications of the metaleptic quality of the communication, as signalled in the multiple discourse deictic uses of spatial and person references, highlight both the ontological differences between speaker and reader and the various conventional illusions that otherwise disguise those differences.

Initially, given the lack of speech marks or reporting clauses to signal otherwise, these words seem to be spoken by the story's narrator. However, the next paragraph begins "Having let off this barrage of rhetorical or at least unanswered questions [. . .] he concluded" (p. 127), which clarifies that the words were in fact spoken not by the narrator but by the central character, referred to here with "he". This prompts a kind of ontological regrading of the prior paragraph: it was not narrator-to-reader communication, but character-to-reader communication. However, the narrator then continues with "why do you suppose— you! you!—he's gone on so, so relentlessly refusing to entertain you [. . .]?" (p. 127) and so we do, ultimately, get an instance of narratorial address of the reader. This address insistently repeats the second-person pronoun, echoing the implications of the words "it's you I'm addressing, who else" within the preceding "barrage", almost as if to counter a hypothesised response on the part of the reader akin to Katz's narrator in the prior example—"who me?" This suggests a further kind of metaleptic awareness on the part of both the narrator and character—awareness of the deictically problematic aspects of use of second-person address in fiction (potentially perceived as singular and personal or plural or general, as immersive or alienating, etc., as discussed in Herman, 2002).

This last example from 'Life-Story' raises the matter of the possibility of metaleptic communication from extradiegetic narrator to reader, of which many more conventional examples can be found in Brophy, Coover, Fowles, Katz, and Johnson. As mentioned, the thorniest issue with regards to metaleptic communication is how far, or perhaps what kinds of, narratorial address of the reader can be perceived as metaleptic. This is also the area of greatest overlap with metanarration (see Chapter 3). As briefly discussed in section 4.2, all narration arguably entails a metaleptic awareness in its implicit or explicit address of a reader. Following this argument, all narration can be considered metaleptic, in that its textually inscribed speaker is a narrator at the extradiegetic level, or a character-narrator at the diegetic level, and the discourse is directed towards an actual addressee at the extrafictional level, albeit arguably via the textually inscribed role of the narratee. Thoss argues that "there is usually nothing metaleptic about the narrator addressing the reader, since they do so as part of the discourse, whose function it is to relate information about the storyworld to recipients" (2015, p. 31). Despite this function, the reader exists in reality, whereas the narrator is a fictional, textual construct, and so a narrator addressing a reader is arguably just as metaleptic as a character addressing a reader (which, incidentally, Thoss does categorise as metalepsis, within his category of "storyworld-reality metalepsis", pp. 28–31). In this view, all of fictional narration is therefore metaleptic communication, in a sense (as implied by Genette, 2004). The metaleptic quality of conventional narrative discourse is covert and does not disrupt the suspension of disbelief. Narratorial discourse which foregrounds its 'vertical' direction to the reader, by second-person address and the like, however, can be considered more overtly metaleptic.

In establishing his stance on metaleptic communication, McHale begins by discussing second-person address (1987, pp. 223–227). Describing the use of "you", he writes, "the most reliable sign of narratorial 'voice', it compels the reader, by its very presence in a text, to hypothesize a circuit of communication joining an addressor and an addressee" (1992, p. 89). For McHale, the second-person pronoun

> presupposes two parties to the communicative act, the one to whom *you* is addressed (the referent of the *you*) and the one doing the addressing. Wherever *you* occurs in a text, there (if nowhere else) the reader is justified in seeking to identify these two parties, and in reconstructing the communicative circuit that presumably joins them.
>
> (p. 90, italics in the original)

McHale argues that

> any instance of *you* may function in any of several difference communicative circuits, located on different narrative levels or planes of the text. The reader's first challenge is thus to determine, for any instance of *you*, on which plane it functions.
>
> (p. 90, italics in the original)

McHale identifies the conventional levels of narrative at which particular communicative acts usually take place: for example, at the extrafictional level, the author addresses the reader; at the extradiegetic level, an extradiegetic narrator addresses an extradiegetic narratee; and at the storyworld level, characters address other characters, or characters address themselves (which, presumably, narrators can also do at the extradiegetic level) (1992, pp. 90–92).

McHale goes on to describe cases of metaleptic communication—specifically, "violations [. . .] of narrative level and communicative logic". Because of their "transgressive" nature, he finds them to be "impossible", and therefore feels they can only be described as cases of " 'pretended' address" (p. 93), which in some ways testifies to the power of the intra-textual ontological structure at work in fiction, illusory though it is. McHale notes that, like metaleptic movements, metaleptic communication can be " 'downward' [. . .] that is, a communicative circuit in which the addressor is located on a level superior to that of the addressee", or it can be "an 'upward' violation (addressor inferior, addressee superior)" (1992, p. 93). He offers examples in which "an extradiegetic narrator pretends to address one of 'his' or 'her' characters", and others in which "an extradiegetic narrator pretends to address the empirical reader directly", more overtly and radically so, it seems, than the address implicit in the act of narration.

Fludernik (2003b) proposes a category of metalepsis which she calls "authorial metalepsis" which is essentially metanarration by a pseudo-authorial narrator, but metanarration without necessarily involving explicit terms of address such as 'you' or 'dear reader'. Notably, McHale's discussions of examples of metaleptic communication to the reader all focus specifically on the use of 'you' in such address, and it is perhaps this use of the deictic pronoun, in foregrounding the discourse participants and in turn their ontological positions, which for him enhances the perceived metaleptic quality (1992, pp. 93–94). Kukkonen likewise includes narratorial address of a reader within her summary of metalepsis (2011, p. 1), which she specifies as occurring through the use of what she calls "verbal deixis" (2011, p. 9). She later clarifies this as use of deictic terms of address or reference such as 'dear reader' or 'you' (p. 16).

The view of narratorial address of the reader outlined here is based on conceiving of the narrator as always present in the act of narration (a view not subscribed to by Hamburger, 1973, Banfield, 1982, and others), as a textually inscribed entity, as the 'speaker', and as distinct and different from the author. Another view would perhaps regard the conceptual construct of the narrator as less important, and would argue that all textual communication is essentially author-to-reader, in the real world, and so no metaleptic communication is involved. Such a view would, however, underplay the apparent significance of the conceptually constructed ontological levels of fictional worlds and the role they play in interpretation and in readers' perceptions of more conventional (e.g. realist) and less conventional (e.g. metafictional) writing.

Another slightly different view might regard both the authorial and narratorial roles as significant, but might conflate the two: that is, a pseudo-authorial narrator might be considered not as a fictional version of an author, but rather as a blend of author and narrator. This would have consequences for the level at which this figure is perceived as being positioned, ontologically, which would in turn have a bearing on whether or not communication from that figure to the reader was regarded as metaleptic.

There are suggestions of this blurring of author and narrator in critical reception of Coover and Johnson, for example. Evenson describes the pseudo-authorial narrator of 'The Magic Poker' as both the "narrator" and "the author/narrator" (Evenson, 2003, p. 56). Alfonso refers to him as "the narrator" (1995, p. 128) and as "the narrator-creator" (p. 127), but also describes "the absence of mediation by a fictional narrator between the reader and the characters" in the story (p. 128), and writes "I assume that it is Coover himself who is, through the first person used by [the] fictional narrator's voice, directly addressing the reader in his abundant self-conscious remarks" (p. 136). Gordon describes the narrator(s) of all of Coover's alternarratives in his collection as the "author-narrator" (1983, p. 89), but also describes the narrator of 'The Magic Poker', specifically, as "Coover's writer-magician" (p. 96) and as "the Coover-narrator" (p. 98). Regarding Johnson, White describes the metanarrative comments in *Christie Malry's Own Double-Entry* as "'authorial' statement[s]" (2005, p. 95). Mengham identifies the narratorial voice in Christie as that of the author, using Johnson's interest at the time in the bomb attacks of the Angry Brigade as justification (2014, p. 130). Splendore refers to the pseudo-authorial narrator as "the author" and "the writer". For example, describing the final metaleptic move in the novel, he writes "the nurses ask the author, not knowing who he is, to leave the room" (1984, p. 96). Tredell likewise describes the narratorial figure in these metaleptic encounters as "the author" (2000, p. 135). Arguably, this phrasing could be short-hand for 'the character who is portrayed as the author', but this is not clearly the case. Critics' identification of the narrator with the author does not confirm the reality of the blending of author and narrator, however. A narrator is unavoidably a sum of textual marks met with a reader's cognitive schemas and anthropomorphising projections. Rather, these examples are testament to the power of the illusion of the pseudo-authorial narrative style as constructed through high frequencies of metanarrational cues.

The nature of the relationship between the author and self-referencing narrator seems less theoretically problematic than the relationship between the reader and a possible extradiegetic narratee role, where again different conceptualisations of the relationship would have consequences with regards to metaleptic communication. Assuming the narrator is identified as the speaker, in the case of a work of fiction with an extradiegetic narrator there seem to be three possible ways of understanding the reader's ontological position and the relative metaleptic quality of the narrative communication. In the first, in the act of reading the text the reader conceptually projects 'downwards' to adopt the position of the textually inscribed narratee role at the extradiegetic level, in which case the communication itself is not metaleptic, but from narrator to narratee within the extradiegesis. The metalepsis involved here is a conceptual metaleptic move on the part of the reader, as will be discussed further in section 4.4. In the second, no such conceptual projection takes place and the reader is always and only at the level of the ontologically real, in which case all narration is 'upward' metaleptic communication, albeit usually covertly so. In the third, like the first, in the act of reading the text the reader conceptually projects downwards to adopt the position of the textually inscribed narratee role at the extradiegetic level, but instances of overt direct address such as narratorial use of 'you' directed at the reader, or use of 'dear reader', etc., foreground for the reader her actual position in the real world at an ontological remove from the fiction, and so create the felt effect of upward metaleptic communication. This third understanding of the reader's processing and positioning would align with some cognitive poetic conceptualisations of reading involving deictic "pushing" and "popping" and the shifting attentional priming and neglect of positions (Macrae, 2012; McIntyre, 2006; Stockwell, 2002, 2009).

The length and depth of this discussion of narratorial address of the reader is a necessary foundation for the analysis of the many instances of such address which have metaleptic effects in Brophy, Coover, Fowles, Johnson, and Katz. Of the five texts, narratorial reader address is most tightly thematically integrated within Brophy's *In Transit: An Heroi-Cyclic Novel* (2002 [1969]). As in the stories from Barth's collection discussed previously, the story attributes to the reader (at least co-)creative responsibility for actualising the narrator. An "interlocutor" figure is introduced in the first pages—"the imaginary interlocutor who is entertained [. . .] by all self-conscious beings" (p. 9). For the character-narrator, this "interlocutory injunction" (p. 15) first manifests in the form of her earliest beloved soft toy, but this is slowly revealed to be a projected form of an internal psychological 'other' through which one's consciousness is expressed and actualised. The narrator then goes on to describe a hypothetical scenario in which the narrator imagines what the reader would do in a particular circumstance (e.g. "What do I think you do? [. . .] I imagine you dramatize your decision"). This ends with "I click my fingers, bite my castanet thumb at you. Got you. That's what I think you do, hypocrite (let me alienate you) lecteur/interlocutor" (p. 18). The character-narrator not only overtly metaleptically directly addresses the reader as "you", and playfully reverses the situation of the reader imagining the character, but also identifies the role of the reader as that of the interlocutor, the force by which the "I" of the character-narrator is brought into being.

A new section, numbered "4", immediately continues in the present tense and addressing the reader as "you [. . .], interlocutor" (p. 18), but then shifts from present tense to past tense and from second-person address to third-person reference: "An airport, I told my interlocutor, is one of the rare places where twentieth century design is happy with its own style" (p. 19). The playful reversal is picked up again on page 73, however, within another passage of metaleptic communication involving direct address in which the character-narrator states

> Suppose for the sake of argument that I am a fictitious character or at least one who appears so to you. I have invited from you a certain temporary identification. I am prepared to be taken over, possessed, by you. In your own eyes, I don't doubt, you are a very real part of the real world. But please remember that, to me it is you who are the fictitious—the, indeed, entirely notional—character. [. . .] I don't even know, for example, what sex you are.

Maack finds that in this passage "Brophy's narrator finally robs the reader of his or her ontological status by presenting him/her as an invention, a fictive character created by the narrator, and this entirely reverses the levels of reality and fiction" (1995, p. 42). While the ontological hierarchy is not, in actuality, reversed, the character-narrator's couching of the reader's ontological reality as a matter of subjective perception—"in your own eyes"—does have the effect of threatening to undermine the reader's certainties about the nature of distinctions between reality and fiction. Meanwhile, the description of the reader's potential identification with the narrating 'I' implicitly suggests a kind of conceptual metalepsis, on the reader's part, entailed in such identification.

In addition to these moments of metaleptic reader address, the character-narrator also interrupts the narrative with several short letters (graphologically laid out as such), all of which constitute overtly metaleptic communication. The first, which the character-narrator describes as an "(at last openly) Open-Letter", includes the following:

> I've muttered you, my dear Reader, several asides on the subject of the technique of fiction, including some about alienation effects—one of which I am indeed practising on you now [. . .]. I want, though I may fail to win, your sympathy for me as narrator as well as for me as character. [. . .] Has it occurred to you there may be a specific determining reason why this narrative should be in the first person? [. . .] So much for the strategy of this narration. [. . .] Pray you, Reader, read on.
>
> (pp. 66–67)

This 'letter' is densely packed with discourse deictic references signalling the character-narrator's ontologically impossible metaleptic awareness of the discourse and its conventions, its fictional nature, and the participant roles involved: the character-narrator directly addresses the reader as "Reader", refers to her/himself as a "narrator" and as a "character", and refers to "this narrative" and to "this narration" being in the "first person". The second, third, and fourth letters involve fewer discourse deictic references of these types, but each explicitly addresses the reader *as* reader: "Yes, dear clever as cartloads of monkeys on parapets Reader [. . .] dear Sir/Madam" (p. 71); "you [. . .] dear Reader" (p. 102), and "I [. . .] address to my Reader-coroner, [. . .] my suicide note" (p. 115) (see also p. 162 and p. 195).

Brophy's character-narrator is keenly aware of, and concerned with, what Kacandes calls the "duplicitous" nature of 'you' as a form of reader address (1993, pp. 148–149; see also Fludernik, 1995; Herman, 2002, pp. 331–371). 'You' is an "empty" pronoun, designating a deictic centre open to occupation by any addressee (Benveniste, 1971 [1966], p. 220). The narratee role in fiction can be conceptually adopted by many potential readers. The impression of direct, personal address from character-narrator to any particular reader is therefore illusory on this basis, as well as the basis of the character-narrator, the speaking 'I', being a conceptual entity reliant upon the reader for actualisation. The description of the first letter as an "Open-Letter" and the second as an "Open memo", the mention in the first quote of the character-narrator not knowing what sex the reader is, and the mention in the first quote and the first letter of alienation effects all foreground this illusion.

The novel closes with an instance of metaleptic communication in which the speaking 'I', the dependence of that 'I' upon the reader for realisation, and the simultaneous general and particular deictic potential of 'you' are all foregrounded yet further. True to the novel's 'cyclic' subtitle, the final paragraph includes the words "I desire You to locute me" and also, finally, "I am coming out now [. . .] to and for You [. . .] the both of You" (p. 236). The capitalisation of the second-person pronoun, and its position as the final word of the text, attracts attention. The reference to "both of You" perhaps connotes both male and female readers (given the prior mention of the reader's sex, and given that the gender identity of the protagonist, unresolvable as male or female, has been a central theme of the novel). Alternatively, it perhaps connotes both the singular and specific reader, and the general 'you' which accommodates the plural—that is, the individual 'you' now encountering the text, and all of the other potential 'yous' who might read it. The character-narrator's "coming out now" could mean coming out (i.e. disclosing) as male or as female, or coming "out" of the fiction ('coming' being a verb bearing deictic directionality, usually away from the current deictic centre of the speaker and towards the deictic centre of the addressee, and 'out', as discussed previously, suggesting a movement from 'inside' to 'outside', potentially out of the conceptual realm of the storyworld to the reality at which the "You" is located). The temporal deictic "now" gives a sense of a shared temporal locus (shared by character-narrator and reader), supporting the illusion of immediacy which can be one of the side-effects of direct address. It is a highly unconventional and ambiguous metaleptic close.

Of Coover's stories, the one involving the most pronounced and thematically integrated narratorial metaleptic address of the reader is 'The Magic Poker' (as discussed in Chapter 3). The story involves frequent metanarrative commentary from the outset, implicitly addressed to the reader, but potentially a kind of self-addressing narratorial interior monologue. On page 19, however, the metanarration employs the second-person pronoun in a more overt direct address to the reader. This occurs within what is presented as a later version of the pseudo-authorial narrator interrupting an earlier version of himself in the middle of a metanarrative comment. It reads

> (I interrupt here to tell you that I have done all that I shall do. I return here to bring you this news, since this seemed as good a place as any. Though you may have more to face, and even more to suffer from me, this is in fact the last thing I shall say to you. But can the end be in the middle? Yes, yes, it always is . . .)
>
> (2011 [1969], p. 19)

The spatial deictic "here" locates this version of the pseudo-authorial narrator with the reader at a shared textual deictic centre within the linear textual sequence. The declaration of a "return" is suggestive of some kind of ontologically impossibly time-travelling or text-travelling potential, paradoxically within the context of an assertion of an authorial and thereby ontologically real function. The pseudo-authorial narrator is seemingly metaleptically aware of the end of the story, and indeed has already reached it, and is likewise metaleptically aware of narrative conventions regarding endings. He makes several self-references (using the first-person pronoun six times) in voicing what he is "here" to "tell you", "do", "bring you", and "say to you". The odd nature of the communication as a parenthetical aside from the pseudo-authorial narrator's future clouds its ontological status in some ways, but its presentation as a metaleptic address of the reader is explicit.

A second instance of narratorial metaleptic communication with the reader using "you" occurs towards the end of this story.

> I am disappearing. You have no doubt noticed. Yes, and by some no doubt calculable formula of event and pagination. But before we drift apart to a distance beyond the reaches of confessions [. . .], listen: [. . .] my invented island is really taking its place in world geography. [. . .] I have invented you, dear reader, while lying here in the afternoon sun, bedded deeply in the bluegreen [sic] grass like an old iron poker.
>
> (pp. 25–26)

The narrator's claim that he is "disappearing" and doing so "by some calculable formula of event and pagination" may be a reference to the fact that the story is coming to an end. This is presumably noticeable to the reader via her schemas of plot arcs (the two main characters, having arrived at the island at the beginning of the story, are now leaving it) and her potential awareness of the page on which the story ends. There is perhaps, then, an implicit reference to the narrator and reader's shared textual deictic centre at this point as well as their shared deictic centre relative to the progression of the conceptual evolution of the storyworld. The references to pagination, to the reader as reader, and implicitly to narrative conventions are evidence of the narrator's apparent metaleptic awareness. The quote goes on to confuse the ontological structure of the fiction in a manner echoic of Brophy's undermining of storyworld-reality distinctions. The iron poker the narrator refers to is a storyworld object, and the grass and sun are described in the same way that the grass and sun in the storyworld have been described (i.e. as "bluegreen" (p. 11), "hot midday" sun (p. 7), etc.). His spatial deictic "here" implicitly and impossibly locates the pseudo-authorial narrator within the storyworld that he has invented, seemingly having shifted from the extradiegesis to the diegesis, or having been within the diegesis all along. At the same time, though, the narrator is maintaining the claim regarding his authorial role, asserting that the storyworld has become real and proposing that the reader is his invention. These lines are arguably merely foregrounding truths about the ontology of the fiction and its participants: the storyworld has been realised within the reader's imagination in her process of following the story; the narrator is equivalent to a fictional character in the sense that the boundary between diegesis and extradiegesis is illusory; and the reader is solely imagined by the author at the point of writing, prior to an actual reader stepping into the narratee role. In tandem with the story's metanarrative commentary (as discussed in Chapter 3) and disnarration (as discussed in Chapter 5), this final ontological confusion may be the tipping point which, as in Barth's 'Title', creates an effect of perceived metaleptic collapse.

Katz use of pseudo-authorial narrator address of the reader is particularly unusual, with interesting ontological implications. One instance of such address occurs soon after the quote, discussed previously, in which Linda Lawrence exhibits various kinds of metaleptic awareness, saying to her co-character Philip Farrel "Of course if you're sick of the whole thing you can just walk out through Gottlieb's Exit on the next page, don't worry" (p. 120). As mentioned previously, a diagram of a double-door exit covers the next page. On the page after that, the narrator states "Those of you who are already worn out by this book, I don't blame you. You can turn back a page and go out through Gottlieb's Exit" (p. 123). "Those of you" suggests that this "you" is plural, and that the pseudo-authorial narrator is addressing several potential readers (specifically, a particular group among his potential readers). His discourse deictic reference to "this book" foregrounds his metaleptic awareness of the physical material form of the end product of the discourse. This impression is furthered by his discourse deictic reference to Gottlieb's Exit "back a page", relative to the textual deictic centre on page 123 of the linear text-continuum, which the narrator implies he and the reader currently share. The spatial deictics involved in the combination of "turn back a page" and "go out through" are strange, though, in that they position the reader first in relation to the text-continuum and second as 'inside' the physical text, implicitly alongside Philip Farrel, as if immersed both in the conceptual storyworld and the tissue of print.

Whereas this example suggests a blurring of the textual and ontological dimensions and suggests an ontological repositioning of the reader, other instances of pseudo-authorial narrator address of the reader in Katz's novel maintain the impression of the reader as positioned external to both the storyworld and extradiegesis. Following a section of alter-narration in three parallel columns (as discussed in Chapter 5), Katz's narrator states

> By now I'm sure you want to know what's really happening, where it's really at, what's actually going on and where. I'm going to tell you. [. . .] First of all where am I? This is an air-conditioned library study. [. . .] As you may be able to tell from the way this book looks, the light here is fluorescent.
>
> (p. 74)

Later, on page 168, he states "I do suggest that you finish this book, if you haven't already started it that way, under fluorescent light" (p. 168). The narrator here is at pains to explain to the reader details about the context of his act of composition. In the words "This is an air-conditioned library study", the pronoun "this" functions as a proximal demonstrative foregrounding the narrator's deictic centre within a fictional space. He appears to be effectively fleshing out the extradiegesis, albeit to a limited degree. The portrayal of his act of creation as that of the real author— that is, of this extradiegetic space as the real-world context of the book's creation—is undermined by the playful and surreal implication that the fluorescent lighting in the room is somehow perceptible in the appearance of the final production (again, of which the narrator is metaleptically aware, hence "the way this book looks").

In both examples from Katz, the narrator voices hypotheses, assumptions, or recommendations about the reader's concerns or behaviour. This highlights the fact that, despite the impression of communication, the discourse context is split (as discussed in Chapter 2, section 2.4) and the narrator has no way of receiving actual information about or communication from the reader. Johnson's pseudo-authorial narrator performs the same trick. For example, at one point he states " 'Where', you must be screaming, 'did Christie find his gelignite? I can't obtain gelignite. Not that I want to, of course' " (p. 106). This largely functions as a projected metanarrative comment, implicitly projecting a degree of dubiousness about the plot upon the reader to justify then explaining the plot development in question. The specificity of the comments, voicing an "I" on the reader's behalf, and humorously also suggesting that the reader suddenly recognises that what she is 'saying' might seem suspicious, highlights the difference between this hypothetical "you" and the actual reader, with the potential effect of alienating the real reader from any felt address. Another example appears within one of the depictions of a table of double-entry bookkeeping. This is seemingly 'written' by the pseudo-authorial narrator, as Christie is referred to within it by name. Regarding one of his acts of "recompense", the narrator has added "you will be relieved to hear" that there was "negligible damage to property" (p. 151). Some of the chapter titles also suggest this hypothesising: Chapter XVII is titled "The No Doubt Welcome Return of the Shrike" (p. 135), and, in a more Shandean move, Chapter I is titled "The Industrious Pilgrim: an Exposition without which You might have felt Unhappy" (p. 9) and Chapter XXI is titled "In which Christie and I have it All Out; and which you may care to Miss Out" (p. 163). These instances of pseudo-narratorial reader address arguably hover between Lawrence Sterne and George Eliot in their effects. However, in the context of the novel's insistent metafictionality, it is hard not to find, as Ryf does, that the portrayed act "of speaking directly to the reader reinforces the sense of artifice" (1977, p. 71)—that is, it foregrounds the illusions at play in the novel's use (and abuse) of such conventions.

The pseudo-authorial narrator in Fowles's *The French Lieutenant's Woman* metaleptically addresses the reader throughout the novel in his frequent metanarrative commentary, as discussed in Chapter 3. Three examples of this address, from the densely metanarrative Chapter 13, are "Perhaps you suppose that a novelist has only to pull the right strings and his puppets will behave in a lifelike manner" (p. 97); "Oh, but you say, come on—what I really mean is that the idea crossed my mind" (p. 98); and "But this is preposterous? A character is either 'real' or 'imaginary'? If you think that, *hypocrite lecteur*, I can only smile" (p. 99, italics in the original). All three examples express the kinds of hypotheses and assumptions about the reader's concerns or behaviour suggested in Johnson, and have the same effect of highlighting the split discourse context, creating tension between the illusion of direct address and the ontological impossibility of real communicative exchange.

The last example here is particularly notable in this regard. Fowles's narrator's use of the phrase "hypocrite lecteur" as a term of address to the reader echoes Brophy's use of the same phrase in the first concentrated example of overt reader address in *In Transit*, as discussed previously: "That's what I think you do, hypocrite (let me alienate you) lecteur/interlocutor" (p. 18). Both authors are intertextually recalling the last line of

Baudelaire's poem 'Au lecteur' ('To the reader'): "hypocrite lecteur,—mon semblable,—mon frère!" (1961, p. 6), echoed also by T. S. Eliot in part 1, line 76 of *The Waste Land* (2002 [1954], p. 43) and in Nabokov's *Lolita* ("Reader! *Bruder!*", 1995 [1959], p. 262). Indeed, Brophy goes on to use the words "mon semblable, mon frère" only two pages after her use of "hypocrite [. . .] lecteur". One of the dominant themes of Baudelaire's poem is humankind's collective, perversely committed belief in things we know not to be true and failure to acknowledge what is known to be the case. The intertextual appropriation of this phrase brings its implications to bear on the perverse suspensions of disbelief entailed in reading fiction.

Most of the examples of overt narratorial metaleptic communication with the reader in Barth, Brophy, Coover, Fowles, Katz, and Johnson are brief passages, often presented as asides. Fowles's metanarrative Chapter 13 is one exception. Another significant exception, of a different kind, though, is Coover's 'Panel Game' (pp. 62–70) which is narrated wholly in the second person. According to Fludernik (2011), in the case of second-person narration, when the 'you' is recognised as referring to a character—that is, "after the referent has been established as a character in the story ('not-me, actually she or he')"—the 'you' becomes non-deictic and loses its "address-function" (pp. 107–108). Herman (2002) also differentiates between the deictic value of 'you' in what he calls "apostrophic address", in which "the address operates vertically [. . .], directed toward and actual (storyworld-external)" addressee (p. 361), and in "fictionalized address", whereby 'you' is used "as a reference (or address) to a fictional character" (p. 360). For Herman, unlike Fludernik, the use of 'you' to refer to a fictional character does not lose its deictic value or address function. Arguably, once the 'you' is recognised as consistently referring to a character in storyworld, it loses its potential effect of making the reader feel directly addressed (for more on this, see Macrae, 2012). However, in such cases the deictic value of the 'you' is not lost: 'you' is inherently deictic and is meaningful relative to the implicit 'I' of the speaker, and in the context of metafiction this meaning gains further specifically discourse deictic value in signalling discursive positions and roles in relation to the fictional discourse. In 'Panel Game', and perhaps in all cases of second-person fiction (at least, all cases in which the use of 'you' is not identifiably that of self-address, which Herman calls "$I \rightarrow you$ transfer", 2002, p. 367, italics in the original), the second-person narration constitutes metaleptic communication downwards, from extradiegetic narrator to character as referent and addressee. The mode is marked perhaps precisely because direct communication between the discursive roles of extradiegetic narrator and diegetic character constitutes a radical breach of the conventional ontological configurations of fiction.

The second-person mode is perhaps also marked because of the tension between an initial perception of extradiegetic narratorial uses of 'you' as often referring to and addressing the reader, and so 'upward' in direction, and the evolving realisation that the reader is in fact not the addressee but an overhearer. In 'Panel Game' the tendency and drive to conceptually occupy the position of the "you" is particularly confronting due to the extremely surreal, bizarre, and uncomfortable experiences of the "you"-character in the story, ending with "you" being hanged (p. 70). In other, longer works, where the effect can become naturalised over time, this use of 'you' may become less jarring. However, initially, at least, and in short works such as 'Panel Game', use of the deictic 'you' in fictionalised address foregrounds the conventional communicative circuit of fictional discourse, the tendency of readers to conceptually occupy the position designated by 'you', the ontological impossibility of that identification in such circumstances, and the reader's real ontological position outside of the storyworld.

This section has explored different forms of metaleptic communication and how discourse deixis contributes to the demarcation of participant roles and ontological positions in that communication. As mentioned at the start of this section, metaleptic communication relies upon the entities involved remaining at their different ontological levels. The next section investigates what happens when entities move ontological levels and analyses the role of discourse deixis in these moves.

4.4 Metaleptic Moves

Metaleptic moves are the most critically discussed form of metalepsis. Different critical views on metalepsis variably allow for objects, characters, narrators, narratees, authors, and readers to be portrayed as physically appearing at a narrative level different from the level at which they were previously located (cf. Bell and Alber, 2012; Fludernik, 2003b; Genette, 1980; Hanebeck, 2017; Nelles, 1997, 1992; Ryan, 2015, 2006; Thoss, 2015). One of the chief markers of metaleptic moves is the spatial deictic language through which the dislocated entity is signalled as situated within its new level. Person deixis can also play a role, particularly in signalling changed narrative modes and participant relations. Other markers include discourse deictic references to, for example, narrative levels—i.e. in narratorial description of the shift, or within the startled comments of other characters who have witnessed the shift (those characters thereby functioning as Wolf's 'reception figures', as mentioned in section 4.1).

A narrator shifting levels is the most common kind of metaleptic 'move'. Stereotypically, in this kind of metalepsis, a narrator is established as an extradiegetic entity and then at some (or several) point(s) in the narrative the narrator disrupts this narrative situation by metaleptically shifting 'downwards' to adopt a narratorial position within the diegesis. Characters can also be portrayed as crossing this diegesis-extradiegesis divide. Cohn refers to metaleptic crossing of this divide (by characters or narrators, in either direction) as "exterior metalepsis", in comparison to a metaleptic crossing of the hypodiegesis-diegesis divide, where this occurs, which he calls "interior metalepsis" (2012, p. 106).

The extradiegesis–extrafictional reality divide is subject to metaleptic transgressions as well. Thoss (2015) also explores metaleptic transgressions between extrafictional reality and the diegesis which leap over both divides and the extradiegesis altogether (see section 4.1). A fictitious version of the reader can be represented as appearing within the diegesis, for example, as in Federman's *Take It or Leave It* (1976). As described in Chapter 2, section 2.5, a delegation of readers is referred to, who nominate a different narrator to take over the narratorial role of the first-person narrator-protagonist. As mentioned in Chapter 1, section 1.3, though, the situation gets more radical when two different representative readers appear in the storyworld, one of whom is presented as seducing and having a sexual liaison with the protagonist. Hanebeck proposes what he calls second-person metalepsis "in which a protagonist (in second-person fiction) or the [fictive] narratee, addressed by narrative *you*, moves from one diegetic level to another" (2017, pp. 97–98, italics in the original, drawing on Fludernik's (2003b) "lectorial" ontological metalepsis). However, it is hard to find examples beyond Federman's fictive narrative audience. Of course, these are fictional character representations of readers, and, unlike the ontological divide between the diegesis and the extradiegesis, the ontological divide between those two levels and the level of reality is very much real, and so this kind of metalepsis is artificial in a slightly different sense to narrator or character metalepsis between the diegesis and the extradiegesis.

Ryan stresses the protection of the extrafictional level from physical metalepsis: though some impact upon the reader and her relationship with reality is expected and often sought from engagement with and realisation of literary worlds (see Malina, 2002), metalepsis can never break the boundary between the real and the fictional, but is, "rather, a breaking of boundaries that operates strictly within the diegetic levels of a fictional world" (Ryan, 2015, p. 372; cf. 2006, p. 209). The division between extrafictional reality and the extradiegesis cannot be transgressed in a physical sense, even if some conventional fictive illusions suggest the contrary. The extradiegesis can be fleshed out with details in mimicry of the extrafictional reality (e.g. historical references), but it remains, nonetheless, part of the fiction. In the case of the pseudo-authorial narrator, an extradiegetic narrator is given to adopt the identity and compositional responsibility of the extrafictional author. However, in such cases, the author is not portrayed as transgressing an ontological boundary; rather, the narrator and author are portrayed as being one and the same, and the extradiegesis is portrayed as the extrafictional reality. Behind the illusion (which prompts descriptions such as the 'Coover-narrator', discussed in section 4.3), the distinction between the textual narrator and the real author, and the boundary between the extradiegesis and extrafictional reality, remain intact. Cowley raises this distinction in discussing the first metanarrative comment in *The Exagggerations of Peter Prince*, in which the pseudo-authorial narrator appears to address himself as Katz the author, by name, in exasperation, saying "Enough! Katz, you're making this all up. It doesn't make a bit of sense" (p. 4). Cowley makes the point that the real author and narratorial voice are not the same: "such intrusions are familiar in recent fiction, but of course it is the name, not the author, that has really entered the text. 'Katz' shares the same verbal reality as 'Peter Prince' and his companions" (1986, p. 131). Only extradiegetic and diegetic participants can achieve actual physical metalepsis.

However, as suggested by the figure of the pseudo-authorial narrator in examples such as the previous quote from Katz (and tens of other examples discussed elsewhere in this book) the real ontological distinction between the fictionally constructed levels and reality does not prevent the illusion of author metalepsis in fiction (if the pseudo-authorial narrator figure is regarded as such). Furthermore, as with narratorial address of the reader, this kind of metalepsis can be constructed as overt, radical, transgressive, and breaking the suspension of disbelief or as an extension of the mimesis to the extradiegetic level to further support the suspension of disbelief (cf. Nünning's "mimesis of telling" as discussed in Chapter 3, section 3.6, and also McHale, 1987, pp. 197–198). The former tends to serve metafictional functions.

Bell and Alber's (2012) concepts of 'transworld identity' and 'counterparthood', drawn from Possible Worlds theory, offer a means of reconceptualising potential moves across narrative levels. Bell and Alber distinguish between two kinds of metaleptic moves. In one type, a literary participant (a character, narrator, reader, author, etc., or in some cases an inanimate entity) gains a "counterpart" in a level different to the level in which the original version of that literary participant exists. In this type of move, the literary participant undergoes a kind of doubling to appear in more than one level, with "ontological simultaneity". While this might not be considered 'moving', exactly, Bell and Alber nonetheless describe it as such. In the other type, a literary participant more properly moves, in that the participant has a transworld identity—a single identity which moves from one ontological level to another, with existence in one nullifying (or coinciding with a lack of) existence in the other (2012, pp. 173–174). The term 'transworld identity' is also used by Dannenberg with reference to alternarration (see Chapter 5, section 5.3) and by McHale (1987, pp. 203–204, though McHale seems to use it to describe both what Bell and Alber see as counterparthood and what they see as transworld identity).

Bell and Alber follow Ryan in proposing these types, building on her suggestion that metalepsis occurs "when an existent belongs to two or more levels at the same time, or when an existent migrates from one level to the next" (2006, p. 207). However, while Ryan proposes that either the latter kind, or both kinds, of metalepsis "opens up a passage between levels that results in their interpenetration, or mutual contamination" (p. 207), Bell and Alber argue that both types "rel[y] on the separation rather than the entanglement or blending of ontological domains" in that "in each case, an individual (i.e. only *one* part of a given world) moves from a domain to another whether by possessing a transworld identity or by existing as a counterpart" (2012, pp. 173–174, italics in the original).

In the light of this thinking, the extradiegetic pseudo-authorial narrator could arguably be considered a metaleptic counterpart of the extra-fictional author—a version of the author existing within the fictionally constructed discourse and with a different ontological status. Furthermore, the extradiegetic narratee, and/or diegetic second-person protagonist (as in Coover's 'Panel Game'), could be considered a metaleptic counterpart of the extrafictional reader. This conceptualisation would accommodate the difference between the nature of the boundary between the extradiegesis and extrafictional reality, which could be subject only to counterparthood type metaleptic 'moves', and the boundary between the diegesis and extradiegesis, which could be subject to both counterparthood and transworld identity type metaleptic moves. This conceptualisation would also allow for the kinds of readings which conflate the author and the narrator, as described previously, and those which conflate the narratee or second-person protagonist and the reader, and/or it may more properly acknowledge the felt effects of the illusion of such conflations.

One consequence of considering the narratee as a metaleptic counterpart of the reader is that narration by an extradiegetic narrator (pseudo-authorial or otherwise, and overt, e.g. metanarration and/or using direct address, or otherwise) would not qualify as metaleptic communication, as the communication would be from one position within the extradiegesis to another position within the extradiegesis. This would require reconsideration and possible recategorisation of some of the examples discussed in section 4.3.

The concept of counterparthood may or may not be considered a convincing account of any seeming metaleptic aspects of the figures of the pseudo-authorial narrator and/or narratee (i.e. as counterparts of the real-world author and reader). The concepts of counterparthood and transworld—or perhaps more properly, or in the instance of the parameters of this study, trans*level*—identities do, nonetheless, seem to be useful in exploring the various instances of upward and downward metaleptic moves made by narrators and characters and in analysing the discourse deixis which marks those moves.

It is perhaps significant that apart from the pseudo-authorial narrator in *The Exagggerations of Peter Prince* using "Katz" in self-address, as mentioned previously, the other pseudo-authorial narrators are *not* given the same names as the authors, or indeed given names at all. The name

Brigid Brophy does, however, appear twice in *In Transit*, first attached to a review of the embedded erotic story of Oc—" 'straightforward commercial pornography: and what's wrong with that?'—*Brigid Brophy*" (p. 100)—and later when captions appearing on a TV report "programme devised by Brigid Brophy" (p. 138). As discussed in Chapter 2, section 2.3, proper names have a deictic function similar to definite reference (i.e. this Brigid Brophy, the Brigid Brophy most proximal or relevant to this context). Arising within the novel as they do, in association with the creation of (further) fictional worlds presented as real within the main storyworld, the uses of her name evoke fictional, counterpart versions of the real author Brigid Brophy. The ontologically impossible nature of these brief and unexplained references is both jarring and playful, drawing the reader's attention to the fictionality of the discourse.

Unusual and ontologically confusing though these uses of Brophy's name are, they do not feel like fully fledged metalepsis. A similar feeling surrounds the other form of what might be considered a metaleptic move in this novel (i.e. that it hovers at the edges of metalepsis proper). About halfway through the novel, the narratorial mode in the novel overtly and significantly alters. As mentioned in section 4.1, in discussing examples from Balzac and Proust involving narratorial shifts from first to third person or vice versa, Genette writes that "the reader unfailingly takes [. . .] transition from one status to the other—when he perceives it—as an infraction of an implicit norm" (1980, p. 245). Up until this point in *In Transit* the narration has been in the first person. Following the fourth of the letters directly addressed to the reader, discussed in section 4.3—this one a 'suicide note'—the narrative mode changes from first person to third. The story of the protagonist continues with "O'Rooley ran lithely down the steps" (p. 115) and the character continues to be referred to in the third person. A central theme of the novel is gender identity (the gender of the protagonist, the gendering within languages, etc.), and the narrator has suggested at various points that the narrative mode can be in third person only once her/his gender is identified (i.e. prior to this identification occurring, the narrator states "Has it occurred to you there may be a specific determining reason why this narrative should be in the first person?", p. 66), which, along with the direct continuation of action for that figure designated with "I" and then "he", suggests that the entity remains constant and it is simply the pronoun designation which has changed. The shift from first to third person nonetheless deictically 'others' the protagonist from the narrator.

Considering the storyworld protagonist and the narrating persona as counterparts of one another is one way of attempting to ontologically rationalise the situation. That attempt is stymied somewhat by both the "suicide note" preceding this change and the nature of further person-switching at the close of the novel, however. As discussed in Chapter 5, the second half of the novel shifts between gendering the protagonist as male and as female, and splits at times into parallel narration, simultaneously following essentially intradiegetic counterpart versions of the protagonist—one male and one female. At the end of the novel, discussed in section 4.3, we get a brief moment of first-person narration again, beginning with "It no longer matters a damn of course whether 'I' is masc. or fem. or whether 'you' is sing. or plur. [. . .] I crawled out from the control tower" (p. 234). The previously extradiegetic narrator has apparently re-assumed the position and voice of the protagonist figure within the diegesis once more. And yet, this shifts again on the next page, returning to the parallel, third-person narratives, with "Neatly Patricia swung her legs over the side of the girder" on the left and "Convinced by his interlocutors [. . .] Patrick decided to come out of his perilous predicament" on the right (p. 235). The narrative voice then returns back to "I" for the final three paragraphs, after both "he" and "she" have died (p. 236). If it were not for the apparent deaths of each entity at particular junctures in these transitions, metaleptic counterparthood could potentially account for the deictic relationship between the sometimes extradiegetic and sometimes diegetic narrating 'I' and the diegetic Patrick and Patricia. As it is, though, the narrative resists any resolution in the form of an ultimately clear hierarchical ontological structure. Perhaps, as with other specifically anti-conventional, cyclic drives in the novel, the hierarchical structure on which metalepsis is fundamentally based is being subverted and dismantled through an ontological cycle of death and rebirth instead.

The shift in narratorial pronoun use in apparent self-designation is also one of the most interesting, and yet least discussed, aspects of the metaleptic moves in *The French Lieutenant's Woman*. Fowles's novel has been seen as metaleptic by Cohn (2012), Hanebeck (2017), Kukkonen (2011), Onega (1989), Nelles (1992, 1997), Ryan (2006), Thoss (2011), Waugh (1984), and Wolf (2005). The narrator persistently asserts that the storyworld characters and objects exist on the same ontological plane as the pseudo-authorial narrator and the reader, creating the illusion of historical realism as if to hide the ontological boundaries between the levels of narrative. For example, he claims to have bought a toby jug once owned by Sarah (p. 268), and reports that Ernestina lived to 93 and died on the day that Hitler invaded Poland (p. 33) (discussed by Waugh, 1984, p. 33, and Onega, 1989, pp. 73–75). However, there are two instances in the novel in which the extradiegetic pseudo-authorial narrator metaleptically appears within the storyworld, and both of these instances are presented in such a way as to overtly foreground the ontological paradoxes involved.

In the first of these metaleptic episodes, the narrator joins Charles, the protagonist, in a train carriage. This seems to be an example of what Fludernik terms "the narrator-turned-witness", the phenomenon of a narrator appearing as a character in the fictional world and observing and/or interacting with characters within that storyworld (2003b, p. 395).

During this episode the narrator initially introduces the figure in the train carriage using the third person, but then reveals the figure to be the narrator himself, and from then on refers to him(self) in the first person, until he and Charles part ways. In the second episode, the narrator appears in the street outside the house in which Charles and Sarah have their last exchange in the novel. During this episode, the figure in the street, though presented as the pseudo-authorial narrator, is referred to by that same narrator in the third person, and so is deictically othered from the seemingly still simultaneously extradiegetic narratorial deictic centre. These metaleptic episodes can be conceived of as involving translevel identity on the part of the narrator in the first instance and a narratorial counterpart in the second. This conceptualisation of the situation is blurred, though, by various textual contributors to metafictional and ontological confusion.

As mentioned, in the first episode the narrator initially presents his metaleptic entry into the storyworld train carriage using the third person. Charles has been staring at a stranger, speculating about him, has been caught in the act, and so has turned away and subsequently fallen asleep. The narrator then states

> For a while his travelling companion took no notice of the sleeping Charles. But as the chin sank deeper and deeper [. . .] the prophet-bearded man began to stare at him. His look was peculiar: sizing, ruminative [. . .]. You may one day come under a similar gaze. And you may—in the less reserved context of our own century—be aware of it. [. . .]
>
> It is precisely [. . .] the look an omnipotent god—if there were such an absurd thing—should be shown to have [. . .] one of a distinctly mean and dubious [. . .] moral quality. I see this with particular clarity on the face, only too familiar to me, of the bearded man who stares at Charles. And I will keep up the pretence no longer.
>
> Now the question I am asking, as I stare at Charles, is [. . .] what the devil am I going to do with you?
>
> (pp. 388–389)

The narrator continues with some metanarrative and existential rumination on his choices with regards to Charles's future, eventually saying "as we near London, I think I see a solution" (p. 390) and he tosses a coin to decide Charles's fate. The metaleptic episode then ends with

> So be it. And I am suddenly aware that Charles is looking at me. [. . .] he perceives I am either a gambler or mentally deranged. [. . .] We draw under [. . .] the roof of Paddington station. We arrive, he steps down to the platform [. . .]. In a few minutes [. . .] he turns. The bearded man has disappeared in the throng.
>
> (p. 390)

The "prophet-bearded man", initially deictically othered from the extradiegetic narrator, is situated within the train carriage with Charles. The extradiegetic narrator then directly addresses the reader with "you" and deictically refers to "our own century", suggesting that he and the reader share a temporal deictic locus in reality. Furthermore, in the middle of this metaleptic episode, following his revelation of the "pretence", and his switch to the first person and present tense, he says "I have pretended to slip back into 1867; but of course that year is in reality a century past" (p. 390). The temporal deixis of this sentence affirms the impression that the century in which this train travel is taking place is chronologically prior to ours, and is part of the pseudo-authorial narrator's and reader's supposedly shared "reality" and history. At the same time, the claim to have "pretended" to "slip back" exposes the illusion *as* an illusion. This exposure of the impossibility of time-travel within one plane of reality paradoxically disguises the ontological shift across different planes of reality, and yet the person-switching foregrounds exactly that ontological shift.

The ontological confusion of the passage is confounded again and again. To recap, first, the reader encounters direct address and the suggestion of a shared temporal locus with the extradiegetic narrator. Second, she encounters the revelation of the first "pretence", that is, the revelation that the bearded man is in fact the narrator himself. Third, she encounters the revelation of the second pretence, suggesting that the narrator has *not* in fact time-travelled "back" through history to this point, while this claim nonetheless implies that this storyworld scene is a moment in the history of the reader's real world. Yet, towards the end of that passage, that illusion of time-travel is reaffirmed, with the person and spatial deictics of the phrases "we near London" and "we draw under [. . .] the roof" firmly locating the narrator and Charles together in the train carriage as it arrives at its destination.

Bell and Alber argue, on the basis of this incident specifically, that "this novel exemplifies counterparthood rather than transworld identity since its author exists in two realms at the same time: as an author figure in the storyworld of the protagonists and as an author writing the novel in the actual world" (2012, p. 180). Bell and Alber (2012) and Klimek (2010) notably read the storyworld pseudo-authorial narrator as a counterpart to Fowles himself, rather than as a counterpart to, or translevel manifestation of, the extradiegetic version of that pseudo-authorial narrator (though for Klimek this disqualifies the extract from being considered metaleptic since "metaleptic transgressions are fiction-internal phenomena that cannot involve extrafictional reality", Hanebeck, 2017, p. 29, n. 33, citing Klimek, 2010, p. 44). Though McHale describes this metaleptic move as "the author [. . .] shar[ing] a train compartment with his character", and as an example of instances in which "the author enters the fictional world and confronts his characters *in his role of author*",

McHale is careful to include the caveat that this is only what "at least *appears* to happen" (1987, p. 213, italics in the original). Phelan and Rabinowitz more explicitly identify the moving participant as the narrator, rather than the author, in asserting that "Fowles has his extradiegetic narrator [. . .] enter the diegesis" (2005, pp. 547–548). Despite the narrator's initial and final third-person reference to the storyworld manifestation of himself, and in particular given that this reference is cast as a "pretence", this episode does seem to be one of downward metalepsis endowing the otherwise extradiegetic narrator with a translevel identity.

In discussing the metafictional implications of this passage, Bell and Alber argue that

> this descending metaleptic jump differs from Genette's authorial metalepsis insofar as the novel represents the author as actually descending into the world of a character who can also see him. Nevertheless, their functions seem to converge in this case: according to Fludernik, 'authorial metalepsis' closely correlates with 'the baring of the mimetic illusion by undermining the realistic expectations that the narrator merely tells a story over which he has no power'. We read the descending metaleptic jump [. . .] as a similar display of control or, more simply [. . .] a form of narcissism that allows the author to brag about his abilities in relation to the tales that he tells.
>
> (2012, pp. 179–180, citing Fludernik, 2003b, p. 384)

Bell and Alber's discussion of this extract seems to miss the fact that within this scene the pseudo-authorial narrator does not consistently present himself as having "control". For example, the narrator seems surprised by Charles's noticing him upon waking, as though Charles's sudden awareness of the narrator is not something that the narrator has orchestrated. Interestingly, Charles in some ways functions as a reception figure (Wolf, 2013) in that his lack of recognition of the narrator as narrator, and his minimal reaction to his presence, beyond slight suspicion, helps this metaleptic move seem in some ways unremarkable in the context of this novel. Rather than straightforwardly reflecting a theme of authorial godlike control, this extract—like Chapter 13 of the novel—contains complex ludic contradictions with respect to the pseudo-authorial narrator's role, his relation to his story (across various deictic dimensions), and his agency.

The other metaleptic move in this novel occurs between the two final endings, discussed in detail in Chapter 5, section 5.3. As mentioned previously, the pseudo-authorial narrator appears once again within the storyworld, outside the building in which Charles and Sarah are having their heated final conversation in the novel. The narrator states "It is a time-proven rule of the novelist's craft never to introduce any but very minor characters at the end of a book" only in order to affirm that he has not broken this rule through the presence of "the extremely important-looking person that has, during the last scene, been leaning against the parapet of the embankment across the way from 16 Cheyne Walk" (p. 440). The pseudo-authorial narrator seems to begin by overtly fore-grounding the fictional quality of the discourse and affirming the illusion of his role as author (implicitly metaleptically aware of the discourse as a book, nearing its end), thereby positioned ontologically outside of the invented storyworld and its "scene[s]". The person he then introduces is spatially located very much within the storyworld, relative to the house, for example, from which he later "draws briskly away" (p. 441). The narrator explains

> I did not want to introduce him; but since he is the sort of man [. . .] for whom the first is the only pronoun, [. . .] and since I am the kind of man who refuses to intervene in nature [. . .] he has got himself in *as he really is*. I shall not labour the implication that he was pre-viously got in as he really wasn't, and is therefore not [. . .] a new character.
>
> (p. 440, italics in the original)

If this is not a new character, then this is the same narrator who has been narrating throughout (and continues to do so now), though strategically othering himself in the form of a new version. The narrator goes on to report that this figure's "once full, patriarchal beard has been trimmed down to something rather foppish and Frenchified" (p. 440), implicitly (though with no explicit metadiscursive reference) signalling the narra-tor's current embodiment of the author in the style of an author of the French *nouveau roman* rather than the style of the Victorian realist patri-archal author-god. We are told, though, that in some significant aspects he "has not changed: he very evidently regards the world as his to possess and use as he likes" (p. 441). The metafictional connotations here are confusing, but the implication is that, despite the deictic othering, this author-god character is the same figure who metaleptically appeared in the train carriage and is therefore a metaleptic third-person counterpart of the very same narrator who is currently referring to this figure in the third person.

The two downward narratorial metaleptic moves in Johnson's *Christie Malry's Own Double-Entry* are more simple instances of translevel iden-tity. The narration has, throughout the novel, been in the third-person mode, albeit with occasional narratorial first-person self-references within some of the many metanarrative comments. In both metaleptic instances, towards the end of the novel, new chapters open with the pseudo-authorial narrator and the main character, who is now hospitalised, conversing about the book. In the first episode, both the narrator and the charac-ter flaunt all manner of metaleptic awareness through discourse deictic references to "this novel", "another twenty-two pages", the narrator hypothesising about what "reader[s] may wish me to invent", Christie arguing that "most readers won't read it", etc. (p. 165). It is not initially clear that the narrator is actually within the storyworld space with the character, and that the two are not, instead, metaleptically communicating across the extradiegesis-diegesis divide. However, near the end of the first episode, the narrator states "Christie smiled gently, turned back to me" (p. 166), which could suggest they are in the same space, on the same ontological level. This is much more conclusively communicated in the second episode, however, in the narrator's description of this event as "what [Christie] must have seen as my last visit to him" (p. 178) and in the final sentence of the chapter: "And the nurses then suggested I leave, not knowing who I was, that he could not die without me" (p. 180). The narrator consistently foregrounds his authorial agency throughout these episodes, despite at the same time being within the very fictional world he claims he is inventing.

As in scholarly discussion of Fowles, some critics map out the relationship between the real author and the narrator in Johnson differently to the depiction of metaleptic relations presented here. Bell and Alber describe the first metaleptic move as an instance of authorial counterparthood, arguing that "the author's counterpart realizes that his novel is almost complete and the character accepts his fate" and asserting that at the end of the novel there is a "positive relationship between creator and created" (2012, p. 182). Levitt's assertion that "the author himself appears as a character at Christie's deathbed" similarly suggests that the storyworld figure is a counterpart of the real author, rather than a narrator possessing translevel identity (1982, p. 582). Johnson's texts tend to involve pseudo-authorial narrators keen on metanarrative commentary. Levitt elsewhere talks of Johnson's "authorial intrusions" (p. 575) and talks of another of Johnson's protagonists, Albert Angelo, as "B. S. Johnson and Albert Angelo blurred" (p. 577). (Levitt justifiably notes the more complex relationships between narratorial figure and author in Johnson's fictionalised autobiographical work *See the Old Lady Decently*, 1975; see Gibbons, 2017, on fictionalised autobiographies). Whether the figure manifesting in the storyworld is considered a counterpart of the author, thereby crossing both the extradiegesis-extrafictional reality divide *and* the diegesis-extradiegesis divide (if, indeed, the extradiegesis is part of these theorists' conceptualisations), or is considered a translevel pseudo-authorial narrator, thereby crossing only the diegesis-extradiegesis divide, there is apparent agreement that these episodes are metaleptic moves.

Finally, Katz's *The Exagggerations of Peter Prince* presents five equally unusual metaleptic moves, all of which appear to involve translevel identities. In the first of these examples, the narrator explains that one of his "hired hands", Philip Farrel, has been in need of reassurance regarding the behaviour of his companion, Linda Lawrence, and so the narrator has "dropped in on her" to talk things over. He narrates everything he says to her, but also reports her apparent lack of reaction, for example "She wouldn't look me in the face all the time I talked so I think I was getting to her. It must have been a real shock to her to have her own author walk in while she was cooking" and

> she blushed [. . .] when I said "confusion" and cried a little, partly because she was slicing onions. I did drop in near dinner-time. [. . .] She didn't even have time to answer me. All she said once when she burned her finger was "Oh shit" and then she looked up at me, [. . .] so I'm sure my little lecture made its impression.
>
> (p. 112)

The narrator's discourse deictic reference to himself as "her own author" foregrounds his pseudo-authorial role, which in turn highlights his pur-portedly more 'real' ontological status and the consequent impossibility of this metaleptic move. The spatial prepositions in "walk in" and "drop in" affirm that he is very much "in" her storyworld space. That said, the deictics of her looking "up" at him evoke the conventional hierarchical ontological arrangements explicitly signalled in the deictic directionality of Peter Prince's metaleptic communication to the narrator discussed in section 4.3, such as the narrator's description of Peter Prince waving a "letter above his head toward me" (p. 289). The humour of the passage, though, lies in the combination of the assuredness of the narrator that his "little lecture" is having an effect and there being no real evidence that Linda Lawrence can actually hear him. In terms of the functioning of possible reception figures, Linda Lawrence's role here seems chiefly to be to signal that though the narrator may be "in" the storyworld space she inhabits, he may still not be sharing the same ontological reality, as if he is at most an imperceptible, ghost-like witness.

In the second example from Katz, the protagonist is presented as mov-ing metaleptically upwards into the extradiegetic narrator's level. The narrator explains

> He leans toward me over the table. "There you are. So. Well. There you are. [. . .] I've got you pegged, you know [. . .]". Don't think that doesn't hit me right in the nerves. [. . .] I didn't plan on the materiali-zation of Peter Prince just at this moment.
>
> (pp. 202–203)

(Note Peter Prince's subsequent dematerialisation is discussed in Chap-ter 5, section 5.2.). Three deictic aspects of the language here suggest that this is communication in the canonical situation-of-utterance— i.e. the speaker and hearer are together in the same space at the same time: Peter Prince is presented as leaning "toward" the narrator (that is, relative to the narrator's deictic centre); Peter Prince's use of the demonstrative pronoun "there" in "there you are" signals the narrator's position as visibly identifiable and (so) relatively proximal; and Peter Prince directly addresses the narrator using "you". With "I've got you pegged", Peter Prince voices not only metaleptic awareness of the narrator but also a perception of the narrator's character, and gives the impression that this awareness and character assessment has been going on for some time. It is the narrator who functions as a reception figure of sorts, clarifying that "that"—the metaleptic "materialization of Peter Prince"—shocks him. In a metacompositional comment to the reader, the narrator explicitly denies planning (and, by implication, disclaims agency over) the move. The deictic reference to "this moment" implicitly refers to the narrator's deictic centre within the ongoing process of composition. Both of these two last sentences thereby foreground the narrator's pseudo-authorial guise while paradoxically simultaneously foregrounding his lack of authorial control and the penetration and extension of the fictional world into his narrative level.

Katz's characters Linda Lawrence and Philip Farrel are usually presented as existing at an ontological level higher than that of central protagonist Peter Prince (as briefly mentioned in Chapter 3, section 3.4). In the third example, these characters are metaleptically present in his storyworld. This is announced with the statement "Linda Lawrence and Philip Farrel [. . .] stand beside the bed where Peter Prince sleeps" (p. 208). A little further into the scene, the narrator explains that Philip Farrel protests to Linda Lawrence

> "You know I have to wake him up. I mean it doesn't make any difference to me or anything, but . . ." and he points off the page to where I am sitting. "I just have no choice [. . .]". Philip Farrel points my way again. Linda Lawrence winks at me, as if we have some secret understanding.
>
> (p. 209)

The narrator is spatially located "off the page" (i.e. off *the current* page on which this episode is narrated), signalling Philip Farrel and Linda Lawrence are both, in contrast, 'on' that page. As in examples of metaleptic awareness and communication in Katz discussed previously, this seems to blend the conceptual reality of the storyworld with its physical, textual form, and positions the pseudo-authorial narrator as outside of that textual space. The implicit reference to the narrator's authorial control and the explicit discourse deictic reference to "the page" foregrounds the fictive nature of the discourse and its textual medium. Both characters exhibit metaleptic awareness—Philip Farrel in his gesture, and Linda Lawrence in her wink (which constitutes metaleptic communication). Despite these cues that the narrator is positioned at an ontologically separate level, however, the pseudo-authorial narrator's claim that he and Linda Lawrence share an understanding, foregrounded in his use of the first-person plural pronoun "we", paradoxically entails that they share an ontological reality.

The episode continues with " 'O.K. with me'. Philip Farrel shrugs, and he leaves the scene" (p. 209). The discourse deictic "the scene" (i.e. *this* scene) references the compositional unit; the narrator does not say, for example, "leaves the room", but instead again subverts any realist illusion and highlights the constructedness of the storyworld. A little further, the narrator reports Linda Lawrence waking Peter Prince, and she and the narrator exiting:

> "Please wake up", she urged him by rocking the mattress on its springs. He twisted, and moaned a little, on the brink of rising. I [. . .] did a joyous fade-out, and so did Linda Lawrence fade out, but she in a different direction.
>
> (p. 210)

Linda Lawrence is portrayed as physically interacting with the objects in the storyworld she has metaleptically entered—she is no mere intangible otherworldly witness, despite the connotations of the process of "fad[ing] out" which announces her and the narrator's seemingly metaleptic withdrawal. The preposition "out" could suggest a deictic directionality outward from a position inside, but from inside to outside of what? Is this out of the compositional unit of "the scene"; out of the diegetic storyworld, on Linda Lawrence's part, and some kind of extradiegetic surveying space "off the page", on the part of the narrator; or perhaps out of the physical text? And out to what or to where? The conventional representation of the ontological levels is, as discussed in section 4.1, a vertical hierarchy, hence Pier's categorisation of 'ascending' and 'descending' metalepsis. It is, however, also organised as a Chinese box layering of levels. A downward metaleptic move might be expected to be followed by an upward metaleptic return to the former ontological position. The narrator's assertion that he and Linda Lawrence fade out, implicitly metaleptically, perhaps emphasises the Chinese box arrangement of levels rather than a vertical hierarchy, but the suggestion that they fade out in different directions, specifically, perhaps presents more of a challenge to this model of the ontological structure of fiction.

In the fourth example, Peter Prince seems to have moved metaleptically upwards, though the level to which he has moved is a little unclear:

> There has been some confusion about how Peter Prince got here. He's here, and I didn't expect him. [. . .] On his lap lay a book that confused him. [. . .] Linda Lawrence, herself, was surprised to see

him sitting there out of context scanning a book. [. . .] At first she wanted to cross the street, go around a couple of blocks and never admit that she'd spotted him. Who can blame her? It's a bore when you run into those people in real life that you're forced to spend time with in novels. [. . .] I remained out of it, waiting elsewhere for what was going to turn up.

Linda Lawrence spent a day outside this novel [. . .].

(pp. 319–320)

The passage begins with the possible implication that Peter Prince has appeared at the ontological level of the narrator, in that one could logically expect the narrator's (repeated) use of the spatial deictic "here" to refer to his own location. Also, the last time the narrator reported being surprised by the materialisation of Peter Prince (on pages 202 and 203, discussed previously), Peter Prince had apparently moved upwards to the extradiegetic level. In both episodes, the narrator functions as a reception figure, his surprise helping to mark the metaleptic quality of the move whilst also undermining the logic of authorial control. However, it becomes apparent that this metalepsis is of a different kind, as Peter Prince has seemingly joined the level at which Linda Lawrence exists (in that she can "see" him sat "there" and considers walking a different route to avoid him). Confusing things further, this is apparently not the level at which she conventionally exists, but rather the level of her "real life", Linda encountering him on a day that she has spent "outside this novel", hence her surprise at his manifestation too. The narrator, meanwhile, remains "out of it [. . .] elsewhere", where "it" is interpretable as the novel, or as the ontological level of Linda Lawrence's 'reality' in which she is encountering the novel's central character. Just as the depictions of the narrator at a table, or sitting in a library, in previous examples, suggest a person and place, giving the extradiegetic level more detail than is conventional, here "elsewhere" also implies a physical place. Yet more confusingly, in the fifth example, the novel ends with the narrator seemingly joining Peter Prince in the realm in which he and Linda have encountered each other, and conversing with Peter Prince, the protagonist ultimately telling the narrator to "just get the fuck out of here" (p. 346). As with previous examples, the preposition 'out' (in "outside this novel", "out of it" and "out of here") may foreground the concentric aspect of the ontological structure of narrative levels over the vertically hierarchical.

The emphasis within the metaleptic moves in the novel upon outward and inward directionality rather than ascending or descending is potentially part of a broader thematisation of an anti-hierarchical model of realities, in favour of, or simply mirroring, a postmodern, pluralist conception of subjective constructions of the world. The frequent interpenetration of levels, meanwhile, often presented as beyond the control of the pseudo-authorial narrator, suggests the fragility of conventional conceptual structures of understanding, and the indistinguishability of discursively mediated and mediating realities. While several theorists (e.g. Bell and Alber, 2012; Thoss, 2011) find themes such as "escapism", "control", "a challenge to the creator", and/or "a loss of control over the creation" (2012, p. 176) to be at the heart of metalepsis, and Peter Prince is presented as surprising the pseudo-authorial narrator and circumventing his authorial control at times, Katz's metalepses seem to be much more directly engaged with what Hanebeck (2017) and McHale (1987) identify as the epistemological crisis created by postmodern challenges to systems of narrativisation and sense-making.

This section has examined some examples of metaleptic moves in Brophy, Fowles, Johnson, and Katz. It has discussed some of the potential implications of considering the roles of the author and the reader in the text in relation to the concepts of counterparthood and translevel identities, and has applied these concepts, along with the notion of reception figures, to characters' and narrators' metaleptic moves. This section has drawn out uses of person, spatial, and temporal deixis in the service of discourse deictic marking of characters' and narrators' positions relative to, for example, each other, the storyworld space and extradiegetic realm, and the text-continuum, along with more directly discourse deictic references to compositional units (e.g. 'the scene'), aspects of the physical form of the book (i.e. 'the page'), and traversals upwards and downwards (or inwards and outwards) across ontological boundaries.

4.5 Conclusion

Explorations of metaleptic awareness, metaleptic communication, and metaleptic moves bring to the fore some complex narratological issues, such as the nature of the boundaries between levels within conventional conceptualisations of the ontological structure of fiction. This chapter has explored the antithetical notions of narration as metaleptic communication and of reading as entailing a conceptual metaleptic move. It has also considered the relevance of translevel identities (revising 'transworld') and counterparthood to understandings of pseudo-authorial narrators and to metaleptic moves more broadly. The analyses of examples have drawn out the significant contribution of discourse deixis to the linguistic construction of all forms of metalepsis and to their diverse metafictional implications. The discussions have also illustrated the value of examining discourse deixis to help better understand some narratological issues and evolving concepts. For example, the use of person deixis in the service of determining the ontological positions and discursive roles and relations of different literary participants has been shown to be a crucial aspect of the distinction between metaleptic counterparthood and translevel identity. The metalepses explored in the texts have involved different kinds of disruptions of conventional ontological distinctions, amounting to near metaleptic collapse within Barth and Coover, while Katz seems to sometimes side-step the hierarchical model to foreground the Chinese box structure, and Brophy subverts the vertical with the cyclic. Just as metalepsis plays with the vertical conceptualisation of fiction's ontological structure, disnarration plays with linear models of fiction's composition, form, processing, and conceptual realisation. It is to disnarration that the next chapter will now turn.

References

Alfonso, R. M. (1995). "Fictional self-consciousness in Robert Coover's *Pricksongs and Descants*". *Revista Alicantina de Estudios Ingleses* 8: 123–137.

Appel, A., Jr. (1980). "Lost in the Funhouse". In *Critical Essays on Barth*. Ed. J. J. Waldmeir. Boston, MA: G. K. Hall & Co. 179–182.

Balzac, H. de (n.d.) [1842]. *Autre Étude de Femme*. Geneva: Skira.

Banfield, A. (1982). *Unspeakable Sentences: Narration and Representation in the Language of Fiction*. Boston, MA: Routledge & Kegan Paul.

Bareis, J. A. (2008). *Fiktionales Erzählen: Zur Theorie der Literarischen Fiktion als Make-Believe*. Gothenburg: Acta Universitatis Gothoburgensis.

Baron, C. (2005). "Effet métaleptique et statut des discours fictionnels". In *Métalepses. Entorses au Pacte de la Répresentation*. Eds. J. Pier and J-M. Schaeffer. Paris: Ed. de l'EHESS. 295–310.

Barth, J. (1988) [1968]. *Lost in the Funhouse: Fiction for Print, Tape, Live Voice*. New York: Doubleday.

Baudelaire. C. (1961). "Au lecteur". In *Les Fleurs du Mal*. Ed. A. Adam. Paris: Éditions Garnier Frères. 5–6.

Bell, A. (2016). "Interactional metalepsis and unnatural narratology". *Narrative* 24.3. 294–310.

Bell, A. and Alber, J. (2012). "Ontological metalepsis and unnatural narratology". *Journal of Narrative Theory* 42.2. 166–192.

Benveniste, E. (1971) [1966]. *Problems in General Linguistics*. Trans. M. E. Meek. Coral Gables: University of Miami Press.

Booth, W. C. (1961). *The Rhetoric of Fiction*. Chicago, IL: University of Chicago Press.

Bridgeman, T. (2007). "Time and space". In *The Cambridge Companion to Narrative*. Ed. D. Herman. Cambridge: Cambridge University Press. 52–65.

Brophy, B. (2002) [1969]. *In Transit: An Heroi-Cyclic Novel*. Chicago, IL: Dalkey Archive Press.

Chatman, S. (1978). *Story and Discourse: Narrative Structure in Fiction and Film*. Ithaca, NY: Cornell University Press.

Cohn, D. (2012). "Metalepsis and *mise en abyme*". Trans. L. S. Gleich. *Narrative* 20.1. 105–114.

Coover, R. (2011) [1969]. *Pricksongs and Descants*. New York: New American Library.

Cortàzar, J. (1985) [1967]. "Continuity of parks". In *Blow-Up and Other Stories*. Trans. P. Blackburn. New York: Pantheon. 63–65.

Cowley, J. (1986). "A disintegrating song: The fiction of Steve Katz". *Critique* 27.3. 131–143.

Dannenberg, H. A. (2008). *Coincidence and Counterfactuality: Plotting Time and Space in Narrative Fiction*. Lincoln, NE: University of Nebraska Press.

Duchan, J. F., Bruder, G. A. and Hewitt, L. E. (Eds). (1995). *Deixis in Narrative: A Cognitive Scientific Perspective*. Hillsdale, NJ: Lawrence Erlbaum.

Eliot, T. S. (2002) [1954]. *Selected Poems*. London: Faber and Faber.

Evenson, B. (2003). *Understanding Robert Coover*. Columbia, SC: University of South Carolina Press.

Fauconnier, G. (1994). *Mental Spaces*. Cambridge: Cambridge University Press.

Feyersinger, E. (2011). "Metaleptic TV Crossovers". In *Metalepsis in Popular Culture*. Eds. K. Kukkonen and S. Klimek. Berlin: De Gruyter. 127–157.

Fillmore, C. (1985). "Frames and the semantics of understanding". *Quaderni di Semantica* 6. 222–254.

Fludernik, M. (1995). "Pronouns of address and 'odd' third person forms: The mechanics of involvement in fiction". In *New Essays in Deixis: Discourse, Narrative, Literature*. Ed. K. Green. Amsterdam: Rodopi. 99–129.

Fludernik, M. (2003a). "Metanarrative and metafictional commentary: From metadiscursivity to metanarration and metafiction". *Poetica* 35.1–2. 1–39.

Fludernik, M. (2003b). "Scene, shift, metalepsis, and the metaleptic mode". *Style* 37.4. 382–400.

Fludernik, M. (2011). "The category of 'person' in fiction: *You* and *we* narrative multiplicity and indeterminacy of reference". In *Current Trends in Narratology*. Ed. G. Olsen. Berlin: De Gruyter. 101–141.

Fowles, J. (1996) [1969]. *The French Lieutenant's Woman*. London: Vintage.

Gavins, J. (2007). *Text World Theory: An Introduction*. Edinburgh: Edinburgh University Press.

Genette, G. (1980). *Narrative Discourse: An Essay in Method*. Trans. J. E. Lewin. Ithaca, NY: Cornell University Press.

Genette, G. (1988). *Narrative Discourse Revisited*. Trans. J. E. Lewin. Ithaca, NY: Cornell University Press.

Genette, G. (2004). *Métalepse: De la Figure à la Fiction*. Paris: Seuil, 2004.

Gibbons, A. (2017). "Contemporary autofiction and metamodern affect". In *Historicity, Affect, and Depth After Postmodernism*. Eds. R. van den Akker, A. Gibbons and T. Vermeulen. London: Rowman & Littlefield. 117–130.

Goffman, E. (1974). *Frame Analysis: An Essay on the Organisation of Experience*. New York: Harper Colophon Books.

Gordon, L. (1983). *Robert Coover: The Universal Fictionmaking Process*. Carbondale, IL: South Illinois University Press.

Hamburger, K. (1973). *The Logic of Literature*. 2nd edn. Trans. M. J. Rose. Bloomington, IN: Indiana University Press.

Hanebeck, J. (2017). *Understanding Metalepsis: The Hermeneutics of Narrative Transgression*. Berlin: De Gruyter.

Herman, D. (1997). "Toward a formal description of narrative metalepsis". *Journal of Literary Semantics* 26.2. 132–150.

Herman, D. (2002). *Story Logic: Problems and Possibilities of Narrative*. Ohio, NE: Ohio State University Press.

Hofstadter, D. R. (1979). *Gödel, Escher, Bach: An Eternal Golden Braid*. Hassocks: Harvester Press.

Hutcheon, L. (1988). *A Poetics of Postmodernism: History, Theory, Fiction*. London: Routledge.

Jahn, M. and Nünning, A. (1994). "A survey of narratological models". *Literatur in Wissenschaft und Unterricht* 27.4. 283–303.

Johnson, B. S. (1971). *House Mother Normal*. Glasgow: William Collins, Sons & Co. Ltd.

Johnson, B. S. (1975). *See the Old Lady Decently*. New York: Viking.

Johnson, B. S. (2001) [1973]. *Christie Malry's Own Double-Entry*. London: Picador.

Kacandes, I. (1993). "Are you in the text? The 'literary performative' in postmodernist fiction". *Text and Performance Quarterly* 13. 139–153.

Katz, S. (2017) [1968]. *The Exagggerations of Peter Prince*. Singapore: Verbivoracious Press.

Klimek, S. (2010). *Paradoxes Erzählen: Die Metalepse in der Phantastischen Literatur*. Paderborn: Mentis.

Kukkonen, K. (2011). "Metalepsis in popular culture: An introduction". In *Metalepsis in Popular Culture*. Eds. K. Kukkonen and Sonja Klimek. Berlin: De Gruyter. 1–21.

Kukkonen, K. and Klimek, S. (Eds.). (2011). *Metalepsis in Popular Culture*. Berlin: De Gruyter.

Levitt, M. P. (1982). "The novels of B. S. Johnson: Against the war against Joyce". *Modern Fiction Studies* 27.4. 571–586.

Maack, A. (1995). "Concordia discors: Brigid Brophy's *In Transit*". *Review of Contemporary Fiction* 3. 40–45.

Macrae, A. (2012). "Readerly deictic shifting to and through *I* and *you*: An updated hypothesis". In *Texts and Minds: Papers in Cognitive Poetics and Rhetoric*. Ed. A. Kawaitkowska. Frankfurt am Main: Peter Lang. 41–56.

Malina, D. (2002). *Breaking the Frame: Metalepsis and the Construction of the Subject*. Columbus, OH: The Ohio State University Press.

Margolin, U. (2007). "Character". In *The Cambridge Companion to Narrative*. Ed. D. Herman. Cambridge: Cambridge University Press. 66–79.

McHale, B. (1992). *Constructing Postmodernism*. London: Routledge.

McHale, B. (1987). *Postmodernist Fiction*. London: Routledge.

McIntyre, D. (2006). *Point of View in Plays*. Amsterdam: John Benjamins.

Mengham, R. (2014). "Antepostdated Johnson". In *B. S. Johnson and Post-War Literature: Possibilities of the Avant Garde*. Eds. J. Jordan and M. Ryle. Houndmills, Basingstoke: Palgrave Macmillan. 121–135.

Nabokov, V. (1995) [1959]. *Lolita*. London: Penguin Books.

Nietzsche, F. (1999). "Truth and lying in a non-moral sense". In *Nietzsche: The Birth of Tragedy and Other Writings*. Eds. R. Geuss and R. Speirs. Trans. R. Speirs. Cambridge: Cambridge University Press. 139–153.

Nelles, W. (1992). "Stories within stories: Narrative levels and embedded narrative". *Studies in Literary Imagination* 51.1. 70–96.

Nelles, W. (1997). *Frameworks: Narrative Levels and Embedded Narrative*. New York: Peter Lang.

Onega, S. (1989). *Form and Meaning in the Novels of John Fowles*. Ann Arbor, MI: U.M.I. Research Press.

Phelan, J. and Rabinowitz, P. J. (Eds.). (2005). *A Companion to Narrative Theory*. Oxford: Blackwell.

Pier, J. (2005). "Metalepsis". In *The Routledge Encyclopedia of Narrative Theory*. Eds. D. Herman, M. Jahn and M-L. Ryan. London: Routledge. 303–304.

Pier, J. (2009). "Metalepsis". In *Handbook of Narratology*. Eds. P. Hühn, J. Pier, W. Schmid, and J. Schönert. Berlin: De Gruyter. 190–203.

Prince, G. (1987). *A Dictionary of Narratology*. Revised edn. Lincoln: University of Nebraska Press.

Proust, M. (1971) [1952]. *Jean Santeuil*. Eds P. Clarac and Y. Sandre. Paris: La Pléiade.

Rankin, R. (1997). *Sprout Mask Replica*. London: Corgi.

Richardson, B. (1994). "I etcetera: On the poetics and ideology of multipersoned narratives". *Style* 28.3. 312–328.

Ryan, M-L. (1991). *Possible Worlds, Artificial Intelligence, and Narrative Theory*. Bloomington, IN: Indiana University Press.

Ryan, M.-L. (2001). *Narrative as Virtual Reality: Immersion and Interactivity in Literature and Electronic Media*. Baltimore, MD: Johns Hopkins University Press.

Ryan, M-L. (2006). "Metaleptic machines". *Avatars of Story*. Minneapolis: University of Minnesota Press. 204–229.

Ryan, M-L. (2015). "Impossible worlds". In *The Routledge Companion to Experimental Literature*. Eds. J. Bray, A. Gibbons and B. McHale. London: Routledge. 368–379.

Ryf, R. S. (1977). "B. S. Johnson and the frontiers of fiction". *Critique* 19.1. 58–74.

Spark, M. (1957). *The Comforters*. London: Palgrave Macmillan.

Splendore, P. (1984). "B. S. Johnson's intransitive performance". *The Review of Contemporary Fiction* 5.2. 93–97.

Stendhal (1948) [1889]. *Lamiel*. Paris: Divan.

Stockwell, P. (2002). *Cognitive Poetics: An Introduction*. London: Routledge.

Stockwell, P. (2009). *Texture: A Cognitive Aesthetics of Reading*. Edinburgh: Edinburgh University Press.

Thoss, J. (2011). "Unnatural narrative and metalepsis: Grant Morrison's *Animal Man*". In *Unnatural Narratives—Unnatural Narratology*. Eds. J. Alber and R. Heinze. Berlin: De Gruyter. 189–209.

Thoss, J. (2015). *When Storyworlds Collide: Metalepsis in Popular Fiction, Film and Comics*. Leiden: Brill Rodopi.

Tredell, N. (2000). *Fighting Fictions: The Novels of B. S. Johnson*. Nottingham: Pauper's Press.

Wagner, F. (2002). "Glissements et déphasages: Notes sur la metalepse narrative". *Poétique* 130. 235–253.

Waugh, P. (1984). *Metafiction: The Theory and Practice of Self-Conscious Fiction*. London and New York: Routledge.

Werth, P. (1999). *Text Worlds: Representing Conceptual Space in Discourse*. Harlow, Essex: Longman.

White, G. (2005). *Reading the Graphic Surface: The Presence of the Book in Prose Fiction*. Manchester: Manchester University Press.

Wolf, W. (1993). *Ästhetische Illusion und Illusionsdurchbrechung in der Erzählkunst: Theorie und Geschichte mit Schwerpunkt auf Englischem Illusionsstörenden Erzählen*. Tübingen: Niemeyer.

Wolf, W. (2005). "Metalepsis as a transgeneric and transmedial phenomenon: A case study of the possibilities of 'exporting' narratological concepts". In *Narratology Beyond Literary Criticism: Mediality, Disciplinarity*. Ed. J. C. Meister. Berlin: De Gruyter. 83–108.

Wolf, W. (2009). "Metareference across media: The concept, its transmedial potentials and problems, main forms and functions". In *Metareference Across Media: Theory and Case Studies*. Ed. W. Wolf. Amsterdam: Rodopi. 1–85.

Wolf, W. (2013). "'Unnatural' metalepsis and immersion: Necessarily incompatible?" In *A Poetics of Unnatural Narrative*. Eds. J. Alber, H. Skov Nielsen and B. Richardson. Columbus, OH: Ohio State University Press. 113–141.

Young, K. G. (1987). *Taleworlds and Storyrealms: The Phenomenology of Narrative*. Dordrecht: Martinus Nijhoff Publishers.

5 Discourse Deixis in Disnarration

Arrange words in abstract patterns and you've got nonsense. Nonsense is right. For example. On, God damn it; take linear plot, take resolution of conflict, [. . .] they may very well be obsolete notions, indeed they are, no doubt untenable at this late date, [. . .] but in fact we still lead our lives by clock and calendar, for example, and though the seasons recur our mortal human time does not; we grow old and tired, we think of how things used to be or might have been and how they are now, and in fact, and in fact we get exasperated and desperate and out of expedients and out of words.

(Barth, 1988 [1968], p. 112)

Of course it happened. Of course it didn't happen.

(Pynchon, 1973, p. 88)

As Prince states, "the hallmark of narrative is assurance. Narrative, which is etymologically linked to knowledge, lives in certainty (this happened then that; this happened because of that; this happened and it was related to that) and dies from (sustained) ignorance and indecision" (1988, p. 4; cf. Cohn, 1999; Hamburger, 1973). Some novels, however, exploit an ontological 'flickering' effect, created by the evocation of entities, states, acts, or events the ontological status of which, as 'actual' within the storyworld, is made temporarily or permanently ambiguous, or ultimately denied (McHale, 1987, pp. 99–111). Prince (1988, 1992) coined the term 'disnarration' to describe various techniques which can create these effects. This chapter starts by exploring Prince's definition (section 5.1), and then examines types of disnarration in examples from Barth, Brophy, Coover, Fowles, Johnson, and Katz. It investigates, in turn, discourse deixis in denarration (section 5.2), alternarration (section 5.3), negation and hypothetical focalisation (section 5.4), and narrative refusal and the antinarratable (section 5.5).

5.1 Defining Disnarration

Prince was the first narratologist to directly address the phenomenon of disnarration (first in his seminal 1988 essay, which he then reworked and republished in 1992). Prince defines the "disnarrated" as "the events that do not happen but, nonetheless, are referred to (in a negative or hypothetical mode) by the narrative text" (1988, p. 2). The concept of disnarration arises in various branches of literary and narratological theory across the twentieth century. For example, Prince notes related observations by Shklovsky in his discussion of negative parallelism and negative or hypothetical comparison in 'Art as Technique' (1965 [1917], pp. 8–9). Disnarration is also a part of Labov's appreciation of comparators in narrative—that is, of the significance, to narrative, of comparison of unrealised and realised events (1972, pp. 383–384). The concept is also drawn upon in Ryan's study of the "virtual embedded narratives" that can be portrayed as occurring within the minds of characters (1986; see also 1991, drawing on the Possible Worlds theory of Doležel, 1988). Prince summarises disnarration as

> terms, phrases, and passages that consider what did not or does not take place [. . .], whether they pertain to the narrator and his or her narration [. . .] or to one of the characters and his or her actions.
>
> (1988, p. 3)

Disnarration, according to Prince's broad definition, thus includes

> alethic expressions of impossibility or unrealized possibility, deontic expressions of observed prohibition, epistemic expressions of ignorance, ontological expressions of nonexistence, purely imagined worlds, desired worlds, or intended worlds, unfulfilled expectations, unwarranted beliefs, failed attempts, crushed hopes, suppositions and false calculations, errors and lies, and so forth.
>
> (p. 3)

The various forms of disnarration described here can be represented within the fiction as rooted in the consciousness of any sentient story-world entities, as the narrator's own thoughts and/or act of narration, or can be attributed to the reader.

Disnarration can be employed in different ways for a variety of effects. Warhol argues that "literary genres can [. . .] be characterized by the degree to which they use disnarration, and the nature of the material their narrators explicitly omit" (2005, p. 221). Prince (1988) notes that disnarration "on the level of story" (i.e. located within the thoughts or speech of characters) is employed in "the realist text, and, more generally, mimetic fiction" to assert the factuality of the narrated events and authenticity of the narration (p. 6), to reassure the reader by demonstration that the narrator knows the difference between what is 'real' within the storyworld and what is not. Within a metafictional context, Prince locates disnarration as most common at the level of discourse (i.e. overtly rooted within the narrating act). At this level, disnarration "foregrounds ways of creating a situation or ordering an experience [and] emphasizes the realities of representation as opposed to the representation of realities", and "multiplies signs of arbitrary power in narrative articulation and signs of contingency in narrative explanation" (1988, pp. 5–6). In this way, disnarration can be used to explore the relationship between the narrator and reader and their relative roles in the discursive construction of the fictional world, and to subvert and so confront the narrativising impulse (the processing and/or construction of events as sequential, causally linked, epistemologically certain and ontologically stable). Prince suggests that there are particular themes with which the disnarrated "has many affinities", for example, "the class of themes governed by contrasts and contraries (lifelikeness and reality, appearance and being, determinism and freedom, imagination and perception)" (1992, p. 37). All of these themes are, of course, at the heart of metafiction.

Despite the breadth of Prince's definition of disnarration, it is quite restrictive in some ways. For example, he argues that "the disnarrated [. . .] is disnarrated only relative to a given diegesis, and only if it designates in that diegesis a possibility that remains unrealized" (1992, p. 34). He gives examples such as "Like everyone else, I believed that Victor could have won but he lost" and "Isabelle got up laboriously to explain her reservations but this effort killed her" (p. 34). This definition of disnarration explicitly excludes things which are, for example, "realized" as (f)actual—as actually happening or existing within the diegesis—but then that status as real within the diegesis is revoked. He also excludes from the category of disnarration things which go "unmentioned" (p. 30)—that which in Genette's terms constitutes narrative ellipsis (1980). Prince distinguishes this from the disnarrated and calls this, instead, "the unnarrated, or nonnarrated" (p. 30). The disnarrated includes events which explicitly "*do not* happen" within the storyworld, but are mentioned in the negative or hypothetical mode (1988, p. 2, 1992, p. 30). He nonetheless excludes from disnarration "the mere negative depiction of a situation or event" and gives examples of this such as "Warren did not close the door" and "Elizabeth remained silent" (1992, p. 33).

Prince's initial work presents many opportunities for further exploration and distillation. Other scholars have added greater nuance to the concept of disnarration, both expanding it and identifying types. Those of particular relevance to the study of metafiction and discourse deixis include 'denarration' (Richardson, 2001); 'counternarration' (Dannenberg, 2008); 'hypothetical focalisation' (Herman, 1994, 2002); and 'narrative refusal' (Warhol-Down, 2010) and the 'antinarratable' (Warhol,

2005). Among this scholarship, only Herman begins to investigate the linguistic workings of disnarration. The miniature metafictional canon explored in this book contains a wealth of examples of these types of disnarration, all of which, to a greater or lesser extent, rely on discourse deixis in their workings. This chapter moves through these types, and draws out and investigates exactly how discourse deixis contributes to their effects.

5.2 Discourse Deixis in Denarration

A key issue raised by disnarration is the relationship between linear, progressive textual narration and dynamic readerly conceptualisation. Richardson (2001) and McHale (1987) identify examples of disnarration which involve a form of narrative 'reversal' explicitly excluded by Prince. Richardson paraphrases 'disnarration' as "[Prince's] term for possible events that, though referred to, remain unactualized in a text" (2001, p. 169). What is left out by this, as suggested previously, are instances of narrative which are narrated in a manner such that the events or characters involved are initially portrayed as 'real' within the world of the story—that is, as possessing the same ontological status as all other elements given to be constituents of the storyworld—only for that status to be later denied. Richardson (2001) calls this latter phenomenon 'denarration'. He provides the following comparison of Prince's notion of disnarration and his own concept of denarration (p. 169):

> in *Vanity Fair* [(1969) [1848]], we find the following fateful non-event: "If Rawdon Crawley had been then and there present, instead of being at the club nervously drinking claret, the pair might have gone down on their knees before the old spinster, avowed all, and have been forgiven in a twinkling. But that good chance was denied to the young couple." (p. 174) Denarration, by contrast, would have affirmed Rawdon's presence in the company of Miss Crawley, and then denied this event.

Denarration is therefore arguably a form of disnarration in which "a narrator denies significant aspects of her narrative that had earlier been presented as given" (Richardson, 2001, p. 168). Note Richardson attributes denarration only to the narrator, not a character. The entities and events of the conceptualised world(s) are denarrated in the sense that they are ultimately "unactualized" within the storyworld (Richardson, 2001, p. 168). They are not, however, merely modalised in some way—hypothesised, for example, as could be included under the broader heading of disnarration—but rather are "given and then taken away" (McHale, 1987, p. 101).

Denarration can be used in metafiction to explore the relationship between the text and the reader's interpretation. It lays bare the text-driven nature of the reader's dynamic mental construction of the storyworld, and the narratorial control over that processing and realisation. Denarration foregrounds the fact that all that is narrated—even if it is later denied—is inevitably and necessarily conceptualised by the reader, in the act of processing, as a constituent of the dynamic realisation of the text. The readerly processing of the narrative entails conceptualisation of all that is linguistically inscribed. The consequence of this is that denarration inevitably highlights the conceptual significance of the denarrated: what can be denarrated in/from the storyworld cannot be erased from the readerly conceptualisation, in that the processing cannot be 'undone'. The denarrated may be relegated to the diegetically unreal (that is, not, ultimately, real within the diegesis), unfulfilled, hypothetical, or ambiguous. It may be latterly re-conceptualised as the contrasting opposite to, or a variant of, what is real within the storyworld. Nonetheless, crucially it contributes to the reader's processing and interpretation of the text, and plays a role in their interpretation, even if only transiently, and/or by contrast to (and therefore affirming) what is determined and maintained as real with the storyworld.

Denarration in this regard functions as a form of literary negation. Hidalgo Downing more explicitly asserts that "negation as a structure involves the formation of a complex structure with regard to the corresponding affirmative" (2000, p. 36). Lakoff likewise stresses that "when we negate a frame, we evoke the frame" (2004, p. 3): cognitive processing of negation necessarily entails conceptualisation of that which is negated, as in the processing of the title of Lakoff's book on the subject, *Don't Think of an Elephant* (2004), or, to offer another example, "I went home. Steve was not there". Lakoff's argument is that examples such as these entail that we initially do think of an elephant, and imagine the scenario of Steve being at the speaker's home, respectively, as part of the process of negating these imaginative conceptualisations. Werth claims that negation possesses world-building properties similar to positive propositions. He asserts that "there are forms of negation [. . .] which not only delete an entity, but also introduce it at the same time" (Werth, 1999, pp. 253–254, cited in Nørgaard, 2007, p. 40).

Various strands of research from psycholinguistics and related fields support the hypothesis that the processing of negation of a proposition involves initial conceptual realisation of that proposition before the subsequent recategorisation of that proposition as negated. That is, something must be first actualised for it to be possible for it to be negated; the actualisation is entailed within the negation. Clark and Clark (1977, pp. 107–108) cite several empirical studies which manifest longer processing times for denials than for affirmatives. They deduce from this that the cognitive processing of the negation is a secondary stage of comprehension subsequent to the processing of affirmative entailments. The view that readers actualise the negated situation when processing a negated sentence is supported by more recent work in experimental psychology and pragmatics (e.g. Israel, 2004; Kaup, Lüdtke, and Zwaan, 2006; Kaup, Yaxley, Madden, Zwaan, and Lüdtke, 2007).

Richardson offers a continuum of denarration, whereby in a weaker form narrated events are very quickly negated without "trespass[ing] beyond the basic conventions of realism" (Richardson, 2001, p. 169). McHale presents as an example a moment in Bennett's *The Old Wives' Tale* where what is represented as a character's speech is quickly followed with a disclaimer, "She did not say this aloud" (1963 [1908], p. 71, cited in Richardson, 2001, p. 169). In the weaker form "the denarration remains distinctly local, indeterminacies are temporary, and the stability of the represented world is not seriously challenged" (Richardson, 2001, p. 171), as may be the occasional result of unreliable narration. Another example would be 'I walked into the room, and found myself face to face with Richard; his glowering eyes looked down at me from the portrait above the fireplace'. In this example an event is implied to have occurred within the reality of the storyworld (the speaker encountering the person named Richard), only for the storyworld reality of that event to be clarified and revoked in some way (here, it being not the person but a portrait of the person that has been encountered), and the reader's comprehension is consequently amended.

More radical denarration is brought about through subsequent denial of events and/or storyworld entities that have been initially conveyed as stable and interpretively significant constituents of the narrative, and (so) have been fully established within the reader's conceptualisation of the storyworld, possibly for longer stretches of text. Such narration may be more duplicitous than unreliable (Richardson, 2001, p. 173). Extreme denarration "is global and undermines the world it purports to depict; very little (if anything) is left over after the assaults of textual negation the narrative performs upon itself" (Richardson, 2001, p. 171). Denarration of the stronger kind foregrounds the discursive foundation of the storyworld, creating "the dual effect of destabalizing the ontology of this projected world and simultaneously laying bare the process of world-construction" (McHale, 1987, p. 101). It therefore offers a neat formal means of engaging with postmodernism's thematic concerns, hence the frequency of denarration in postmodern metafiction.

McHale (1987, pp. 99–111) surveys various uses of this stronger form of denarration within postmodern literature, and offers an example from Katz's *The Exagggerations of Peter Prince* (2017 [1968], pp. 205–206):

The empty dishes fade away, and so does the tablecloth: the chair I am sitting on softens and slowly disappears. I have to stand up in

a dark space. Peter Prince is permeated by the deep, flowing atmosphere and is tugged away in gauzy sections. "WAIT," I shout (too
late, he's disappearing) and I hastily, though reluctantly, begin the
description he demanded.

Here, in a twist of the regular relationship between teller and told,
the character is portrayed as making demands of the narrator regarding how he is narrated, and, when the narrator hesitates to satisfy his
blackmailer, Peter Prince wilfully erases not only himself but also the
narrator's surroundings. Such disintegration of entities draws attention to "the ineluctable writtenness of character" (McHale, 1987,
p. 105). It not only disrupts the suspension of disbelief, the development of realistic characterisation, and any readerly investment of
empathy with the characters, but also draws attention to the broader
fictional and discursive foundation of the text, the dynamic nature of
its construction, and additionally to the portrayed simultaneity of that
construction to the narrating process of the 'I'-narrator (indicated by
the present tense).

This extract from Katz is a questionable example of denarration
proper, however. In it, the preceding existence of Peter Prince, the dishes,
the tablecloth, the chair, etc., is not denied or revoked, and no revision of
the reader's conceptualisation of the narrated world is prompted in those
terms. (Incidentally, this passage does not make clear whether this scene
and the communication between the protagonist and pseudo-narrator is
taking place via a metaleptic intrusion of the protagonist into the level
of narration, or via a narratorial intrusion into the storyworld.) This
character and these entities are erased, but not in a fashion that erases
their previous ontological status within the scene. They do leave in an
unusual way, apparently disintegrating, and at the will of the character
rather than the narrator. This constitutes a radical deviation from both
the norms of conventional fiction and from the heretofore implicit internal logic of the narration, as well as exceeding Richardson's definition
of denarration to suggest that it can be instituted by narrative participants other than the narrator. Nonetheless, in that the ontological status
of the entities is merely ceased, rather than retrospectively negated, it
raises the question as to what truly constitutes denarration. Given the
context—the protagonist making demands of the narrator's choices in
narrating—the disintegration can be interpreted as representative of a
ceasing and reversing of the narrator's work, a direct reversal of those
objects being conceptually realised through the narrator's act of narrating and the reader's processing of the narrative: the dishes and tablecloth
"fade away", the chair "softens and slowly disappears", a "dark space"
surrounds the narrator, Peter Prince "is permeated by the deep, flowing
atmosphere and is tugged away in gauzy sections", as if the entities, created in a conceptual space out of nothingness, leave that same void in

their wake. Denarration therefore occurs here in a *mimetic* sense. None-theless, what has been 'given' in this instance is not now 'denied', but rather simply ceases to exist: its existence in the past of the narrative is not threatened, it simply does not exist any longer.

Another example from Katz, briefly mentioned in Chapter 4, might serve as a better illustration of denarration, along with a similar instance in Barth's 'Life-Story'. In both, within a few pages of the start of the story, the narration is interrupted, the opening criticised, and the story begun anew. The text reads "Enough! Katz, you're making this all up. It doesn't make a bit of sense. It's not a promising beginning. Why can't you follow the instructions? You can't write whatever you want [. . .]. Where's the story?" (p. 4). For the next two paragraphs, the voice contin-ues the critique and proposes other ways to start the story, one of which is then taken up (pp. 4–5).

The deictic "this" in "making this all up" and the subsequent deictic "It" refer anaphorically to the stretch of discourse comprising the open-ing (though, ironically, both could of course equally refer to the current sentences—the interruption). The protest that "this" is all invented is ini-tially confusing, invention being the essence of fiction. This is perhaps resolved, though, by the following references to "instructions" and the need for a "story": these metacompositional references situate the pseudo-authorial narrator's style in relation to narratological conventions, which are, it is claimed, being flouted, the pseudo-authorial narrator presuming too much freedom to "write whatever [he] want[s]". The interruption radically breaks the fourth wall; presents a discourse between the pseudo-authorial narrator and himself, or an editor and the pseudo-authorial narrator, foregrounding the process of literary creation; and discounts the prior three pages from the story.

The denarrating interruption in Barth's 'Life-Story' is more subtle and complex. The story opens with the words

> Without discarding what he'd already written he began his story afresh in a somewhat different manner. Whereas his earlier version had opened in a straight-forward documentary fashion and then degenerated [. . .] into irrealism and dissonance he decided this time to tell his tale from start to finish in a conservative, 'realistic', unself-conscious [sic] way.
>
> (p. 116)

The story continues with metanarrative ruminations about "our author's" story, with mention of his characters, labelled "D" and "E". The next paragraph, though, opens with "What a dreary way to begin a story he said to himself upon reviewing his long introduction. [. . .] Another story about a writer writing a story! Another regress in infinitum!" (p. 117). This is soon followed, mid-paragraph on the next page, with

> C flung away the whining manuscript and pushed impatiently through the French doors leading to the terrace from his oak-wainscoted study. Pausing at the stone balustrade to light his briar he remarked through a lavender cascade of wisteria that the lithe-limbed Gloria, Gloria of the timorous eye and militant breast, had once again chosen his boat-wharf as her basking-place.
>
> By Jove he exclaimed to himself. It's particularly disquieting to suspect not only that one is a fictional character but that the fiction one's in—the fiction one is—is quite the sort one least prefers. His wife entered the study with coffee and an apple-pastry, set them at his elbow on his work table, returned to the living room.
>
> (p. 118)

The twists and turns of this passage are hard to follow, chiefly due to the ambiguity of the person deixis and the contradictory spatial references. C is presumably the character referred to with the third-person deictic "he" thus far, and who is writing a story about D and E. It is often unclear whether at any point we are reading C's manuscript directly, or the narrator's story about C's writing of his (C's) manuscript. In reading this passage, the reader is arguably led to infer that "C" is the same character previously and subsequently referred to as "he", and that he leaves his study. However, the second paragraph of this extract suggests that "he" is in fact still in his study. The fact that "his elbow" is at his work table entails that "he" is, and the verb 'entered' in "his wife entered" possesses a deictic directionality, suggesting a perspectival locus that is within the study. All of this is confused by that fact that "he" seems to observe the fact that he indeed is the "fictional character" C, "in" a fiction (and himself *a* fiction), apparently observing himself inside a fiction (within an embedded storyworld, and on the terrace) from a point outside it (at a higher ontological level, yet still a fictional one, and in the study). The boundaries between the narrative levels are radically disturbed and the distinction between them blurred in a manner approaching the kind of metaleptic collapse discussed in Chapter 4, section 4.1.

The section describing C's exit onto the terrace is in effect denarrated, in that the reader is driven to revise her understanding of it—specifically its ontological status, and the identity of C. The reader may re-situate the event described in these lines at the hypodiegetic level—as a section of "his" manuscript, C being not the character referred to as "he", but a further character within "his" invented story. However, it may be more likely that the reader feels unable to 'resolve' these lines, their ontological status remaining ultimately ambiguous.

McHale discusses a further passage from Katz as an example of denarration which is more emotionally poignant. The most affecting part of Katz's novel is the description of the possibly accidental, or possibly suicidal, asphyxiation of Thwang-Nuc, the protagonist's very young adopted daughter. Directly after the description of Peter Prince's discovery of her body, the narration moves to a conversation between Linda Lawrence and Philip Farrel, the two characters who, as previously discussed, are usually portrayed as existing at an ontological level higher than the storyworld of the protagonist Peter Prince and lower than that of the pseudo-authorial narrator. Philip Farrel is baffled by Linda Lawrence's statement that "everything's O.K." straight after (in his words) "what's happened there" with "Peter Prince and the child". Linda responds:

> You're so gullible. [. . .] Just go back and read that section over, sentence by sentence. There are some nice sentences in it. What more do you want? Some nice style, some neat scenes. It's emotionally packed, but it's well written just the same. Read it some more. What do you have to worry about?
>
> (p. 119)

McHale writes that the reader "has been duped into a degree of emotional engagement, and then deprived of the event that has provoked that engagement", in that the comments by Linda Lawrence "emphasize the unreality, the merely verbal or textual existence, of this event" (1987, p. 103). McHale predicts that, despite the reader's likely preference for evading or suppressing her own reactions to the narrated death, she "will, nevertheless, feel a certain resentment" as a result of the comments, and that "the reader clings to the 'lost', erased sequence as he or she might not to one less highly charged" (p. 103).

The emotionally wrought scene is not being properly denarrated or 'erased', however. Its reality within the storyworld is not being revoked or even questioned. The sudden shift out into the framing world (incidentally, and brutally, at precisely the moment at which Philip Farrel is taking Linda Lawrence's temperature, "both rectal and oral", p. 119) breaks both the narrative tension and the suspension of disbelief which has supported the reader's initial emotional investment in the scene. Rather than denarrate the scene, or alter its ontological status, the anaphoric discourse deictic references to "that section", "there", its "sentences", its "style" and its "scenes", and its being "well written", all work to simply foreground the ontological status of the tragedy, and the storyworld within which it occurs, as fictional invention—as textual and crafted. The ontological status of this storyworld has always been the case, as has been foregrounded many times throughout the novel via frequent metanarrative commentary (as discussed in Chapter 3). It is the timing and the nature of the act of foregrounding here, in combination with the emotional power of the scene, which are so confronting. The swift deflation of tension is confounded by the paradoxical irony of this partly metatextual commentary coming from two characters who are just as much fictional constructs as Peter Prince and Thwang-Nuc. The reference to being able to "read" the scene, and Philip Farrel's spatial deictic reference to it being "there", suggest that they are referring to a unit of physical text. The implication of this is that Linda Lawrence and Philip Farrel have metaleptic awareness of, and access to, the physical text—perhaps (impossibly) even the whole, finished, printed book—that the real reader is reading, and that they themselves are characters within. The playful, fictional, and metafictional quality of the book is foregrounded and the emotional investment facilitated by the suspension of disbelief is disrupted. The deflationary effects of this passage seem to be less those of denarration proper, therefore, and more those of metanarration and metalepsis.

A further example from Katz presents denarration proper, albeit ultimately ambiguous. A long stretch of the story is denarrated both prior to its commencement and throughout its duration. On page 140 of the novel, the narrator announces "There are thirty pages of transition here which I have decided not to write". He continues, summarising some of the things "which were to be described in the thirty pages I decided not to write", adding "all of which could add up to sensitivity galore, but you'll have to take my word for it" (p. 140). Between pages 142 and 189, thirty whole pages are each overlaid with a large 'X'. This section of the story is literally crossed out. The text on these pages nonetheless remains present in the book, and perfectly legible: it has not been cut from the final, printed text.

The announcement of these "pages of transition" with the spatial "here" foregrounds and deictically anchors the reader's position along the linear continuum of the textual discourse. The metatextual reference to "pages" and metacompositional reference to the writing process pull the reader's attention away from the story and towards its construction, highlighting its artifice, and reasserting the authorial guise of the narratorial voice. The passage seems to function as an aside in which the pseudo-authorial narrator directly addresses the reader, as "you". In saying "all of which could add up to sensitivity galore, but you'll have to take my word for it", he interestingly draws attention to narratorial reliability, the conditional "could" suggesting there are no guarantees. The passage is paradoxical and ironic, in that, firstly, the 30 pages of transition do actually follow directly, therefore they were in fact written despite the decision to the contrary, and, secondly, they are perfectly readable, and so the reader *does not* merely have to take the narrator's word for the interpretable sensitivity. The teasing paradox and ambiguous "could" therefore actually function as a further spur to read these 30 pages rather than simply trust the narrator's summary.

There are several pages within this section which are not crossed out. These pages are either blank or contain, within square brackets, further details about and metanarrative comments upon what is narrated and crossed out on the 'pages of transition'. One of the metanarrative comments reads

> Don't worry. I decided to scrap this scene long before I talked to any editors about the book. [. . .] I can't remember now what I had in mind, but it was important to me at the time. Now it makes me yawn. [. . .] At the time I knew I was telling the truth but forget it. Let's X it out and come what will.
>
> (p. 142)

The use of square brackets suggests these passages are narrative 'asides' from pseudo-authorial narrator to reader, as do the frequent first-person references and the informal and familiar tone of the metanarrative comments, e.g. "Don't worry". These asides fit Genette's description of paratextual "notes" (1997, p. 319), in which he highlights the significance of discourse positioning and textual relations:

> A note is a statement of variable length (one word is enough) connected to a more or less definite segment of text and either placed opposite or keyed to this segment. The always partial character of the text being referred to, and therefore the always local character of the statement conveyed in a note, seems to me the most distinctive formal feature of this paratextual element.

The discourse deictic references to "this scene" refer specifically to the scene relayed on the right-hand page. The temporal deictic references to the decision to cut the scene being made "long before" the point at which he spoke to editors, and therefore also long before "now", draw attention to the (lengthy) compositional process. The "now" is presumably a moment in the re-drafting or editing process. This brings to the fore the complex relationship between the linear textual continuum and the less linear, perhaps partially cyclical, process of drafting that ultimately linear textual continuum. This whole section is underscored by an unusual foregrounding of the dynamic nature of that drafting process—usually obscured within the fixed material result—and also of the dynamic nature of the reader's processing and conceptualisation of the text. Furthermore, the use of the term "scene" is more typical in describing fictional events, and therefore sits uncomfortably and paradoxically with the claim that the events described are true. The sentence "At the time I knew I was telling the truth but forget it" works like the conditional "could" on the earlier page in at once making and yet also undermining or mitigating a claim, evoking the reader's curiosity and suspicions about reliability—in effect, again, enticing the reader to read the crossed-out pages.

Later, we get "This was such a great idea when I got it. [. . .] Alas. Here I am X-ing it out" (p. 156). Again, we have foregrounded deictic first-person references to the pseudo-authorial narrator—specifically, within the context of his act of creation (as foregrounded by the reference to the "idea"). Again, too, we have a "then" and "now', or, to be more precise, a moment in the past (and described in the past tense) in the process of initial drafting, and a point "here" (described in the present tense) in the process of editing. Here, the reference to the propositional content of the following crossed-out page as an "idea" presents that material unambiguously as fictive invention, and the pseudo-authorial narrator goes on to discuss his related compositional choices, conveying his authorial agency in narrating and denarrating his text.

The passages of metacommentary also entice the reader to read the crossed-out pages through frequent references to their content, references which only make sense if the reader reads those crossed-out pages. Some of these references are deictic, as in the previous example "This was such a great idea" (p. 156). Others include mention of people or objects that feature on the previous or subsequent crossed-out page, for example "Sorensen's wife deserves all the mention she can get. She's a peach" (p. 180). Others combine the two, for example "This Danish fellow whom I have eliminated over there" (p. 145). Even if these sections in square brackets are to be considered a kind of 'sub-narration' of sorts, asides, like footnotes, "a threshold [. . .] more or less legitimated by the author" (Genette, 1997, p. 2)—optional and supplementary reading content—they are nonetheless present and not crossed out, and so of a higher, or perhaps firmer, ontological status than the denarrated sections to which they refer. This creates an odd and nonsensical ontological hierarchy, and provides more impetus (in the sense of offering a resolution to this conundrum) to retain the denarrated sections within the parameters of the 'actual' in the text.

These pages contain yet other kinds of ontological confusion and complexity. On page 158, the narrator writes "I absolutely back off at the idea of eliminating this little scene [. . .]. I'll not X it out. [. . .] This scene shall remain therefore unscathed" (p. 158). The discourse deictic reference "this little scene" refers to the scene partially described over the next two and a half pages which are not crossed out (though the first sentence of the scene actually begins on the crossed-out page 157, with only its second half being not crossed out on page 159, after the metanarrative interruption). The decision not to excise something from within a section which has otherwise been excised seems almost to be a kind of disnarrated disnarration, and, if one were to ignore the crossed-out pages, leaves "this little scene" adrift and not connected to the most recent non-crossed-out section of the story.

On page 188, alongside the final crossed-out page, the narrator states:

> Alright. Here's the end of my purge, and I feel better for it. [. . .] I feel lighter. It's a loss, but also a gain. I've done something for all of you, made it a little shorter through this book.

The referent of "it" here is not entirely clear. The book is not physically shorter, in that the "purge[d]", crossed-out text remains in the final, published material text. If anything, the book is longer, due to the meta-commentary on the other, intermittently interrupting pages. The *story* is arguably shorter—or, at least, the authorially legitimised story is shorter due to the purging of these pages. Their ontological status as a part of the story has been denied from the section's outset. Yet, the reader is implicitly invited to read this section, through its maintained legible presence and through the cross-referencing discourse deixis in the interrupting and enticing narrative asides, which, by contrast, are not crossed out. The section is simultaneously evoked and negated in a complex structure of paradoxical ontological relations.

Perhaps the most famous example of denarration, and the one which fits Richardson's definition most closely, is Chapter 45 of Fowles's *The French Lieutenant's Woman* (1996 [1969]). Though Frangipane finds it to be an example of Prince's disnarration (2017, p. 573), it is more properly Richardson's denarration, as the events are initially portrayed as 'real' within the diegesis before that ontological status is revoked. Chapters 43 and 44 provide the novel's first of three endings (or, debatably, of four, if taking into account the immediately disnarrated ending in Chapter 55). Chapters 43 and 44 present, the narrator tells us, a "thoroughly traditional" close (p. 327). The 'garden path' nature of these chapters is revealed by the subsequent two-page denarration of this ending, opening Chapter 45. These chapters have received relatively little attention. The ending itself is often critically ignored, overshadowed by the two later endings. For example, consider Scruggs' article 'The Two Endings of *The French Lieutenant's Woman*' (1985). Hutcheon (1978), Onega (1989) and Gutleben (2001) each note only two endings overall, and Holmes (1995 [1981]) and Rankin (1974), though acknowledging three endings, award the first minimal discussion. The two-page narratorial revision at the opening of Chapter 45 is interesting in several respects, however: in the metanarrative situating of the loci of the narrator and reader in relation to the narrative discourse and storyworld, in the manner in which the ontological status of the propositional content of the previous two chapters is revised, in the retrospective reductive portrayal of the conventionalism of the false ending, and in the paradoxical intertwining of realist illusion with this metanarrative strain.

Discourse deixis plays a significant role in how these aspects of the passage are constructed.

Before analysing its negation, the "thoroughly traditional ending" warrants some discussion. Chapter 43 relays Charles's thoughts on his train journey back to Lyme, his resignation to his future with Ernestina. The first half of Chapter 44 tells of their happy reunion. Both scenes are portrayed without overt narratorial intrusion. In the final few pages of Chapter 44, however, the narrator announces "And so ends the story" (p. 324). He claims "What happened to Sarah, I do not know", letting her "drown in the shadows of closer things" (pp. 324–325). He proceeds to state "Charles and Ernestina [. . .] lived together" and "begat what shall it be—let us say seven children" (p. 325). The tale of Sam and Mary is summarised with a brevity to match the narrator's proclaimed lack of interest in "the biography of servants", and Mrs Poulteney, receiving more attention than the other characters combined, is comically cast down to hell (p. 325). The pace, the opinionated and sardonic manner, and the distribution of detail in the narration of these final few pages constitute an overt breach of any realist pretence. The narrator's subsequent summary of these chapters as comprising a "thoroughly traditional ending" therefore ironically downplays his (often metanarrative) narratorial intrusions and implicitly simplifies the 'traditional' through pastiche. Given the critical acceptance of the supposedly Victorian realist tidiness of the sudden wrapping-up (see for example Rankin, 1974, p. 201, discussing "this traditional conclusion"), it would appear that the narrator achieves some residual impact in his generic dupe. Nonetheless, it contributes to the ironic demonstration of the discursive construction of history which accrues over the course of the novel as a whole.

This reflective summary on the "traditional" quality of the ending is only one of several metanarrational discourse deictic references within the opening sentence of Chapter 45, which runs

> And now, having brought this fiction to a thoroughly traditional ending, I had better explain that although all I have described in the last two chapters happened, it did not happen quite in the way you may have been led to believe.
>
> (p. 327)

The narrator shifts from telling the story to discussing the telling of the story, turning directly to the reader, explicitly addressed as "you". The loci of the narrator and reader with respect to progress through the text-continuum are foregrounded with the temporal deictic "now" and by anaphoric discourse deictic reference to the "last two chapters". The metanarrational, metacompositional, and metatextual discourse deictic phrases "this fiction", "a traditional ending", "all I have described", and "the last two chapters" convey a narrating locus external to the fiction and foreground both the text's fictional status and the reader's own extra-fictional context in the act of reading a work of fiction. The narrator also affirms his feigned authorial stance and control over the fiction by asserting his role, with many first-person references, in "having brought" the fiction to a close and in having described all that happened in the last two chapters.

At the same time as the fictionality of the text is foregrounded, though, the narrator stresses the reality of the events relayed, claiming "all that I have described [. . .] happened". A further complicating gap is opened up between what he has narrated and that 'reality' with the statement "it did not happen in quite the way you may have been led to believe". This has several ramifications. The reader's conceptualised version of the storyworld, as directed by the narration, is undermined, and its text-drivenness foregrounded. The deferral of responsibility implied by the deletion of agency in the final phrase ("you may have been led to believe") raises questions about, but does not wholly contradict, the narrator's preceding assertion of authorial responsibility. Attention is drawn to the mediating, potentially distorting, and unreliable nature of his narration, whilst the reality of the events of which he (more or less faithfully) tells is implicitly affirmed. The first sentence of the chapter thus contains within it the extrafictional situating of the narrator and reader in relation to the text, foregrounding of the reader's text-driven dynamic processing and conceptual realisation, metanarrative disruption of the reader's suspension of disbelief, and simultaneous and paradoxical covert affirmation of the reality of the storyworld.

The ontological status of the events relayed in the preceding chapters is revised more explicitly in the following paragraphs, and the paradox furthered. The narrator states

> the last few pages you have read are not what happened, but what [Charles] spent the hours between London and Exeter imagining might happen. To be sure he did not think in quite the detailed and coherent narrative manner I have employed; nor would I swear that he followed Mrs Poulteney's postmortal career in quite such interesting detail. But he certainly wished her to the Devil, so it comes to almost the same thing.
>
> (p. 327)

The metatextual and metadiscursive discourse deictic references within the phrase "the last few pages you have read" explicitly indicate the textual medium of the discourse, its reception through the dynamic act of reading, and the processual locus of the reader in relation to that act. The ontological status of the recently conceptualised events is demoted from the diegetic reality to the hypodiegetic imaginings of the diegetic protagonist (see McHale, 1987, pp. 109–110), and then to yet another remove from the fictional 'reality', being, the narrator admits, a slightly warped version of those imaginings. The narrator acknowledges his own elaboration, metanarratively contrasting his "detailed and coherent narrative manner" and "interesting detail" with Charles's thoughts. In doing so he evokes the reader's extrafictional awareness and assessment of the discourse as narrative fiction (necessarily in relation to other narrative fictions and to the literary context at large). At the same time, he again implies a 'real' (non-fictional) basis (i.e. Charles's thoughts) for his (variably faithful) narrative representation, whilst side-stepping the issue of his thereby ontologically problematic apparent omniscience.

The narrator's assertion that "all I have described in the last two chapters happened" is interesting in that it suggests he credits Charles's imaginings with *some* ontological validity, despite this being implicitly undercut by the following contrary assertions "it did not happen quite in the way you may have been led to believe", and then "the last few pages you have read are not what happened, but what he spent the hours between London and Exeter imagining might happen". This is perhaps suggestive of the fact that though by the end of the third paragraph of Chapter 45 the events relayed in these pages have been denarrated in terms of their diegetic actuality, they retain significance in terms of both Charles's future diegetic path (as we are told), and the reader's interpretation.

The attentiveness of that readerly processing and conceptualisation of the now negated storyworld events is explicitly referred to in the next paragraph. The narrator continues,

> Above all he felt himself coming to the end of a story; and to an end he did not like. If you noticed in those last two chapters an abruptness, a lack of consonance [. . .] and a small matter of [Charles] being given a life-span of very nearly a century and a quarter; if you entertained a suspicion [. . .] that the writer's breath has given out and he has rather arbitrarily ended the race [. . .], then do not blame me; because all these feelings [. . .] were very present in Charles's own mind. The book of his existence, so it seemed to him, was about to come to a distinctly shabby close.
>
> (pp. 327–328)

The reader is here again directly addressed with the second-person pronoun "you". Whilst engagingly mimicking direct exchange, the pronoun can have alienating undercurrents in its plural deictic potential, undermining that illusory immediacy. The narratorial hypotheses of the reader's thoughts, within which the two instances of address occur, mirror those elsewhere in the novel (see section 5.4). In this instance the narrator imposes upon the reader not only a literary-critical aptitude but also a particular assessment of the false ending as slightly weak in places, indicating a lack of authorial skill. The negative imperative "do not blame me" encodes an anticipation of the reader's blame for this, and, in effect, presumptuously *imposes* this opinion upon the reader (see the discussion of negative sentences in section 5.4). The narrator's deferral of this blame to Charles's feelings again heightens the impression of the reality of the protagonist.

The paragraph as whole is nonetheless predominantly metanarrative: the narrator metatextually refers to the narrative sequence ("those last two chapters"), both foregrounding the linear, concrete textuality of the discourse and again deictically situating the loci of reader and narrator in relation to a point of progress through the text-continuum. He also refers to apparent deviation from implicitly conventional standards of fictional narrative (e.g. pace, 'consonance', characterisation, realism) and metacompositionally refers explicitly to "the writer" and the writing process (e.g. "the writer's breath has given out"). This again foregrounds the literariness of the text and intertextually evokes comparison with the broader literary context. The common metafictional metaphor of the world as a book (Waugh, 1984, p. 3) is also made most explicit, but its ramifications restricted to Charles in this instance, covertly backgrounding the mutually constructive nature of the reader's processing of the text that underscores other elements of the paragraph. The paradoxical pushing and pulling of the passage—at one point foregrounding one narrative and discursive agent of the fictionality, and at another point foregrounding another, and at one juncture undermining realism and at another upholding it—is thus in several ways enhanced.

The paradoxical assertion within these paragraphs of both the narrative act and the reality of the diegesis has thus far supported the impression of the extrafictional reality of the pseudo-authorial narrating 'I'-persona. His relation to the story is radically complicated by the following paragraph, however, in which he asserts that

> the 'I', that entity who found such [. . .] specious reasons for consigning Sarah to the shadows [. . .], was not myself; it was merely the personification of a certain massive indifference in things—too hostile for Charles to think of as 'God'—that had set its malevolent inertia on the Ernestina side of the scales; that seemed an inexorable onward direction as fixed as that of the train which drew Charles along.
>
> (p. 328)

With the phrase "the 'I', that entity", the narrator employs literary-critical terminology for discussing the narrating voice and persona, foregrounding its status as a literary motif, and conveying an expectation of readerly literary-critical awareness. The use of the definite article and the inhuman connotations of "entity" further suggest the 'I' is a textual construct, a fictitious discursive role, a mere mimicry of any real authorial persona. The potential deictic fluidity of the first-person pronoun is drawn attention to, and its referential value in the discourse so far slightly destabilised: along with the deictic use of the definite article ("the" I as opposed to, for example, 'my' I), the deictic demonstrative "that" distances the narrator, previously designated as "I", from the entity who/which drew together the "shabby close". Though the narrator initially appears to attribute to this "I" a consciousness (in the suggestion of reasoning and motivation), he then posits it as a mere personification, apparently on the part of Charles, of the omnipotent presence he feels is determining his path (the reality of the diegesis again affirmed). This "I", then, is Charles's invention within his hypodiegetic imaginings, portrayed by the pseudo-authorial narrator from his supposed extrafictional stance. The negative assertion "the 'I' [. . .] was not myself" counters and 'denarrates' the interpretation that is textually prompted by the preceding pages, an interpretation which (unlike the projected "blame" discussed previously) the narrator therefore might legitimately anticipate the reader may hold.

This instance serves to show a further interesting facet of denarration: denarration reveals the comprehensive nature of text processing, in that the text directs, and interpretation requires, imaginative conceptualisation of elements of the narrative discourse including and beyond the textually delimited storyworld (e.g. conceptual realisation of narratorial intertextual references, of the figure of the narrator her/himself, etc.). This returns us to the permeable nature of the membrane between the diegetic and the extradiegetic—the (equally) fictive nature of the discourse through which the storyworld is mediated.

The narrator follows his foregrounding of the illusory nature of the prior fictive 'I'-persona with an immediate 'self'-reference. Through this, the narratorial voice is instantly portrayed as more 'real', by contrast. That is, this juxtaposition, and the paragraph as a whole, paradoxically affirms the impression of the narrator's own reality in contrast to the overtly acknowledged unreality of "the 'I', that entity".

However, and perhaps inevitably, there is a further ironic twist to this denarration of the attribution of the "I". In the opening of the next paragraph, the narrator seemingly contradicts any readerly reconceptualisation of the narratorial voice in the last two chapters that has been prompted by his overt deferral of "the 'I' ". He now claims

> I was not cheating when I said that Charles had decided, in London, that day after his escapade, to go through with his marriage; that was his official decision [. . .]. Where I have cheated was in analysing the effect that three-word letter continued to have on him.

> (p. 328)

The narrator here firmly re-anchors the first-person pronoun to his own deictic locus as the speaking participant. He also reasserts his identity with the narrating voice in Chapter 43 (in which Charles's decision was relayed). The reader's interpretive revision of the ontological status of the narrator of the false ending, as directed by the preceding paragraph, is now revised again, and can be restricted to the self-referring and intrusive narration of the final few pages of tying-up in Chapter 44 (from the juncture previously referred to explicitly—the point at which the 'I'-speaker intrudes and consigns Sarah to the shadows). The narrative-determining authority of the pseudo-authorial narrator is emphasised not only by the repeated narratorial self-reference but also by his claim to have manipulated the facts. The narrator's assertion that he has "cheated" portrays narration as a game with rules, rules he has broken in misleading the reader with regard to what is actual within the diegesis. This (like the discourse deictic reference to "the 'I', that entity") metanarrationally foregrounds the notion of machinations through which fiction operates and conveys an expectation of the reader's understanding of those machinations. The implied rule, that the narrator must be faithful to the diegesis, however, is in itself an illusory code: like any attestation of narratorial reliability, it covertly supports the chimera of a real, factual basis underlying the narration. Whilst the narrator's pseudo-authorial stance and responsibility for the narrating act is reaffirmed, so, too, is the realist illusion.

The narrator finally turns back to the progress of the storyworld events, picking up the sequence from the diegetic instance preceding the two denarrated chapters. As he does so, however, he encompasses the reader within first-person plural references, implying a shared process of evolving insight into the diegesis, as well as, paradoxically, a shared role in determining that diegesis:

> But above all it seemed to set Charles a choice; and while one part of him hated having to choose, we come near the secret of his state on that journey west when we know that another part of him felt intolerably excited by the proximity of the moment of choice. He had not the benefit of existentialist terminology; but what he felt was really a very clear case of the anxiety of freedom [. . .]. So let us kick Sam out of his hypothetical future and back into his Exeter present. He goes to his master's compartment when the train stops.
>   Are we stayin' the night, sir?
>
>   (p. 328)

In using the deictic first-person plural pronoun "we" the narrator both addresses and identifies with the reader. Within the words "we come near the secret of his state on that journey west when we know that another part of him felt intolerably excited by the moment of choice", this use of "we", together with the present tense of the verbs "come" and "know", conveys a shared dynamic progression, albeit led by the narrator, to greater knowledge of the diegesis (the reality of which is again affirmed). In pointing out, in the next sentence, that Charles "had not the benefit of existentialist terminology", the narrator again evokes both further shared knowledge (in co-joined opposition to Charles) and an extrafictional awareness of the postmodern context of the literature's composition. Returning to the story with the words "let us kick Sam out of his hypothetical future", however, the narrator suggests a shared responsibility also for the determination of the diegesis, both undermining the realist dimension of the passage and bestowing a greater significance upon the reader's conceptual engagement in that determination than is suggested in the preceding passages.

These instances of implied intimacy between narrator and reader are brief, and the following narration continues without narratorial intervention (swiftly returning to the retrospective tense). Nonetheless, the suggestion of collaboration works towards the overall effect created by the passage's denarration, best described by Goffman as

> insider's folly: When a construction is discredited—whether by discovery, confession, or informing—and a frame apparently cleared, the plight of the discovered persons tends to be accepted with little reservation, very often with less reservation than was sustained in regard to the initial frame itself.
>
> (1974, p. 473)

Having denarrated the "traditional ending", the narrator overtly incites readerly engagement in the ensuing diegesis, the reality of that diegesis newly legitimated just as its fictive discursive frame is paradoxically asserted.

This analysis has drawn out the paradoxical strands of the opening pages of Chapter 45 and has drawn out the significant role of discourse deixis in much of the paradoxical effect. Discourse deictic references situate the narrator and reader in particular relations: relations to the development of the diegesis, to each other in the discursive dyad, to the text-continuum, and to the extrafictional context. The narrator's occupation of the position of the speaking 'I' is briefly problematised, foregrounding both the literary motif of the narrating persona and the deictic fluidity of the first-person pronoun. The traditional Victorian realist quality of the two preceding chapters is discursively constructed in retrospect, simplifying elements of the Victorian novelistic genre in the process. These chapters are denarrated to the extent that their ontological status is demoted from diegetic actuality to the hypodiegetic level as the protagonist's imaginings. The illusion of the reality of that diegesis is affirmed, and yet discourse deixis is repeatedly exploited to emphasise its discursive frame, not least through denarrated attribution of the speaking 'I'.

The de- and disnarrated events, along with the narrator's overt assertions of authorial (and readerly) godlike control, the imperatives to the reader, and the reference to the dependence of the storyworld upon imaginative conceptualisation all covertly signal the significance of the narration to that imaginative conceptualisation over and above the final resultant storyworld (should an ontologically stable storyworld ultimately remain). That which is narrated is actualised by the reader. It is in this way that denarration can function to explore the relationships between the discourse and the story—between reader, narrator, text, and storyworld—and confront the nature of the discursive dependence of fictional worlds. As shown, the deictic anchoring of participants to loci within the discourse, its linear flow, and the ontological hierarchy of the narrative levels contribute significantly to these effects.

The forms and uses of denarration explored in these examples share metafictional implications. As Richardson (2001) observes, when the narrator denies and/or negates elements of the storyworld, the subversion of the functioning of the narration foregrounds the conventional conditions by which it operates, and the relationship between discourse and story: in extreme circumstances "the usual separation between story and discourse collapses, and we are left with discourse without a retrievable story. The work's discourse is determinate; its story is inherently indeterminable" (p. 173). Denarration draws attention to the readerly processing of and conceptual engagement with the linear text, upon which the actualisation of the storyworld depends. Denarration highlights the reader's relationship to the story, her role in its construction—"the performative aspect of world making in narrative fiction" (Richardson, 2001, p. 173). Also foregrounded, within this relationship, is the reader's participation in the discourse—through which her relationship to the story is mediated—and the inscribed power dynamic between narrator and reader. Denarration of storyworld entities and narrated events therefore offer a variety of metafictional implications for each of the narrative strata and their interrelations.

This section has explored a 'garden path' kind of disnarration, whereby the ontological status of part of the narrative is denied or left ambiguous. The next section explores a different type—that of 'forked paths'—whereby alternative versions of parts of the narrative are impossibly presented as contrary and yet ontologically equally real.

5.3 Discourse Deixis in Alternarration

In some of the examples of denarration presented previously, an aspect of the storyworld is explicitly disnarrated and a different version of that aspect is then offered in its place. Metafiction often presents a related, but slightly different kind of disnarration, whereby two or more different and mutually exclusive versions of an aspect of the story are presented without any indication of which, if any, is 'real' within the storyworld (McHale, 1987, p. 108). This is disnarration in the form of forking paths. Each narrative path can be taken by the narrator and reader only if the other is not taken, in that the realisation of one depends on and entails the negation of the other: they cannot co-exist within a coherent conceptualisation of the story. Barth's 'Title' offers a brief example: "At this point they were both smiling despite themselves. At this point they were both flashing hatred despite themselves. [. . .] At this point they were both despite themselves" (1988 [1968], p. 112). Because the first two sentences, at least, seem mutually exclusive—they cannot both be true, assuming "this point" in each refers to the same moment—and yet no single version is presented and legitimised as 'real', the reader is left to merely oscillate between acceptance of each, and corresponding negation of its alternative(s), without reaching resolution.

According to Prince, disnarration "makes explicit the logic at work in narrative whereby, as Claude Bremond emphasized, every narrative function opens an alternative, a set of possible directions, and every narrative progresses by following certain directions as opposed to others" (1992, p. 36). Prince is referring to Bremond's 'The Logic of Narrative Possibilities' (1980), in which he deconstructs a purely linear notion of narrative progression and proposes instead a "network of possibilities" (1980, p. 388). Both Waugh (1984, p. 137) and McHale (1987, p. 108) discuss Borges's 'The Garden of Forking Paths' as a seminal text in introducing the principle of "incompatible alternate plots" (Doležel, 1988, p. 491). This kind of narrative configuration, in which versions of the fictional reality sit alongside each other as equally 'real' and 'unreal' in the story, does not just propose that different speakers can perceive and present different versions of the same event, or that progress through life inevitably involves a choice between one path and another (neither of which are too unconventional in narrative). Instead, it more radically counters singularity, linearity, and chronology.

Discourse deixis works interestingly in forked paths, specifically because the reader's perception of the units of narrative as being in parallel, rather than unilinear, often relies on a combination of foregrounded metatextual discourse deixis, slightly ontologically unusual use of person and spatial deixis across the units of narrative (often with metatextual and metadiscursive discourse deictic functions), and a *lack* of the kind of sequential textual deixis (included co-opted spatial or, metaphorically, temporal deixis) that usually communicates narrative order. The following section builds on the work of Dannenberg (2008) and Ryan (2006) on forked paths to explore and extrapolate the functioning of discourse deixis within forked paths.

Dannenberg writes about counterfactual ontological hierarchies. For Dannenberg, "basic counterfactuals generate a binary of events, in which fact is contrasted with a hypothetical counterfact" (2008, p. 120). Dannenberg seems to be using 'factual' in the sense of 'true' or 'actual' in the world of the novel. The term 'counterfactual' is a little problematic in the context of fiction, as all fiction is in essence 'counterfactual' in the sense that it is other to fact and reality. The term is perhaps more awkward in the context of analysing metafiction specifically, precisely because metafiction flaunts its fictionality in such a concentrated way. 'Counterfictional' might be more appropriate, though 'counter' implies the opposite of or against, so, just as counterfactual may imply fictional, counterfictional may imply factual. The main thrust of historiographic metafiction is not quite counterfactual, for the very reason that it tends to challenge and subvert the concept of History as factual, but one of its chief methods in doing so can be through offering up a version of events which is directly, even if only slightly, counter to History's narrative.

Dannenberg poignantly notes that "counter-counterfactuals—a counterfactual version of a counterfactual proposition—[. . .] already destabilize th[e] binary relationship between fact and counterfact" (p. 120). Of course, Dannenberg is thinking of the fictional world as the original factual world, with a different version of that fiction being the counterfactual, and a further, alternative different version being the counter-counterfactual. The counterfactual, in this view, is a forked path with one path leading away from the heretofore main path. The counter-counterfactual describes the situation in which a further, third path branches off. This third path may branch off the first, or the second, and/or it may become the most 'real' in the story (surpassing the first path with this status). Counter-counterfactuals do not, though, necessarily (or probably) return us to 'fact', in that a proposition which is 'counter' to a lie may not be the truth, but yet another, different lie. This is what Dannenberg seems to suggest in proposing that counter-counterfactuals "destabalize th[e] binary relationship between fact and counterfact", in that they can problematise a kind of understanding of the world which presupposes that there is one true version of events and other false versions, and that any version of events is distinguishably either true or false in a simple binary. This destabalisation relates not only to ontology, with respect to the ontological status of different versions of events, but also to epistemology—ways of seeing and understanding the world and 'reality', and ways of thinking about knowing and knowledge.

Dannenberg proposes that some radical and historiographic metafictions are comprised of "antirealist ontological hierarch[ies]" in which "multiple worlds are not part of a coherent and unified system". She suggests that relationships between these worlds tend to be "analogical as opposed to causal" to the extent that "hierarchical distinctions between these multiple worlds, such as the distinction between fact and counterfact, become fuzzy and disappear altogether" (p. 121). According to Dannenberg, historiographic metafiction "uses historical counterfactuals but with significant alterations to the clear ontological hierarchy of fact versus counterfact" (p. 129), creating "an ambivalent ontological structure" (p. 130). She also notes that in some novels of this type, "if the precise nature of the true facts remains unknown or indeed is unknowable, there can also be no clear counterfactual but only multiple configurations of data" (p. 130).

Dannenberg's understanding of an ontological hierarchy, in this context, seems to entail that the 'real' version of the narrative (the version which is 'true' within the storyworld) has a higher ontological status than other, therefore 'lower', versions. This seems to be how Dannenberg is using the concept of an ontological hierarchy in statements such as "in some narratives the ontological hierarchy is so blurred that it is no longer possible to use the designation *counter*factual" (p. 130). Where Dannenberg does explicitly discuss counterfactual hierarchies within her analyses, however, an "upward" counterfactual is one "would have been better" for the character imagining it, for example (pp. 122–123)—better in the sense of more personally or socially advantageous. The ordering principle in this hierarchical system is one of scalar advantage—specifically, which version is better or worse from the perspective of the character who is the source of the counterfactual—rather than one of ontology in the sense of true and not true, or, for example, a hierarchy with three layers comprised of true, partially false, and entirely false, etc.

This issue exposes some ways in which the concepts of counterfactuals and ontological hierarchies are problematic in the context of metafiction, precisely because they are part of what metafiction overtly works to subvert. The destabilisation of a binary relationship between true and false, within the world of the story, destabilises the very notion of the 'counterfactual', as this implies that one version is factual and another not. Framing counterfactuals within a hierarchical structure specified as ontological (albeit not always applied in that way) suggests that different versions of the narrative can be ordered by some criteria of relative 'reality' within the storyworld. This subscribes to a notion of there being a true representation of events (or a version which is more true), and to a privileging of that truth. One of the main drives of metafiction is to challenge the perception that there is a supremely correct version of events, and to reveal that even information presented as 'facts' (in the real world) is biased and mediated by the discourses of power and knowledge which generate these facts (as per Foucault, 1977). In the context of metafiction, at least, the term 'alternarration' seems more fitting, in that it does not speak to fact (vs. fiction), and does not propose an ontological differentiation in the form of a hierarchy. Incidentally, Prince admits he considered using the term "alternarrated" in the place of disnarrated, but felt disnarrated was more appropriate (1992, p. 137, n. 2). 'Alternarration' can better describe circumstances whereby contrary plots are pursued, each with the same ontological status as each other and (usually) with the same ontological status as the preceding and subsequent story.

Alternarration appears in various forms in Barth, Brophy, Coover, Fowles, and Katz. These forms include presentation of versions of events in sequence and in parallel, those which are wholly mutually exclusive and those which are not wholly mutually exclusive, and those which are clearly distinguished as discrete paths and units of text and those which are not so distinctly discrete. The length of text which is alternarrated can also vary, as can the nature of the text (compare, for example, a critical narrative moment vs. a descriptive bridging passage).

An example of alternarration at sentence level was given previously, from Barth's 'Title': "At this point they were both smiling despite themselves. At this point they were both flashing hatred despite themselves. [. . .] At this point they were both despite themselves" (1988 [1968], p. 112). Here the temporally deictic "this point" refers to a particular instance in the chronology of the story, but three different things are presented as happening at the same instance (if "this point" is interpreted as referring to the same instance in each case). The same pair of characters is referred to in each of the three variants, with the anaphoric person deixis "they" (which, as with all pronouns, signals a shared knowledge of sorts between the narrator and the reader, such that the narrator feels no names are needed for the reader to recognise the referent). The slight differences within the pattern of the repeated syntactic structure "At this point they were [. . .] despite themselves" work to foreground both the parallel nature of the variants and the one difference between them. The mutual exclusivity of the difference between the variants is the key signal of the parallel and contrary ontology. In the final variant there is no main verb following "were", as in the previous iterations. This makes 'were' the main verb, which offers up a possible interpretation along the lines of "at this point they existed, despite themselves". Such an interpretation fits with the metanarrative and ontological play of the story (and collection as a whole), but the repetition in the lead-up adds an element of wry wordplay and metacompositional flaunting to the discourse.

Barth uses alternarration in 'Lost in the Funhouse' too, both at sentence level (as in the example from 'Title') and more substantially. We are told, of the hesitant Ambrose, "Naturally he didn't have the nerve to ask Magda to go through the funhouse with him. With incredible nerve and to everyone's surprise he invited Magda, quietly and politely, to go through the funhouse with him" (p. 90). The adverb "Naturally" presupposes and implies that the pseudo-authorial narrator and reader have a shared understanding of Ambrose. As in the alternarration in 'Title', there is overt syntactic repetition, this time of the close of the sentence. There is no temporal deixis signalling synchronicity (or otherwise), but the mutual exclusivity and therefore parallel nature of the two variants here is more pronounced than in the previous example.

The other, earlier example of alternarration in this story is more complex. The narration runs as follows:

> I'll never be an author. It's been forever already, everybody's gone home, Ocean City's deserted, the ghost-crabs are tickling across the

beach and [. . .] the empty halls of clapboard hotel and abandoned funhouses. A tidal wave; an enemy air raid; *The inhabitants fled in terror.* Magda clung to his trouser leg; he alone knew the maze's secret. "He gave his life that we might live," said Uncle Karl with a scowl of pain, as he. [sic] The fellow's hands had been tattooed; the woman's legs, the woman's fat white legs had. [sic] *An astonishing coincidence.* They hadn't even chased him. He wished he were dead.

(pp. 86–87, italics in the original)

The first two phrases, "I'll never be an author. It's been forever already", are a metanarrative critique on the part of the pseudo-authorial narrator. The "it" seems to refer to the time he has taken to tell the story so far (the narrator having already criticised his slow progress through the plot several times on prior pages, as discussed in Chapter 3). However, the second sentence continues directly with "everyone's gone home", which implies he has been too slow or too late—that the characters have somehow proceeded without him, and he has failed to keep up. The passage then backtracks a little, from a possible post-ending scenario, to the events that may have led up to it—"a tidal wave; an enemy air raid"; references to German World War 2 U-boats and hurricanes have appeared in previous paragraphs, their mark on the resort noted. At this point the fantasy of Ambrose's heroism suggests the focalisation may have slipped into the character's thoughts. The interruption (a sentence being cut off at "as he", and the next sentence likewise grammatically problematic and cut off) could signal the intrusion within Ambrose's thoughts of the memory of the illicit sexual encounter under the boardwalk which he has just witnessed and is seemingly troubled by. The flawed and thereby foregrounded grammar and the italicised news headline style sentences of commentary (e.g. "*An astonishing coincidence*") confuse the sense of this paragraph being anchored with the 'I'-narrator.

Immediately following this passage, the narrator breaks in again and proposes one optional close to the story which is more overtly his own notion (as opposed to a character's fantasy), this path then forking internally into many variants:

One possible ending would be to have Ambrose come across another lost person in the dark. They'd match their wits together against the funhouse, struggle like Ulysses. [. . .] or a girl. [. . .] and it would turn out that [she] was a negro. A blind girl. President Roosevelt's son. Ambrose's former archenemy.

(p. 87)

An explicit metacompositional reference to "a possible ending" introduces the hypothesis, within which five alternative variants are swiftly listed, only one with the word "or" differentiating the path as an alternate parallel possibility: the differentiation of the others as alternative paths is deduced by their (variable) mutual exclusivity and the absence of any spatial or temporal deixis which might suggest a connected sequence. This optional close is disnarration in Prince's original sense of being a modalised hypothesis, not ever posited as 'real' within the storyworld, which the story then moves on from and leaves unrealised. It is not, therefore, alternarration in the sense being described here. That said, together with the narrative's next move—returning to the funhouse and continuing with "Shortly after the mirror room he'd groped along a musty corridor" (p. 87)—the passage does serve to cue the reader's revised comprehension of the preceding, more disastrous close as an alternative, parallel version of the story, now abandoned.

What is notable in these examples, and crucial to their workings, is the lack of discourse deixis, in all but the narrator's overtly hypothetical ending, to signal and thereby delineate the specific section which comprises the alternarration, and to signal it *as* alternarration. As Verdonk argues, the absence of a significant feature can be as salient and significant for meaning as presence (Verdonk, 2013, p. 131; Verdonk, 2002, p. 6). It is the poignant absence of discourse deixis which creates the ambiguity about the boundaries of sections, and the ontological status of and relationships between these sections and others. These circumstances create a relatively high cognitive load for the reader, in the efforts evoked, and ultimately frustrated, to resolve the narrative sections into one coherent path, or indeed a clear ontological hierarchy of paths. The inevitable frustration exposes both the inherent drive to narrativise (on the part of the reader) and the simplification and occasional outright impossibility of narrativisation in the face of postmodern existential and ontological anxieties.

Barth's 'Lost in the Funhouse' involves a few brief instances of alternarration. In Coover's *Pricksongs and Descants* (2011 [1969]), alternarration is embedded more thoroughly throughout stories such as 'The Magic Poker', 'The Babysitter', and 'The Elevator'. As discussed in Chapter 3, 'The Magic Poker' begins with a metanarrative passage in which the pseudo-authorial narrator describes his creation of the story's setting: "I wander the island, inventing it. I make a sun for it, and trees" and so on. This opening paragraph ends with "I impose a hot midday silence, a profound and heavy stillness. But anything can happen" (p. 7). This sets the tone for the story, in which the narrator seems to claim and assert some godlike control over the story on the one hand, but also to relinquish control to apparent chaos on the other.

The alternative narrative paths offered in what follows in the story are interwoven and often difficult to distinguish, proceeding along similar lines, with the same characters and places, but at different paces and involving either slightly or dramatically different events. What can appear initially as a move backward or forward in time along one path slowly becomes discernible as a move to a different path. The shifts are generally unmarked by metanarrative comment, though a few intrude, such as, on page 16,

> A love letter! Wait a minute, this is getting out of hand! What hap-pened to that poker, I was doing much better with the poker, I had something going there, archetypal and even maybe beautiful [. . .]. Back to the poker.

The most overtly distinct paths are two beginning "There is a storm on the lake" (p. 23, p. 26) in which two children play on the green piano that has appeared in other paths. In one version their grandmother stirs embers in the fireplace with the poker (which also appears in other paths), and then runs with her children in terror from the suddenly appearing caretaker's son, seemingly arriving from another path. In the other, sec-ond variant, the grandmother settles down to tell her grandchildren the eponymous story of the magic poker. On pages 26 and 27, four para-graphs, each beginning with "Once upon a time", offer further, differ-ent, and distinct variants of the story—three summarising a whole story in that one paragraph, and one just beginning a story. The repetition of the opening phrase and the shared referents (the island, the sisters, the magic poker, etc.) but mutually exclusive content of each paragraph leaves them resolvable only as alternative variations, together subverting coherence and closure (Alfonso, 1995, p. 131). Evenson writes, "Which is the correct version? None of them. Or perhaps all of them. Coover is not interested in allowing the reader to puzzle out what *really* happened" (2003, p. 58, italics in the original). Evenson's appraisal reveals that not uncommon desire for a singular "correct" version of what "really" happened—a master-narrative that much of postmodernism seeks to confront as problematic and illusory, as epitomised by Coover's several alternarrative stories.

'Quenby and Ola, Swede and Carl' is another story in Coover's collec-tion in which several mutually exclusive alternative paths are run through at different points in the narrative. Each of the paths are seemingly on the same ontological level and no single path is discernible as the 'real' plot within the storyworld (see McHale, 1987, pp. 106–109). Kennedy describes the story as without "plot, coherent transition, explanation, or resolution" (1992, p. 54). In 'Quenby', the lack of temporal anchors combines with, on this occasion, very little repetition of phrases, and so the reader's inability to locate herself as following one path or another is compounded. One or two paths are discernible, such as one character's apparent sexual pursuit of and intercourse with the daughter of the other characters. This path is roughly discernible via the connectable sequence of events, albeit interrupted by paragraphs from other paths. The paths are not mutually exclusive, however, and quite what has and has not happened in each, and to which path each individual paragraph may belong, remains ambiguous.

'The Elevator' and 'The Babysitter' are slightly more systematic collections of alternarratives. In 'The Elevator', a male protagonist, Martin, is reported as entering an elevator in his workplace and having different experiences, most of which involve being bullied by colleagues or having sexual fantasies about one of his female co-workers. The experiences are not offered in a clear series. That is, in the series of passages subtitled "7", "8", and "9", for example, we cut from Martin entering the elevator alone for a suspense-stricken and surreal episode in which he gets out on a floor which does not exist, to him being in the elevator with his bullying colleagues, to him having sex with his female co-worker in the elevator while it is crashing to the ground. Because the shifts are marked by the breaks between the numbered subsections, the alternarratives are more easily distinguished and trackable than those in the previous examples. As in 'The Magic Poker', some of the passages do seem to fit together potentially as part of the same alternarrative path (e.g. 2 and 8, in which the bullying colleagues tease Martin, and 3, 6, and 9 in which Martin and his female colleague are alone in the elevator), and follow an (albeit interrupted) linear progression.

'The Babysitter' is the most famous story of the collection. A range of alternarratives follow the course(s) of one evening in which a couple leave a babysitter minding their children. The alternarrative paths are cut up into short paragraphs which are intermingled and arranged without clear logic beyond the apparent (though not conclusive) temporal progression of each path. Some paragraphs do not clearly belong to one path over another, and many are not mutually exclusive. One feature which recurs in most of the paragraphs is the television, featuring a discordant array of different things on different channels, usually in the background.

For Evenson, the story "offers a critique of the concerns of contemporary life, [and] points out the superficialities of lives whose most intense relationships seem to be with the TV" (2003, p. 94). Besides escapism, the experiential mode offered by the television seems to be an analogy for the story as a whole, and in turn, arguably, for contemporary existence. The television offers a series of channels running in parallel which one can freely move between, each of which presents an incoherent schedule of disconnected programmes. The characters' engagement with what is on the screen tends to involve either ignoring it or watching it with unfeeling detachment and disinterest, just as the narrative traces the sometimes horrific events within the paths without emotional investment or persistence.

Dannenberg interprets the coldness and frequent shifting in 'The Babysitter' as an absence of character development. She argues that "the lack of any clear markers concerning an ontological hierarchy sabotages the reader's ability to interact with the narrative world. The emphasis is on the antirealistic *exaggeration* of plot, while the detailed depiction of character [. . .] is avoided" (2008, p. 131, italics in the original). When later noting that "all the versions are given actual status" (p. 216) she adds that "the story's characters remain undifferentiated puppets", by which she means that "there is no or little transworld differentiation between characters across the different story versions" (p. 216; see Chapter 4, section 4.4 on transworld identities). This reading of the story ignores the stark differences in the behaviour of, for example, the babysitter between the paths: in one, for example, she is presented as proactively encouraging a threesome with her boyfriend and his friend, and in another explicitly refusing to allow them to even visit the house. By turns, the threesome narrative seems to be her boyfriend's fantasy, then a mutually consensual reality within the storyworld, then rape. The differences in the babysitter's attitude in these moments in the narrative are crucial to the significance of the differentiation between the parallel paths.

Dannenberg continues her discussion of 'The Babysitter', holding it up as an example of what she calls the "radical metafictions" of "the 1960s and 1970s", which she feels "use contradictory story versions to sabotage the teleological linearity of closure" (p. 215), but often at a cost. She believes that the "concerted sabotaging of narrative immersion" by "narratives like 'The Babysitter'" has "not rendered them sufficiently interesting for readers", which she in turn believes "indicates that the character-cognitive dimension and human experientiality [. . .], which are missing in the representation of alternate worlds in these texts, are indeed key features that contribute to qualitative narrativity" (p. 216). The intertwined alternarratives do interrupt narrative immersion in any one path, but each path is nonetheless lengthy enough to allow for, and in fact does involve, depiction of character. Extra work is required of the reader in trying, unaided by discourse deixis, to distinguish the different narrative paths and connect the different paragraphs in relation to those paths, and to recognise and accommodate the parallel but overlapping and ambiguous nature of the paths, resisting cohesive linear narrativisation. These increased cognitive demands arguably increase immersion rather than detract from it, however, and the absence of discourse deixis, which often 'breaks the fourth wall', conceivably helps to facilitate this immersion.

For Ryan, 'The Babysitter' is an example of what she calls the "do it yourself" type of "parallel universe" narratives (2006, p. 671, p. 668), a type which here features a "circus of possibilities" and "spiral of variations" (Kennedy, 1992, pp. 61–62). With this type, Ryan claims, the reader initially feels challenged to resolve the "multiple, mutually incompatible stories" into one coherent thread, but cannot as this proves to be "impossible". Instead, Ryan argues, the text fragments should be regarded as "a construction kit that inspires free play with its elements": the contrary stories "are offered to the readers as material for creating their own stories" (p. 671). Dannenberg offers a different strategy through which to rationalise alternarratives of this kind, suggesting that "in the radical postmodernist alternate story text, the reader can only impose coherence on the story fragments by identifying the causal-manipulative role of an extradiegetic author who must ultimately be seen as the source of the contradictory story fragments" (2008, p. 132). She states that "the chaotic alternative worlds of radical metafiction can only be recuperated into a coherent narrative by explaining them as fragments penned by the real-world author" (p. 216). Stories such as 'The Babysitter' do not, however, seem to be accommodated by either of these approaches. The plural, parallel narratives of the 'The Babysitter' can certainly be rationalised within the context of the broader metafictionality of the collection (and of postmodern metafiction as a whole), but this rationalisation does not allow the reader to 'impose coherence': the relationships between the paragraphs and alternarrative paths still resist both logic and clear distinction. Similarly, the story does not offer 'free play', in the sense that the paragraphs are, of course, inevitably sequentially ordered within the physical text and connected through shared characters, events, and settings, and some perceivable continuation of events and cause and effect.

The issue of linear presentation is brought to the fore in Ryan's proposal of a further, different subtype of forked path narratives, which she describes as the "meta-textual", whereby "the characters did not lead parallel lives; rather, these lives are different draftings of a novel in progress, different developments that the author is contemplating" (2006, p. 670). Fowles's two final endings are the example Ryan uses for this subtype, though she argues that "most postmodern narratives fall into this category" (p. 670). Furthermore, with regards to sequentiality in general, she argues that "the second of the two branches is the one that tends to survive in the reader's mind as the ending in which 'the author got it right'" (p. 670). Her argument here is apparently not based on this second ending offering the more fitting and coherent close for that particular narrative; rather, she cites Bordwell's (2002) observation that "in branching films, the branch shown last tends to be regarded as the true version" and states that "this observation holds for [. . .] meta-textualism" (p. 670).

The use of Fowles as a chief example throws an interesting light on this issue. The functioning of Fowles's two final endings, in relation to the postmodern and metafictional meanings of the novel, has been much debated. For the few critics who, at least at the time of publication, found his text to be predominantly a retrograde Victorian realist pastiche, the first ending would seem the more satisfactory, as implied by Allen (1970) and Ricks (1970), in that it offers something akin to traditional Victorian closure, and a particular realisation or 'awakening' in Charles: "And he comprehended: it had been in God's hands, in His forgiveness of their sins" (p. 438). The second ending, in which Charles does not achieve the same kind of realisation but rather faces a new future of chaos and uncertainty, is more quintessentially postmodern. This ending suggests to Acheson that Charles "may finally attain to existential authenticity" (1998, p. 47), while for Dannenberg, the first version "tames Sarah's behaviour", but the second "empowers" her (2008, p. 217). For these reasons and others, Hutcheon (1978, p. 92), Onega (1989, p. 90), and Rankin (1974, p. 205), among others, find the second of these two endings more fitting for the novel as a whole.

Despite the wealth of critical attention the two final endings have received, the actual form of this disnarration does not seem to have been discussed in detail. The textual mechanics of the disnarration here are worth exploring, not least because the first of these endings is not explicitly retrospectively denied (unlike the ending in Chapter 44, discussed in section 5.2). Retrospective denial would require the kind of metatextual or metacompositional discourse deixis which is in fact overtly missing in the bridging pages: the disnarrated section, and the act of disnarration, are not referred to explicitly here at all.

Where discourse deixis does occur in these two pages, it is in relation to metalepsis. As discussed in Chapter 4, section 4.4, the narrator, referred to in the third person, appears within the storyworld, outside the building in which Charles and Sarah are talking. The actual act of disnarration which this narrator performs is covert. At no point is the preceding section of the story referred to. All we are told in relation to this is that the narrator makes "a small adjustment to the time" on his pocket watch, for "it seems [. . .] that he was running a quarter of an hour fast" and departs (p. 441). The next page, page 442, then begins with a line of dialogue from the previous scene, on page 433: "No, it is as I say. You have not only planted the dagger in my breast, you have delighted in twisting it". We are seemingly thrust back into Charles's and Sarah's conversation—but this time the conversation takes a different turn, and leads towards a different ending.

As suggested, the main marker in the bridging pages that disnarration is occurring is the narrator winding back his watch (just as the Stationmaster winds back the clock in Coover's 'In a Train Station', implicitly to run its tortuous scene again, seemingly having done so many times). The reader is left to work out the significance of this watch-winding retrospectively, having been cued by the description of this act to think there may be a mere fault with the watch—it going fast—rather than to think that the narrative is being re-wound. The narration within the bridging pages, of course, continues to run chronologically despite this act. The reader is able to comprehend the watch-winding as disnarration only once she encounters the repeated words, recognises them from the previous scene (without the benefit, even, of reporting clauses to clarify who is speaking), and realises that a different version of that scene is now proceeding. The absence of discourse deixis in these bridging pages increases the cognitive load for the reader, and heightens the sense of surprise and confusion, and then the satisfaction of recognition and comprehension, evoked within the course of her processing the disnarration.

Partly because of this absence of discourse deixis in introducing the disnarration, the *nature* of the disnarration—that is, whether this is a case of alternarration or denarration—remains in question. The final two endings have been critically read as alternarration, in the sense that, for example, McHale feels "both are equally 'authoritative'", and their "coexistence [. . .] produces a kind of permanently unresolved hesitation between two alternatives" (2013, p. 177). Frangipane argues that "we are left with two equally plausible endings and no reason to believe one over the other" (2017, p. 574). For Dannenberg, likewise, they exist as "alternate narratives" (2008, p. 217). Arguably, however, Fowles's forked endings constitute a case of denarration rather than alternarration, in that the narrative is seemingly reversed, as the clock is wound back to a particular juncture, and the narrative follows a different path. Temporal progression and the narrative path are presented as inextricably linked, here, in a way that they are not linked to the linear, physical text (which is not literally reversed, or, as in Katz, crossed out, etc.) or to the sequential progression of the reader's conceptualisation of the text (which likewise cannot be 'undone').

This returns us to the issue of narrative ordering. As mentioned previously, according to Ryan and Bordwell, where there are two mutually exclusive paths, the one presented second is deemed the authoritative version. As well as discussing how well each ending 'fits' the preceding novel, and what kind of "retrospective patterning" each evokes (Scruggs, 1985, p. 98), Fowles's critics have also debated the consequences of the sequencing and the related, relative authority of the final ending (as suggested by Ryan). Significantly, the narrator explicitly raises this issue during his metaleptic instruction in Chapter 55 (see Chapter 4 in this book). Here, ruminating on the fate of Charles, he comes to the realisation that "The only way I can take no part in the fight is to show two versions of it", but continues "That leaves me with only one problem: I cannot give both versions at once, yet whichever is the second will seem, so strong is the tyranny of the last chapter, the final, the 'real' version" (p. 390). He then proceeds to flip a coin, and, with "So be it" (without telling us the outcome), continues with the story.

This "tyranny of the last chapter" is felt by Hutcheon, who argues that, given this, "the flipping of a coin or the turning back of a clock do not have any final effect on the reader", who will ultimately read the closing words as the authoritative version of events (1978, p. 92). Gutleben also feels that due to "the spatial constraints of the novel's linearity the second ending appears as the final—and therefore genuine?—close of the narrative" (2001, p. 117). Sequentiality does not eradicate the "effect on the reader" of disnarration, and Gutleben notably hesitates around notions of "genuine" narration (presumably vs. 'inauthentic', either on the part of the narrator or author), but this feeling that positioning a narrative segment last endows it with authority aligns with Ryan's opinion.

Several other critics, however, including Holmes (1995 [1981]), Palmer (1974, p. 74), Scruggs (1985), and Waugh (1984, pp. 42–43), feel the reader is left to choose an ending, as part of an authorial resignation of author-god-like control and resistance to closure, and to involve the reader in "a collective creation rather than a monologic and authoritative version of history" (Waugh, 1984, p. 43). Rankin feels that the ordering does not lead readers either way, but argues that any notion of choice is nonetheless an illusion, not because the penultimate ending is superseded by a second ending, but because the second ending offers the only "logical" ending through which Fowles "construct[s] a meaningful world" (1974, pp. 205–206). While the interpretation that the second ending is the 'right' ending does not necessarily entail a conceptualisation of the disnarration as denarration (rather than alternarration), this interpretation and conceptualisation may coincide. That said, the interpretation that one can 'choose' the ending does seem to entail a conceptualisation of the disnarration as alternarration (rather than denarration).

Where discourse deixis does finally contribute to communication of the disnarration is at the close of the second ending, within the three penultimate paragraphs on the very last page of the novel. For most critics, this does not offer direction regarding the issue of denarration vs. alternarration, however. The narrator draws attention to his metaleptic presence again, referring to himself in the first person this time (in contrast to the third-person reference to the narrator figure in the bridging passages). He states that Sarah "is too far away for me to tell" whether or not she is crying, the light reflecting on the windows she stands behind (p. 445). He then moves into metanarrative commentary, urging the reader not to think "that this is a less plausible ending to their story" than the first. The "this" of "this [. . . not] less plausible ending" is the first discourse deictic reference within these final chapters. It refers to the segment of the narration comprising the current ending (i.e. ongoing at this juncture in the text). Through implicit comparison, the phrase also refers to the prior ending, though notably not explicitly—the onus is put upon the reader to work this out. For some, the narrator's act of urging the reader "not [to] think that this is a less plausible ending" may support the impression of alternarration, and indeed may also be felt to support the impression that the reader has the freedom to choose an ending, though neither necessarily follow.

For Acheson (1998) and Rankin (1974), other discourse deictic elements contribute to a different interpretation. The narrator opens the next paragraph with a claim to have "returned", with the second ending, to his "original principle: that there is no intervening god" (p. 445), which recalls his proclamation in the bridging pages, cited earlier, that

"I am the kind of man who refuses to intervene" (p. 440). However, this precedes the description of a narrator figure, in the third person, doing exactly that, and hence this second ending occurs. On the one hand, he draws attention to his compositional principles, and yet on the other, in this same paragraph he talks of Sarah as if she is real (e.g. with her own principles). He also goes on to deictically refer to "the first epigraph [of] this chapter", and also to the second, which he metacompositionally points out that he chose and "set". Thus, while decrying divine will, discussing life as only "made [by] ourselves", and implying Sarah is independent of authorial invention, he at the same time foregrounds his own pseudo-authorial and compositional control.

Poignantly, in discussing the second epigraph, he refers to its author: Matthew Arnold. Arnold is also, though, the author of 'To Marguerite', the poem which Charles has committed to heart, cited in Chapter 58 (p. 409), the final line of which is repeated as the words of this final chapter. 'To Marguerite' is a poem which explicitly evokes an omnipotent God. Acheson (1998, p. 47) and Rankin (1974) find that this foregrounding of Arnold, via the explicit deictically anaphoric, metatextual, and metacompositional reference to epigraphs, and the embedded intertextual reference to the previously cited poem, undermines any equating of the final ending with a postmodern will to freedom. Rather, this suggests instead that the second ending may ultimately reinforce the idea of the author as the all-powerful god who decides on his characters' fates, and, for all the facade of the coin toss, decides which ending comes last and is more 'true'. This interpretation is based on a particular reading—of the inter- and intratextuality and of a form of anaphora, specifically—which presents a different kind of retrospective patterning and thematic 'fit'.

The chapter actually ends with the same strategy with which it begins, repeating words from previous pages. The repeated lines from Sarah and Charles's prior conversation and the quote from Arnold both function as endophoric, intratextual references, though the embedded quote from Arnold is additionally intertextual. Both instances are anaphora in its rhetorical sense—as repetition—but both also function like discourse deictic anaphoric reference in the sense of calling back (Halliday and Hasan, 1976). This repetition works slightly differently to, for example, proper anaphoric pronoun reference. While both this repetition and anaphoric reference in general evoke the prior reference and cue the reader to draw on that prior reference to comprehend the meaning of the second reference, repetition creates a new version of the reference, and this second version can be meaningful (if not offering the 'ideal' or 'full' meaning) independently of the first.

The second ending's first line, "No, it is as I say. You have not only planted the dagger in my breast, you have delighted in twisting it" (p. 442), of course, only carries the additional interpretative weight of its significance *as* repetition in this second iteration; its original iteration on page 433 is less loaded. There are other side-effects of the linear textual presentation upon the inferences available to the reader in the second ending. For instance, the first ending may be initially interpreted as ontologically stable (in that the earlier coin-flipping scene does not actually promise two endings will be provided: the resolution of the problem, in the face of the "tyranny of the last chapter", and the question decided by the coin toss, may have been to not present two endings). The second ending, though, once recognised as such, is inevitably read in contrast with the first, and in the conditional. It has the double function of being offered up as potentially ontologically 'real' within the storyworld and, by implication (even without explicit discourse deixis signalling disnarration), as challenging the ontological status of the first ending. Also, as it is the first ending in which Lalage is revealed to be Charles's daughter, his walking away from the baby in the second ending is, for the reader, imbued with tragic dramatic irony—an effect which relies entirely on the sequencing. The impact of the tragic ending is made all the more forceful having just read the 'happy ending'. For Evarts, "however we yearn for the fulfillment of the happy ending, we know that the tragic one is the real one; we acknowledge it, but the desire in the other direction remains. In this sense, the tragic emotion is full of tension and profound questioning" (1972, p. 66).

Ryan draws out the fact that for Ts'ui Pen (the author of the semi-mythical book *The Garden of Forking Paths* described in Borges's eponymous story, 2000 [1998]), forking paths present "a fundamentally temporal phenomenon" (2006, p. 653), but one that is comprehended, metaphorically, spatially: "narrative must limit itself to a subset of all possibilities and [. . .] its *branches* must be *presented sequentially rather than simultaneously*" (pp. 653–654, my italics). However, in a direct challenge to this temporal and linear governance of narrative which so troubles Ts'ui Pen, some of the authors explored in this book try to break through its strictures as his did and present alternative paths simultaneously.

The presentation of (at least partially) contrary narrative paths simultaneously (e.g. in parallel columns), rather than sequentially, offers some advantages. In cases of sequentially presented disnarration, the boundaries of and distinctions between the disnarrated sections are not always clear (as in Coover's 'The Babysitter', for example). This distinction is one of the affordances of the graphology of parallel presentation. Also, unlike sequential presentation, simultaneous presentation of alternarratives avoids leading the reader to process one version of events as 'real' and then to revise that understanding. It also seemingly side-steps 'the tyranny of the last chapter' or of the final segment in a sequence. However, in the circumstances of simultaneous presentation, the reader faces a different processing challenge, that of choosing her own sequence by which to process the different paths—as her processing must, inevitably, still be singular and linear, in that it is only possible to comprehend one section of text at a time. Whichever segment the reader chooses to read first, her interpretation of that which she processes second (assuming she does so) will inevitably be informed or influenced, however subconsciously, by the first.

The foregrounded, deviant graphology of parallel presentation also influences the reader's interpretative experience. As McHale writes, "the reader, forced to *improvise* an order of reading [. . .] remains constantly aware of the spatiality and materiality of the page and the book. This awareness tends to eclipse, if only sporadically, the projected fictional world" (1987, p. 192). Whereas sequential disnarration allows for immersion in the storyworld at least for the duration of each alternative narrative segment, the layout of parallel alternarration adds to the reader's processing the need for a choice. This choice may need to be made several times per page, and made again with any turn of the page which reveals continuation of columns, for should "the complete left-hand" section be read "first, then the right-hand one, or vice-versa? Or page by page? Or some combination of these reading patterns?" (McHale, 1987, p. 193). Even if this decision about the order in which to read only needs to be made once, the overtly unusual graphology penetrates perception, and so the reader's immersion in the storyworld is continually disrupted, and the 'surface' of the text continually foregrounded.

Brophy involves parallel narration in *In Transit* (2002 [1969]) even at the level of lexis. She sometimes provides two options, in smaller font, for particular letters or syllables within a word, or presents puns or translations, placing one version directly above the other within a line of type, inserted within braces. Each version of the word gives the containing sentence as a whole an alternative meaning, and each version always neatly fits, but differently expresses, the themes of the novel. This wordplay has occasionally been considered a little too frequent and the puns "feeble" (Brooke-Rose, 2002, p. vi), but it is strategically enmeshed in the novel's extreme lexico-(poly)semantic self-consciousness, and is part of Brophy's insistent disruption of linearity, singularity, certainty, and interpretative closure. It is also an expression of the narrator-protagonist's "linguistic insecurity" (Maack, 1995, p. 41) which is deeply intertwined with her/his crisis of gender identity (Stephenson, 1991).

Brophy's most substantial parallel alternarration in *In Transit* serves to present the novel's transgender oscillations. The novel starts in the first-person narrative mode, with a pseudo-authorial narrator, but moves, in section 7 of part 2, into third-person narration, gendering the protagonist (now distinct from the narrator) as male (see Chapter 4). Two pages later the protagonist's gender is revised as questionable once more, from whence the narrative continues to oscillate between gendering the protagonist as female and as male, as confusion about her/his sex abounds. On pages 161 to 165, the male version of the protagonist (Patrick O'Rooley) meets the female version of the protagonist (Patricia), introduced at this point as his assistant, in what is described as "a work-ing relationship that may also be erotic, and, if so, is probably incestu-ous" (p. 166). From pages 165 to 177, the narrative divides into two columns, which Maack refers to as the novel's "twin-track discourses" (1995, p. 43), each following the journey of one of the versions of the protagonist. The two narratives run counter to each other, however, as in both versions each protagonist arrives at the same agreed rendezvous at the agreed time, but finds the other not there—a situation not possible if they shared the same storyworld 'reality'. Here Brophy is exploring, she claims, "whether Aristotelian logic might disintegrate, whether we are mistaken in thinking that a thing cannot be both X and not-X" (Dock and Brophy, 1976, p. 166).

The close of the book presents antithetical parallel narration again, but here explicitly asks the reader to select one of the narrative paths— *either* X *or* not-X. As the book reaches its end, the narrative has latterly been following O'Rooley (in the third-person mode). The final chapter, though, opens in the first person, 'ego' having broken apart in the last words of the preceding chapter—literally: "there really was nothing else left: 'Eg—o', 'Eg—o' 'E . . .'" (p. 233). This first-person voice is that of the protagonist, which is clarified when she is addressed by another char-acter as "Pat" (p. 234). The protagonist and pseudo-authorial narrator have become one again (as discussed in Chapter 4), with metanarrative comments expressed in this first-person voice: "I warned you I wouldn't play god, disliking as I rigorously do that old fraud's authoritarian tem-perament. So You'll [sic] have to make the choice" (p. 234). And at this point the narrative bifurcates into two columns again, one following 'Patricia' and the other 'Patrick', Patricia killing herself by throwing her-self off a girder, plummeting to her death in the transit lounge below, and Patrick contemplating this, deciding not to, but falling over the edge of girder and dying anyway.

The pseudo-authorial narrator's comment here—"I warned you I wouldn't play god [. . .] So You'll have to make the choice"—echoes Fowles's narrator in his final chapter, in that the narrator makes an implicit reference to herself in her pseudo-authorial role and to her compositional principles, and recalls, too, prior parts of the narrative (not with specific, repeated lines, but here more generally, to the many deferrals made to the reader's interpretative decisions throughout the novel). However, here we also have explicit metadiscursive reference: the endings are to be chosen between, and the narrator refuses to determine that "choice". There is no ontological hierarchy between the two endings, unless one could suggest that the 'tyranny of the last chapter' transposes also onto a tyranny of the right-hand column, given the left-to-right reading pattern of English. Again, there is no explicit discourse deictic reference to the sections of narration to be chosen between, but the immediate bifurcation is cue enough. Unlike denarration, no one path is presented as less 'real' within the storyworld than another. Also unlike denarration, where the pseudo-authorial narrator asserts control over what is legitimised and what is not (as in Katz's crossing out, discussed in section 5.2), here the reader is explicitly given responsibility for the selective realisation of the story.

A more extensive instance of column-formed alternarration occurs in Katz's *The Exagggerations of Peter Prince*. The prose divides into two columns on page 28, only for one of those columns to then itself fork into two on page 53. All three columns, given equal width, then continue for a while, ceasing at different points until the text of the last-running column ends on page 59 (with two empty columns beside it), at which point the text returns to conventional pages of prose. The graphology of column-formed alternarration arguably removes the need for discourse deixis to signal what is occurring and/or how it should be processed, as is the case for this and most other instances in which columns appear in Katz, and also for some elsewhere in Brophy (e.g. pp. 165–177). A more 'directing' instance of ontologically 'equal' alternarration in Brophy is introduced as "two simultaneous trains of idea", one column beginning "(i)" and the column to its right beginning "(ii)" (pp. 93–101). The direction is, though, graphological rather than deictic: these columns are predominantly laid out in such a way as to direct one's reading between one and the other, zig-zagging attention from text running down the left column while the right column is blank, and then on to a passage on the right where there is none on the left.

These are all cases of typically 'independent' alternarratives. Where multiple channels of text occur in the style of text-and-translation (e.g. Brophy, 2002 [1969], pp. 50–59) or 'main'-text-and-commentary (e.g. Katz, 2017 [1968], pp. 241–255), the ontological and referential relationship between the columns is different. For example, a column of erotica in Brophy is accompanied by a column of commentary alongside (pp. 103–104), the commentary full of discourse deictic references to the erotic text (e.g. "The double quotes around *He* may be a mistake", p. 103). However, these are not instances of proper alternarration or even disnarration, but rather metanarration, as discussed in Chapter 3.

Simultaneous, parallel narration is perhaps the ultimate expression of postmodern metafictional alternarration. Prince ruminates on the possibility of a "transgressive, self-conscious, and self-critical history", stating it "would aspire to no ordering other than temporary, no synthesis other than provisional". He adds that "without renouncing narrative it would substitute openness for closure; problematize communicational circuits; question beginnings, middles, ends; favor rupture instead of continuity, simultaneity and not succession" (1992, p. 110). Disnarration in the form of simultaneous alternarration may offer the most ideal textual means of performing these ruptures of which metafiction is so fond. Its (general) lack of a reliance on discourse deixis is both a consequence of the clarity of distinct paths within the graphological form, and strategic means of refusing and resisting provision of authorial (or pseudo-authorial) direction: responsibility for the path taken, and the resultant interpretation, is left squarely with the reader.

5.4 Discourse Deixis in Negation and Hypothetical Focalisation

As mentioned in section 5.1, for Prince the disnarrated includes events which explicitly "*do not* happen" within the storyworld, but are mentioned in the negative or hypothetical mode (1988, p. 2, 1992, p. 30), and yet he excludes "the mere negative depiction of a situation or event" and gives examples of this such as "Warren did not close the door" and "Elizabeth remained silent" (1992, p. 33). According to Labov,

> Negative sentences draw upon a cognitive background considerably richer than the set of events which were observed. They provide a way of evaluating events by placing them against the background of the other events which might have happened, but did not.
> (1972, p. 381, cited in Herman, 2002, p. 58)

As highlighted by Nørgaard, negation can be considered more informative than positive alternatives in that it is used "to indicate something different, unusual or contrary to the expectations of the addressee" (Jordan, 1998, p. 714, cited in Nørgaard, 2007, p. 38). Clark and Clark assert that "denials are equivalent to suppositions plus their cancellations"; for example, "It wasn't John who hit Bill" equates to "[I believe that] you [. . .] believe it was John who hit Bill, but that [- the belief that John hit Bill -] is false" (1977, p. 108). Negation encodes the speaker's expectations regarding what *needs* to be explicitly countered, based on what she perceives to be the likely beliefs of the addressee (because of the speaker's previous utterance or otherwise). Negation therefore has a discourse-pragmatic function, in the sense that (among other things) it implies or projects the speaker's assumptions about the addressee's knowledge and/or views. In a relationship between narrator and reader, this can work in part to project, impose, or construct the nature of the reader. The extent to which this is either effective in imposing attitudes, or instead alienating and discomforting, will vary depending on the reader. In the context of metafiction, this discursive dynamic of negation can foreground the discourse and the narrator-reader relationship—the act and issues involved in the telling—rather than facilitating immersion in the story told.

Affirmative narration and negative/negating disnarration can be seen as occupying two poles of a scale of modalised narration. Hypothetical focalisation is situated more centrally on that scale, but with complex effects constituting forms of disnarration. Herman's detailed study of hypothetical focalisation addresses a significant gap in narratological understanding of the technique (1994, see also 2002, and see Genette, 1980, pp. 202–203 and Rimmon-Kenan, 1983, p. 79 for earlier discussions). Herman defines hypothetical focalisation as "the use of hypotheses, framed by the narrator or a character, about what might be or have been seen or perceived—if only there were someone who could have adopted the requisite perspective on the situations and events at issue" (1994, p. 231), as in the example 'If only I had come into the room a few moments earlier, I would have seen Richard in person'. In such circumstances, the focaliser and/or the act of focalisation are to some degree counterfactual within the world of the story. Broadly, hypothetical focalisation is "the formal marker of a peculiar epistemic modality" (1994, p. 231), which Frawley describes as an "epistemic version of deixis" (1992, p. 387; see also Herman, 2002, p. 326), from which both the likelihood of actualisation of the expressed proposition and the speaker's commitment to that likelihood are difficult to reconstruct (1994, p. 232).

Herman demonstrates the use of hypothetical focalisation across a variety of literary genres, constituted via a range of linguistic cues and with various effects. He identifies 'direct' (explicit) and 'indirect' (inexplicit, inferable) hypothetical focalisation in both 'stronger' and 'weaker' forms. In the stronger form of direct hypothetical focalisation, the focaliser and (so) the act of focalisation are both hypothetical, or 'virtual'— not actual (real) within the storyworld. As an example of strong and direct hypothetical focalisation, Herman offers an extract from William Faulkner's *As I Lay Dying*, in which the character Darl Bundren narrates

> Jewel and I come up from the field, following the path in single file. Although I am fifteen feet ahead of him, anyone watching us from the cottonhouse can see Jewel's frayed and broken straw hat a full head above my own.
>
> (1987, p. 3, cited in Herman, 2002, p. 312)

Here Darl's hypothesis about the prospect from the (storyworld-actual) cottonhouse is modalised by the adverb 'can', and filtered through the perspective of a possible (non-storyworld-actual) onlooker. In weaker direct hypothetical focalisation, the focaliser is a narrator or character actual within the fiction, and only the act of focalisation is hypothetical, as in the following instance from Russell Banks's *The Sweet Hereafter*: "The snow continued to fall, and from the perspective of Risa and the others back at the accident site, I [Ansel] must have disappeared into it, just walked straight out of their reality into my own" (1991, p. 72, cited in Herman, 2002, p. 315). Both narrators offer hypotheses about another's view of them, but whereas the lack of an identified focaliser in Darl's hypothetical focalisation emphasises the two men's isolation, the uncertainty and ambiguity Ansel can only suppose to have been felt by his onlookers regarding his movements supports the surreal drama of the accident and the idiosyncratic and unreliable nature of the experiences of it, as otherwise implied by the language, among those involved.

The indirect form employs the same variety of modal operators in expressing the hypothetical focalisation but does not explicitly designate any focaliser; the seer is left merely inferable from, for example, an explicit act of seeing—more explicit, and "less doubtful" (Herman, 2002, p. 322) in the case of stronger indirect hypothetical focalisation than in weaker indirect hypothetical focalisation. The example Herman offers from Nadine Gordimer's *A Guest of Honour* (1970) echoes the passage from Faulkner, but lacks a specified hypothetical focaliser: "Mweta was smaller and more animated than Bray, and seen from the distance of the house, as they got further away their progress would have been a sort of dance" (pp. 73–74; cited in Herman, 2002, p. 319). Further, in a more complex series of removes from the storyworld-actual, the act of focalisation may be embedded within a counterfactual conditional context, as in Herman's example from Salman Rushdie's *Haroun and the Sea of Stories*: "Miss Oneta was standing on her upstairs balcony, shaking like jelly; and if it hadn't been raining, Haroun might have noticed that she was crying" (1990, p. 21, cited in Herman, 2002, p. 321). Alternatively, it may be the temporal instance of the act of focalisation which is in question. As Herman states,

> In hypothetically focalized narrative descriptions, doubt attaches now to the status of narrative agents (are they there or not?), now to that of their thoughts and behaviour (do they do/think/perceive that or not?), now to that of their circumstances (is their world like that or not?). The stronger and weaker versions of direct and indirect [hypothetical focalisation] mark different distributions of doubt and doubtfulness with respect to the situations and events being focalized—different ways of ranking the components of the narrated according to their place on the continuum of epistemic modalities.
>
> (1994, p. 246)

Analysis of hypothetical focalisation, Herman argues, reveals the "array of epistemic modalities" (p. 234) operating within focalisation, and so can contribute to a more nuanced account of focalisation and the texture of narrative worlds.

Certain aspects of hypothetical focalisation merit further discussion here. While instances of each of the four main forms of hypothetical focalisation vary in effect depending on their constitutive cues and contexts, Herman offers a broad generalisation: hypothetical focalisation "marks more or less severe, more or less pervasive diegetic indecision over what counts as the actual versus what counts as merely possible worlds built up over the course of a narrative" (2002, p. 311). Hypothetical focalisation can be utilised to particular ends in realist texts, as in Herman's example of the following passage from Thackeray's *Vanity Fair*:

> [Becky Sharp's] dress, though if you were to see it now, any present lady of Vanity Fair would pronounce it to be the most foolish and preposterous attire ever worn, was as handsome in her eyes and those of the public, some five-and-twenty years since, as the most brilliant costume of the most famous beauty of the present season.
>
> (Thackeray, 1963 [1848], pp. 547–548, cited in Herman, 1994, p. 245)

In this context, the proposed hypothetical focalisation, with the reader designated, by the deictic "you", as focaliser, serves to support the claim to historical accuracy. Hypothetical focalisation often functions in Victorian realist texts to affirm the authenticity of the representation of a purportedly real, if not always fully knowable, storyworld.

Within a metafictional text, however, the relationship between what is 'actual' within the storyworld and the version(s) of events presented by narrative discourse "form part of the very subject-matter of the novel" (Herman, 1994, p. 239), and hypothetical focalisation can thus be exploited to foreground and explore that relationship. The indecision imbued in hypothetical focalisation gives rise to a kind of ontological uncertainty and foregrounds the storyworld-actual and its construction in relation to the possible. Herman argues that more careful exploration of hypothetical focalisation may therefore reveal it to be significant "among the repertoire of narrative devices typically exploited by texts that question or resist the norms and presuppositions of realistic genres" (p. 239). By way of demonstration, Herman notes how the high frequency of epistemic modal operators in Kafka's *Der prozeß* contributes to a metafictional effect:

> the *sjužet* works to de-differentiate, as it were, the modal structure of the *fabula*, eroding the grounds on which we might distinguish actual from merely possible situations and events in the world(s) constructed over the course of Kafka's novel. The format of Kafka's discourse encodes, at every turn, reference to the difficulty or even impossibility of knowing exactly what happened at the level of the story.
>
> (p. 232)

Herman also discusses an example from A. S. Byatt's *Possession* in which instances of hypothetical focalisation serve to reinforce the ontological uncertainty established by the novel. In Byatt's text, we are told "An observer might have speculated for some time as to whether they [Roland and Maud] were travelling together or separately, for their eyes rarely met, and when they did, they remained expressionless" (1990, p. 297, cited in Herman, 2002, p. 314). Here, the uncertainty constructed appeals to the relationship between the nineteenth and twentieth century frames of reference, which is a main concern of the text. Like Kafka's novel, then, "the format of Byatt's text therefore encodes that same proliferation of possible frames of reference—and *eo ipso* the multiplication of candidate models of a given situation or event—which is also its chief topic" (Herman, 2002, p. 314).

Summarising his thesis, Herman states

> In writers like Brontë and Thackeray [. . .] [hypothetical focalisation] does not compromise basic epistemological presuppositions and norms. Debatably, [. . .] it helps keep the virtual in the service of the actual, marking momentary derangements of a modal structure in which the known and the real vastly exceed the unknown and the irreal. Such derangements are edifying; readers pass through salutary doubts to achieve greater certainties. But in texts of a different sort or genre—and this in part contributes to their recognizably different generic status—[hypothetical focalisation] helps put the actual in the service of the virtual, formally marking doubts about whether human beings can determine, in every case, where they stand in a world they only thought they knew.
>
> (2002, p. 329)

Hypothetical focalisation can thus serve metafictional ends as an ideal resource for postmodern exploration of the relationship between discourse and reality.

Herman's discussion of hypothetical focalisation reveals some of the complicating ramifications of its use with regard to the ontological structures of fiction and the agency of focalisation—ramifications which warrant further analytical attention. A précis offered by Herman of one example of hypothetical focalisation can be applied to all cases: the storyworld is described "as if" the hypothesised focaliser(s), act(s) of focalisation, conditions, etc., "are in fact included in the ontology of the narrated, as if such things formed part of the inventory of the actual [. . .] troubl[ing] the border between actuality and virtuality" (1994, p. 243). However, hypothetical focalisation does not only trouble the border between the storyworld-actual and the storyworld-virtual, nor does it merely "mark [. . .] diegetic indecision" (2002, p. 311). Hypothetical focalisation directs readerly construction of that which is not actual within the storyworld but is nonetheless part of the narratorial delineation of that world, and which therefore contributes to the reader's comprehension and interpretation of the fiction. Though not actual within the storyworld, hypothetical focalisation is part of the narrative discourse and contributes to the development of the storyworld just as much as non-modalised description. Further, the hypothesisation does not necessarily simply indicate *indecision* regarding the actual vs. non-actual: rather hypothetical focalisation enables various expressions of suggestion, doubt, hedging, prediction, possibility, (im)probability, etc., for a variety of effects, not least the development of the representation of the narratorial speaker's relations to the narrated. Also, the particular agency and ownership of the hypothesised focalisation must not be overlooked. Whilst usually *about* the diegetic, hypothetical focalisation is often instigated from an extradiegetic narratorial position: though the different gradations of strong/weak and direct/indirect hypothetical focalisation allow for different degrees and forms of distancing of the focalisation from the speaker, hypothetical focalisation (like all focalisation) nonetheless originates from and is deictically anchored to the narrator, she/he albeit projecting to a viewpoint of another entity and/or in another circumstance. As Herman states, "at issue are narratives focalized such that we gain as it were illicit access to the materials of the story—materials not in fact focalized, or not focalizable even in principle, in the world(s) of the narrative" (1994, p. 236). Hypothetical focalisation can create interesting deviations from the established or conventional ontological strata of the fiction, and/or troubling transgressions across and foregrounding of the boundaries between the diegetic, the extradiegetic, and the extrafictional.

With this in mind, let us turn back to a section of Fowles's novel. Chapter 13 of *The French Lieutenant's Woman* has been much discussed, including in Chapter 3 of this book, but the ending of Chapter 12 is less explored. Yet, it is metafictionally significant, not least in the many ways in which it sets up the metanarrative flourish of the celebrated Chapter 13, but also in the metafictional implications of its hypothetical focalisation and negation. Chapter 12 ends with a passage in which Sarah is portrayed at her bedroom window, staring out to sea. The manner in which she is represented brings into question the ontological status of the storyworld, foregrounding both the reader's and narrator's role in its construction. Through a combination of negation, deictically directed hypothetical focalisation, and discourse deixis, narratorial responsibility for the conceptual realisation of Sarah at the windowsill is paradoxically both denied and asserted, and the historical reality of the storyworld is in turn affirmed and undermined. The following analysis draws out the deictic contribution to these metafictional effects and explores the thematic ramifications.

The passage begins as follows:

> Later that night Sarah might have been seen—though I cannot think by whom, unless a passing owl—standing at the open window of her unlit bedroom. The house was silent, and the town as well, for people went to bed by nine in those days before electricity and television. It was now one o'clock. Sarah was in her nightgown, with her

hair loose; and she was staring out to sea. A distant lantern winked faintly on the black waters out towards Portland Bill, where some ship sailed towards Bridport. Sarah had seen the tiny point of light; and not given it a second thought.

(pp. 95–96)

The narration is dominated by temporal contextualisation of the narrated moment, and by objectifying focalisation of Sarah. It begins by switching narrative attention from another character to Sarah, along a shared timeline—a strategy which often functions to affirm the realism of the storyworld. The initial temporal locative "Later that night" constructs a deictic temporal relation between this storyworld incident and the preceding storyworld chronology. However, it does so via an anaphoric co-textual reference—the demonstrative "that". This could function as a temporally and/or attitudinally distal deictic reference to the night in question. The temporal location of this event is then narrowed to after nine o'clock within the storyworld chronology. Similarly to the use of "that night", but more overtly so, the nature of this temporal contextualisation appeals to the extradiegetic position of the narrator: it implicitly draws a retrospective contrast between "those days before electricity and television" (the perceptual deictic "those" again conveying the distal relation) and the narrator's temporal context, thus located after the advent of electricity and television. This historical comparison, relating to developments in technology, fashion, and art, is a realist tactic used by the narrator frequently throughout the novel, from the very first page. The reference to the changes made to lifestyles by electricity and television implicitly suggests that the narrator (and the reader, who it is assumed will understand the reference) share an ontological and referential context (e.g. a schema of technological developments and lifestyles) and suggests that the storyworld exists on the same ontological plane as the narrator and reader. This passage therefore does some subtle work to affirm the historical reality of the events described, and to indicate or situate the relative temporal locations of the narrator, the reader, and Sarah along the same chronological line. Yet, there are two lines of temporal progression in play. The further specification "It was now one o'clock" combines a deictic past-tense relation, signalling narratorial retrospection, with the present tense deictic adverb "now". Without quashing the illusion of the continuous and shared chronology, stretching from Sarah in 1867 to the reader and narrator in their twentieth century contexts, this "now" could be interpreted as referring to the 'present' moment in the storyworld chronology, and/or the extrafictional loci of the narrator and reader with respect to their progress through the linear sequence of the narrative discourse (e.g. 'now, at this point in the story').

As in the opening pages of the novel, the objectification of Sarah here is mitigated through a hypothetical (epistemically modalised) act of focalisation: "Sarah *might* have been seen" (my italics). This seems to be Herman's weak indirect form of hypothetical focalisation, in that it does not explicitly designate any focaliser, and the act of focalisation is presented as hypothetical. In stating "though I cannot think by whom, unless a passing owl", the narrator disowns this act of witnessing, and (initially, at least) resists attributing it (to, for example, another character). However, despite counterfactual modalisation, the focalisation is relayed, and is actualised in the reader's imagination. The ensuing description focuses upon Sarah at her window against the darkness, and then pans out to the house and next to the town as a whole, allowing the narrator to make the point that all are asleep, foregrounding Sarah's solitude and the otherwise private context into which the observation intrudes. The focalisation is then immediately attenuated upon Sarah once again, with a more intimate portrayal of her "in her nightgown, with her hair loose". In asserting the ability to report historical events that had no contemporaneous witness, the narrator partly undermines the claim to historical authenticity implicit here, though explicit elsewhere (though this is not unconventional even within realist novels). More striking, though, is the effect the intimacy of the image in combination with the narrator's deferral of ownership of the focalising act. In engaging with and processing this description, and creating an imaginative realisation of the scene, the reader necessarily takes on the otherwise seemingly empty position of focaliser and voyeur.

The mention of the ship, along with the information that Sarah had seen it, encourages the reader to infer that these details may be significant to the meaning of the novel. The reader's quickest and easiest way of resolving this is by reference to Ernestina's first description of Sarah (in the opening chapters), when she is seen standing on the Cobb staring out to sea, and is said by the locals to be hopelessly and forlornly awaiting her lover's return. However, the narrator proceeds, eventually, to point out that Sarah "had not given it a second thought". This kind of garden path narration invites the reader to buy into the local gossip and to imagine Sarah to be a fallen, tragic figure, only to then counter that, and force the reader to 'undo' their interpretive inference and potentially feel a little ashamed over their impressionable and uncritical presumption, and/or annoyed over the subtle narratorial misdirection (foreshadowing Charles's similar construction of Sarah, her own misdirection, and his response to her later revelation). This is but one instance in the passage in which the narrator elicits and negates a part of the reader's imaginative construction of the narrative, foregrounding the nature of the reader's engagement with the text—from one view collaborative, from another complicit, in (at least co-)determining the realisation of the story.

The second paragraph of the passage more explicitly situates the reader in the role of the hypothetical focaliser: "If you had gone closer still, you would have seen that her face was wet with silent tears. She was not standing at her window as part of her mysterious vigil for Satan's sails; but as a preliminary to jumping from it" (p. 96). This appears to be an example of Herman's strong, direct hypothetical focalisation, in which the focaliser is explicitly mentioned, but both the act of focalisation and the focaliser are not 'actual' within the storyworld. It seemingly resembles Herman's example from Thackeray's *Vanity Fair*, in which the reader is co-opted as a direct and implicitly corroborating witness, albeit couched within a counterfactual circumstance by "if". The poignant difference though is that Thackeray's narrator suggests that "if you were to see [Becky's dress] now" you, like "any present lady" of the village, "would" think it odd, which affirms a shared reality and continuous chronology from then to now, but does not dislocate the reader from her current temporal context. Fowles's narrator, conversely, uses the pasttense conditional, "if you had" and "you would have". Like other aspects of these paragraphs, the first sentence here is echoic of the passages at the novel's beginning in positioning the reader at a hypothetical locus of focalisation within the storyworld. The evocation of a kind of conceptual metalepsis is here strengthened by the hypothetical motion encoded within the focalisation: the spatial deixis of the verbal phrase "gone closer" furthers the suggestion of the reader's presence within the storyworld. Notably, with the adverb "still" the narrator seems to perhaps be suggesting that the reader has from the outset been the hypothesised storyworld witness to Sarah's woeful pose, though this is ambiguous, creating an added "doubt attach[ing]" to what is actual and non-actual (or at least presented as such) within the storyworld (Herman, 1994, p. 246). In this light, the narrator's earlier deferral and denial of knowledge of the hypothetical focaliser (stating "though I cannot think by whom, unless a passing owl") retrospectively appears to be satiric and knowing—that is, flaunting his manipulative use of the apparatus of narration.

The reader is implied to be more than a mere witness, though: her role in constructively conceptualising Sarah is again foregrounded by the negation—that is, by the linguistic prompting of conceptualisation of states and events which are counterfactual and which do not occur in the 'reality' of the storyworld. The reader is told that "Sarah was not standing at her window as part of her mysterious vigil for Satan's sails", and thus induced to imagine this image in order to negate it, and does all of this before processing the subsequently asserted alternative and 'actual' version: that Sarah is stood at the window rather "as a preliminary to jumping from it". The narratorial denial of the reality of one state of affairs affirms the historical actuality of the other state of affairs. Of course, this is framed by the narrator putting the onus of the act of focalisation of Sarah, in such a personal moment of private trauma, upon the reader, drawing attention to the reader's role in the actualisation of the storyworld and its voyeuristic implications.

In the next paragraph, the negation intensifies, further encouraging the reader to construct mental representations that are not part of the storyworld:

> I will not make her teeter on the window-sill; or sway forward, and then collapse sobbing back on to the worn carpet of her room. We know she was alive a fortnight after this incident, and therefore she did not jump. Nor were hers the sobbing, hysterical sort of tears that presage violent action; but those produced by a profound conditional, rather than emotional, misery—slow-welling, unstoppable, creeping like blood through a bandage.
>
> (p. 96)

She does "not [. . .] teeter", nor "collapse", she "did not jump", "nor" were her tears "hysterical". Yet the negation here, unlike that of the earlier sentences, is overtly framed by an assertion of narratorial responsibility for that storyworld, drawing attention to its fictive status, the dynamic process of its realisation, and the narrator's role in directing that realisation. The first-person pronoun is used in an explicit metacompositional discourse deictic self-reference by the narrator as part of foregrounding his roles as speaker and creator of the discourse. As is briefly discussed in Chapter 3, section 3.3, the claim that he will not "make her teeter" refers to the act of construction through an assertion of pseudo-authorial control over the storyworld. The illusion of the historical reality of the storyworld is broken down, whilst the impression of the reality of the narrator is affirmed in contrast. At the same time, the again detailed and intimate but negated portrayal of Sarah re-emphasises the dynamic evolution of the storyworld and the reader's active conceptualisation of that which is narrated: just as the first sentence of this extract offers images of Sarah teetering, swaying, collapsing to the floor sobbing, and jumping from the window, the final sentence of the paragraph describes her tears with the present progressive, creating the same emphasis on developing processes, her tears "sobbing", her misery "slow-welling, unstoppable, creeping". Unlike the focalisation in the previous paragraph, hypothesised, deferred by the narrator and attributed to the reader, here the narrator takes ownership of the delimited storyworld. However, the narrator stresses that the actions described are what he "will not make her" do, and so culpability for the processual conceptual realisation of this portrayal, for mentally "making her" do these things, is arguably ultimately left with the reader.

The reference to the potential immediate future of the storyworld (in the modal auxiliary "will") draws further attention to the dynamic nature of the construction of this world and situates the narrator's locus in relation to the progression of that act. The next sentence, "We know she was alive a fortnight after this incident, and therefore she did not jump", identifies the reader's processual locus with the narrator's locus through the use of the first-person plural deictic reference "we" and through the implicit anaphoric co-textual reference in determining shared knowledge of the preceding textual discourse (in which Sarah's subsequent acts are narrated). In highlighting the disjunction between the sequence of narratorial representation of the storyworld and the storyworld's chronology, the narrator further foregrounds his discursive compositional control. Also, in referring to details already processed by the reader to point out to her that she should already know the outcome of this event, the narrator halts any suspense developed, draws attention to the ease of manipulation of the reader's participatory engagement with the discursive construction of the storyworld, and, at the same time, enhances the impression of the reader's culpability in imagining such things by emphasising their illogicality.

Paradoxically, however, the narrator's language simultaneously affirms, once again, the historical reality of the storyworld: it is pointed out that Sarah is "alive a fortnight after this incident", disguising her fictive status and suggesting a historically real and fixed sequence of events that cannot be controlled by any narratorial manipulation. The final few lines of the paragraph also offer a non-negated portrayal of Sarah and her emotional state, suggesting some narratorial, albeit limited, insight into Sarah. This in turn suggests she is a character to be known, rather than an entity being created. Despite this, the passage ends with two apparently rhetorical questions: "Who is Sarah? Out of what shadows does she come?" (p. 96). Historically real, or his own construction, the narrator claims not to know Sarah or her origins. She remains a mystery at the brink of tragedy. Ferrebe's answer to his questions here is simple: "like the noir (anti-)heroine she comes direct from the Romantic feminine—from an image of woman as potent, and potentially destructive, mystery" (2004, p. 216). The portrayal of Sarah, Ferrebe asserts, "chimes with Doane's verdict on the noir genre, 'the woman confounds the relations between the visible and the knowable at the same time that she is made into an object for the gaze' " (2004, p. 216, citing Doane, 1991, p. 103). More than this, however,

> her intangible mystery makes her a demonstration of existential contingency. [. . .] As a character, she is represented by a recognizable and well-defined icon (the Romantic heroine, the femme fatale) which is however located at the very margins of representation, merging with the chaos that lies beyond imagery and epistemology.
>
> (Ferrebe, 2004, p. 216, p. 218)

Throughout this passage the narrator directly incites the reader to attempt to understand Sarah, to hypothesise about her nature, whilst implying he is unable to do so and again deferring responsibility for that construction.

The representation of Sarah is ontologically unstable, imagery put forth and negated, constructive responsibility deferred, claimed, and deferred once more. This not only troubles the ontology of the storyworld, but also troubles the norms of pseudo-authorial narrative discourse, in denying aspects of authorial knowledge, agency, and control (as he goes on to do more radically in Chapter 13). Herman's description of the effects of hypothetical focalisation, "formally marking doubts about whether human beings can determine, in every case, where they stand in a world they only thought they knew" (2002, p. 329), gains more radical significance in the context of Fowles's metafiction.

The heteronomous construction of the text, and of Sarah within it, is brought into question in this passage through second-person hypothetical focalisation, in intimate detail, in combination with tactical temporal deixis and narratorial negation. The effect is an unnerving challenge to the conventional and comfortable perception of the reader's role as passive observer, detached and external to the storyworld, a world for which she need claim no responsibility. Here the reader is exposed as voyeuristic, even sadistic, in the eager conceptualisation of private, personal, and tragic affairs beyond that which is actual within the storyworld, the reader's dynamic conceptualisation being an inevitable consequence of— and dependent upon—her engagement with the text.

At the same time, the reader's attention is drawn to that textual and discursive context, and to the necessarily fictitious status of the storyworld, by the foregrounding of the focalising act through the descriptive detail of that which is negated. The reader's conceptual immersion is halted by the overt pseudo-authorial metanarration. Whilst on the one hand asserting historical authenticity, the narrator on the other hand claims constructive authorial control over the storyworld, and points to the dynamic discursive context by which it is brought into being. The claim appears to release the reader from responsibility, only for the pattern of narratorial negation to ensue and implicate her once more. Ultimately, responsibility for the text and for the gaze upon and construction of Sarah is left ambiguous, both the reader and narrator implicated, though the latter more disconcertingly denies, in the final two lines, full knowledge and responsibility. Through temporal and discourse deixis, particularly, the ontological status of the storyworld is problematised anew, with reciprocal ramifications for the ontology and epistemology of narrator and reader engaging in its construction.

This section has explored hypothetical narration and negation as forms of disnarration which create various kinds of (potentially conditional) counterfactuality. The detailed analysis of the close of Chapter 12 of *The French Lieutenant's Woman* illustrates the ways in which hypothetical narration and negation are both exploited here to further the novel's broader metafictional themes. This analysis highlights the significance of these kinds of disnarration to the reader's ongoing comprehension and construction of the storyworld, with respect to the relative ontological (in)stability of that which is described and to the discursive roles and responsibilities of the narrator and reader. The next section explores two final types of disnarration: narrative refusal and the antinarratable.

5.5 Discourse Deixis in Narrative Refusal and the Antinarratable

Hypothetical narration relies on forms of modality. In Johnson's *Christie Malry's Own Double-Entry* (2001 [1973]), the pseudo-authorial narrator co-opts modalisation within some chapter headings to propose hypotheses and create conditionality around not aspects of narration but instead aspects of the reading experience. For example, as mentioned in Chapter 4, section 4.3, the title of Chapter I, "The Industrious Pilgrim: an Exposition without which You might have felt Unhappy" (p. 9), imagines a narration counter to that which occurs—one not including this initial "exposition". This chapter title also involves a hypothesis about the reader's reaction to that alternative version: the pseudo-authorial narrator implicitly presupposes the reader's preferences or expectations regarding narrative structuring. Modality is exploited differently in the title of Chapter XXI, "In which Christie and I have it All Out; and which You may care to Miss Out" (p. 163). Johnson's titular suggestion that the reader skips this chapter should she want to is echoed in his other works (Ryf, 1977 p. 68). Here, rather than presenting the reader with a hypothetical situation in which the pseudo-authorial narrator has missed out a chapter, the narrator explicitly presents the reader with the option of choosing to miss out the chapter. Again, this implicitly presupposes the reader's preferences with regards to what she may or may not want or expect to be part of a narrative. Here, then, we have a hypothetical counterfactual in which the narrator missed a section out including a modalised proposition with regards to whether or not the reader would be happy without this exposition, and a hypothetical proposition in which the reader may choose to miss out a section.

These modalised hypotheses are enmeshed within complex metanarrative functions. Numbered chapter titles by their very nature have an implicit deictic pragmatic function. As discussed in Chapter 2, section 2.5, within the outline of discourse deixis, chapter titles which give chapter numbers effectively signify 'This immediately forthcoming chapter is the *n*th chapter in the sequence'. The referential value of a numbered chapter title is thereby grounded in its spatial and discursive locus in relation to progression through the linear text. The metatextual discourse deixis of numbered chapter titles inevitably foregrounds the physical textuality of the discourse and the reader's dynamic progression through it.

Beyond this implicit discourse deixis, further and more explicit metanarrative and metadiscursive elements are involved. Both chapter titles mention a constituent of narrative: the "exposition" in the first chapter, and, albeit more informally and more ambiguously, "hav[ing] it all out", in the second example, which could feasibly constitute the climax, falling action, or denouement of the story. These metanarrative references combine with metadiscursive person deixis. The person deictic references to the reader (as "you") and pseudo-authorial narrator (as "I"), in relation to their respective roles, foreground the discourse relationship. The second example also specifically announces, from this metanarrative context, that in the chapter in question the narrator, as speaking "I", and Christie, the storyworld protagonist, have a conversation. This is not the first indication of a metaleptic move in the book (it is foreshadowed on page 146, where the narrator mentions something that "Christie told me later"), but it is the most radical so far. Both chapter titles are thus rich in metafictional effects.

These chapter titles describe counterfactual possibilities with respect to the reader missing out on, or deliberately missing out, sections of the narrative. One final form of disnarration to be explored is the case of the reader being not hypothetically but rather being actually denied sections of the narrative. Warhol has extended Prince's ideas to attempt to accommodate this narrative phenomenon, building on his category of the 'unnarrated'—things which apparently happen within the world of the story but go unmentioned (Genette's 'ellipsis'). For Warhol, one subtype of the "unnarratable" is "the antinarratable", that which "shouldn't be told" (2005, p. 222). According to Warhol, the "limits of narratability vary according to nation, period, and audience as well as genre" and "shifts in the category of the unnarratable [. . .] both reflect and constitute their audiences' developing sense of such matters as politics, ethics, and values" (p. 221). A narrator can also express a kind of "narrative refusal", as in "when a narrator says he or she will not tell something" (Warhol-Down, 2010, p. 45). We see both kinds of 'the antinarratable' exploited for metafictional ends in Katz's *The Exagggerations of Peter Prince*.

In a discussion of Philip Farrel and Linda Lawrence, the narrator explains "most of you understand by now that they aren't per se characters in this book, but hired hands, like mercenary muses [. . .] whose real names I can't divulge, but who have agreed to work at a low salary" and who "show up whenever they're needed" (pp. 140–141, see also 4.2). The statement "whose real names I can't divulge" is the first (and most minor instance) of narrative refusal on the part of the pseudo-authorial narrator. It contributes to the creation of a sense of mystery around the two characters in question, who are here seemingly and purportedly clarified as being not characters, and as existing at some unknown and heretofore oblique in-between narratological level (in between the fiction of the storyworld and the level of narration), or able to cross between narrative levels. These characters are present in the much more significant instance of narrative refusal on pages 252 to 255. They are portrayed, in an italicised narrow column of narration on the left-hand side of the page, as watching and commenting on a show on television, which is relayed on the rest of the page, this show being "The Peter Prince Show". The narration has shifted to presenting this show, without much explanation, from an otherwise more conventional portrayal of Peter Prince's travels in Cairo. In this scene of the show, Peter, as the show's protagonist, reveals bugging microphones in his hotel room, puts them inside of the cage of a loudly chirping bird, and begins to have sex with his companion. At this point the narrative text becomes merely the repeated word "beep" for over a page, as the sex, it seems, is censored. Despite this, Linda Lawrence and Philip Farrel can themselves seemingly at least witness the scene on the TV, so within their level of the story it is only the sound which is 'refused'. Alongside the text of beeps, Philip Farrel says to Linda Lawrence "But I can't understand a word of that. They're not audible", to which she responds "Look at them. Read the lips. You know what it's about. We weren't born yesterday. You know what it is" (p. 254). The deictic "that", "they", "them", and "it" all refer to the scene they are watching, neatly foregrounding the relationship (one of metanarrative commentary) between the two parts of the text while the deictic pronouns add to the occlusion in serving in the place of more specific and detailed noun phrases—Linda Lawrence is here refusing to spell 'it' out for him (and the reader). Philip Farrel then switches off the television, seemingly in frustration and disgust, fed up with "the damned [TV] set" and the "Peter Prince show", saying "The public pays the price and gets this" (p. 254). The next page presents only the narrow, left-hand column relaying their conversation.

Philip Farrel's act of switching off the television is not a refusal of narrating on his part, but rather a refusal to watch the scene (or allow it to be watched). In the context of what we've been told earlier, though, about Philip Farrel and Linda Lawrence merely serving as vehicles to do the narrator's bidding (pp. 140–141), the narrative refusal is more directly attributable to the narrator, and therefore can be read as a refusal of narration. Fundamentally, of course, such decisions are attributable to the author Katz himself, though this actual authorial role is deliberately disguised and demonstratively displaced by the multiple levels and figures of purportedly pseudo-authorial narratorial (and other) agency.

Peter Prince's act of obscuring the audibility of the sex with the bird's chirping, and the parallel act of obscuring within the narrative description, via the beeping, is arguably narrative censoring/redacting rather than narrative refusal—that is, rather than simply missing out this sex scene, a page of textual space is taken up, and it is as if the beeps overlay or replace descriptive narration (as would black textual censor bars in 'sanitised' redaction). Nonetheless, the effect is the same: the reader is refused the scene, on the grounds of privacy (on Peter Prince's part) or propriety (on the narrator or author's part, or on the part of the TV production company—the agency of the beeping being less discernible). By contrast, the result of Philip switching off the set is a predominantly blank page—blank but for the poignantly ongoing column of conversation between Linda and Philip—which serves to foreground this refusal: even the beeping, now, is denied to the reader. Altogether, the combination of the metanarrative commentary from the narrator's two "hired hands"; the bugging, censorship, and obscure agency (behind the bugging, the censorship, and the TV production company); and the spectacle of televised casual sex amounts to a playful postmodern expression of the novel's overtly Cold War–era concerns.

Directly following this episode, Peter Prince is arrested and interrogated. Some way into the questioning, the interrogator pulls out "an old manuscript, typed, erased, scribbled over". The narrator then, seemingly shocked, says "I recognized it myself as a scene I had written to use earlier in this novel, but had discarded it" (p. 267). This metafictional comment disrupts the immersive narration. The first-person deictic references (three in close proximity) foreground aspects of the role and discourse position of the narrator; specifically, his temporal locus in relation to the process of his act of writing. This reaffirms the illusion of his pseudo-authorial role and his locus in relation to progressing through the scenes of the novel, witnessing the storyworld—seemingly akin to the reader—and comprehending what's going on.

The narrator purportedly himself regarded this "scene" as 'antinarratable', apparently because it would do something he wanted to avoid, namely "emphasize [a] particular aspect of Peter Prince's boyhood" (p. 267). However, pages 269 to 282 then go on to relay this scene: the interrogator forces Peter Prince to read it, apparently overriding this judgement of antinarratability (note Peter Prince's metanarrative responses to the scene are discussed in Chapter 3, section 3.4). This is different to the parts of Katz's novel described in section 5.2, in which passages are introduced as sections the narrator has decided against, but then goes on to present—not least as the decisions seem to remain his own—and the sections are left literally crossed out and so 'disnarrated' in some way. Here, the section in question is presented without being crossed out, but within a complex contextual frame—as 'antinarratable' from the pseudo-authorial narrator's perspective, but not from the perspective of the interrogator, who seemingly has more editorial power. Despite the metacompositional foregrounding of the pseudo-authorial narrator's prior scene-writing, here he seems to have an ontological relation to the story similar to that of the reader (except, of course, for the retrospective nature of the report of the recognition: to be in line with the reader's ontology and processing experience, the interruption would be in the present tense).

In a further twist, the text relaying the childhood scene is partially occluded by a repeated "z"—a representation of the interrogation room's buzzing fans, which are themselves suggestive of the oppressive heat and windowless containment of the interrogation room. The "z" is mostly marginal but sometimes intrudes upon, overlaps, and obscures the main text. Thus, minor aspects of the childhood scene are effectively residually 'refused'. The reader's access to this scene is therefore subject to the control of multiple agencies—the narrator's, the interrogator's, and even that of the mechanical fans of the interrogation room.

One final minor example from Katz is akin to the second chapter title in Johnson described previously: a form of modalised, optional *readerly* refusal. After a short crude description of a ship deck covered in various kinds of excrement, the narrator states (within parentheses) "The reader may delete this detail if it's distasteful" (p. 290). Unlike the case of Johnson's chapter title, which forewarns the reader that she "may care to Miss Out" the forthcoming section (p. 164), the detail has already been narrated and read by the point at which the narrator presents the option of "delet[ion]". Though various kinds of physical disnarrating deletion have been exploited for metafictional effects in this novel—including crossed-out text, beeps, and blank pages—the text in question here remains intact (assuming the reader chooses not to physically strike it out). Either way, as discussed with regards to the conceptual actualities of negation, that which has been processed and conceptualised cannot be 'deleted' from memory. The resultant effect can only be that the section in question may be downgraded, in the reader's processing of the narration, from any initially inferred status as important to the ongoing story, from the perspective of the narrator, to apparently unimportant to the story. Additionally, as in this case, the disnarrating gesture can have the effect of serving the ongoing characterisation of the narrator and his narratorial style, and his levels of consideration for and presuppositions about the preferences of the reader. Here the preferences in question are not on grounds of narrative coherence, for example, but on grounds of 'taste'.

Disnarrating gestures formulated in this way also therefore contribute to the ongoing development of the narrator–reader discourse relationship. Notably the reader is here addressed more formally and anonymously than 'you', as "the reader", adding to the implications of polite consideration. Ironically, the key factor in the narrator–reader relationship is that of trust, specifically with regards to the ease of gauging the significance of segments of the narrative to the meaning of the story, and indeed also with regards to the meaningfulness of the story (i.e. that there is decipherable meaning worth the investment of reading). While Johnson's chapter titles suggest a pseudo-authorial narrator who is careful in this regard, Katz's disnarration is more chaotically disorienting and distancing, by turns playful and sinister, sometimes more 'actual' and sometimes more superficial (as in this example), and often leaving the reader at a loss with respect to the ever-shifting ontological statuses and relationships of segments and characters of the story.

This section has explored examples of Warhol's narrative refusals and the antinarratable as types of Prince's disnarration, including instances from Katz and Johnson which sit on the edges of or present a motivated twist on those types. The discourse deixis involved, including reader address, metanarrative references to segments of narration, and pseudo-narratorial metacompositional self-reference, all work to both foreground and flounder the reader's positioning in relation to her ongoing conceptualisation of, and ontological relationships to, the fictional world and its participants.

5.6 Conclusion

Discourse deixis is fundamental to the workings of disnarration. This chapter has described the four kinds of disnarration particularly prevalent in metafiction: denarration, alternarration, and the paired negation and hypothetical focalisation, and narrative refusal and the antinarratable. Through illustrative analyses of examples of each type, drawn from Barth, Brophy, Coover, Fowles, Katz, and Johnson, this chapter has shown the complex and multifarious ways in which discourse deixis contributes to their metafictional effects.

References

Acheson, J. (1998). *John Fowles*. Houndmills, Basingstoke: Palgrave Macmillan.

Alfonso, R. M. (1995). "Fictional self-consciousness in Robert Coover's *Pricksongs and Descants*". *Revista Alicantina de Estudios Ingleses* 8. 123–137.

Allen, W. (1970). "The achievement of John Fowles". *Encounter* 35.2. 64–67.

Banks, R. (1991). *The Sweet Hereafter*. New York: HarperCollins.

Barth, J. (1988) [1968]. *Lost in the Funhouse: Fiction for Print, Tape, Live Voice*. New York: Doubleday.

Bennett, A. (1963) [1908]. *The Old Wives' Tale*. New York: New American Library.

Bordwell, D. (2002). "Intensified continuity visual style in contemporary American film". *Film Quarterly* 55.3. 16–28.

Borges, J. L. (2000) [1998]. "The garden of forking paths". In *Fictions*. Trans. A. Hurley. London: Penguin Books. 75–86.

Bremond, C. (1980). "The logic of narrative possibilities". *New Literary History* 11.3. 387–411.

Brooke-Rose, C. (2002). "Introduction". In *In Transit: An Heroi-Cyclic Novel*. Ed. B. Brophy. Chicago, IL: Dalkey Archive Press. i–vii.

Brophy, B. (2002) [1969]. *In Transit: An Heroi-Cyclic Novel*. Chicago, IL: Dalkey Archive Press.

Clark, H. H. and Clark, E. V. (1977). *Psychology and Language: An Introduction to Psycholinguistics*. New York: Harcourt Brace Jovanovich.

Cohn, D. (1999). *The Distinction of Fiction*. Baltimore, MD: Johns Hopkins University Press.

Coover, R. (2011) [1969]. *Pricksongs and Descants*. New York: New American Library.

Dannenberg, H. P. (2008). *Coincidence and Counterfactuality: Plotting Time and Space in Narrative Fiction*. Lincoln, NE: University of Nebraska Press.

Doane, M. A. (1991). *Femmes Fatales: Feminism, Film Studies and Psychoanalysis*. London: Routledge.

Dock, L. and Brophy, B. (1976). "An interview with Brigid Brophy". *Contemporary Literature* 17.2. 151–170.

Doležel, L. (1988). "Mimesis and possible worlds". *Poetics Today* 9.3. 475–496.

Evarts, P. Jr. (1972). "Fowles' *The French Lieutenant's Woman* as tragedy". *Critique: Studies in Contemporary Fiction* 13.3. 57–69.

Evenson, B. K. (2003). *Understanding Robert Coover*. Columbia, SC: University of South Carolina Press.

Ferrebe, A. (2004). "The gaze of the magus: Sexual/scopic politics in the novels of John Fowles". *JNT: Journal of Narrative Theory* 34.2. 207–225.

Foucault, M. (1977). *The Archaeology of Knowledge*. London: Tavistock.

Frangipane, N. (2017). "Two sides to the story: Multiple versions and post-postmodernist epistemology". *Poetics Today* 38.2. 569–587.

Frawley, W. (1992). *Linguistic Semantics*. London: Routledge.

Genette, G. (1980). *Narrative Discourse*. Trans. J. E. Lewin. Ithaca, NY: Cornell University Press.

Genette, G. (1997). *Paratexts: Thresholds of Interpretation*. Trans. J. E. Lewin. Cambridge: Cambridge University Press.

Goffman, E. (1974). *Frame Analysis: An Essay on the Organization of Experience*. Cambridge, MA: Harvard University Press.

Gordimer, N. (1970). *A Guest of Honour*. London: Penguin Books.

Gutleben, C. (2001). *Nostalgic Postmodernism: The Victorian Tradition and the Contemporary British Novel*. Amsterdam: Rodopi.

Halliday, M. A. K. and Hasan, R. (1976). *Cohesion in English*. London: Routledge.

Hamburger, K. (1973). *The Logic of Literature*. Bloomington, IN: Indiana University Press.

Herman, D. (1994). "Hypothetical focalization". *Narrative* 2. 230–253.

Herman, D. (2002). *Story Logic: Problems and Possibilities of Narrative*. Lincoln, NE: University of Nebraska Press.

Hidalgo Downing, L. (2000). *Negation, Text Worlds, and Discourse: The Pragmatics of Fiction*. Stamford, CT: Ablex Publishing Corporation.

Holmes, F. M. (1995) [1981]. "The novel, illusion and reality: The paradox of omniscience in *The French Lieutenant's Woman*". In *Metafiction*. Ed. M. Currie. London: Longman. 206–220.

Hutcheon, L. (1978). "The 'real world(s)' of fiction: *The French Lieutenant's Woman*". *English Studies in Canada* 4.1. 81–94.

Hutcheon, L. (1980). *Narcissistic Narrative: A Metafictional Paradox*. Waterloo, ON: Wilfred Laurier University Press.

Israel, M. (2004). "The pragmatics of polarity". In *The Handbook of Pragmatics*. Eds. L. R. Horn and G. Ward. Oxford: Blackwell. 701–723.

Johnson, B. S. (2001) [1973]. *Christie Malry's Own Double-Entry*. London: Picador.

Katz, S. (2017) [1968]. *The Exagggerations of Peter Prince*. Singapore: Verbivo-arcious Press.

Kaup, B., Lüdtke, J. and Zwaan, R. A. (2006). "Processing negated sentences with contradictory predicates: Is a door that is not open mentally closed?" *Journal of Pragmatics* 38. 1033–1050.

Kaup, B., Yaxley, R. H., Madden, C. J., Zwaan, R. A. and Lüdtke, J. (2007). "Experiential simulations of negated text information". *The Quarterly Journal of Experimental Psychology* 60.7. 976–990.

Kennedy, T. E. (1992). *Robert Coover: A Study of the Short Fiction*. New York: Twayne Publishers.

Labov, W. (1972). *Language in the Inner City: Studies in Black English Vernacular*. Philadelphia: University of Pennsylvania Press.

Lakoff, G. (2004). *Don't Think of an Elephant: Know Your Values and Frame the Debate*. White River Junction, VT: Chelsea Green Publishing.

Maack, A. (1995). "Concordia discors: Brigid Brophy's *In Transit*". *Review of Contemporary Fiction* 3. 40–45.

McHale, B. (1987). *Postmodernist Fiction*. London: Routledge.

McHale, B. (2013). "Fowles and postmodernism: *The French Lieutenant's Woman, Mantissa* and *A Maggot*". In *John Fowles*. Ed. J. Acheson. London: Palgrave Macmillan. 171–185.

Nørgaard, N. (2007). "Disordered collarettes and uncovered tables: Negative polarity as a stylistic device in Joyce's 'Two gallants'". *Journal of Literary Semantics* 36. 35–52.

Onega, S. (1989). *Form and Meaning in the Novels of John Fowles*. Ann Arbor and London: U.M.I. Research Press.

Palmer, W. J. (1974). *The Fiction of John Fowles: Tradition, Art, and the Loneliness of Selfhood*. Columbia, MO: University of Missouri Press.

Prince, G. (1988). "The disnarrated". *Style* 22.1. 1–8.

Prince, G. (1992). *Narrative as Theme: Studies in French Fiction*. Lincoln, NE: University of Nebraska Press.

Pynchon, T. (1973). *Gravity's Rainbow*. New York: Viking.

Rankin, E. D. (1974). "Cryptic coloration in *The French Lieutenant's Woman*". *The Journal of Narrative Technique* 3. 193–207.

Richardson, B. (2001). "Denarration in fiction". *Narrative* 9.2. 168–175.

Ricks, C. (1970). "The unignorable real". *New York Review of Books* 14.3 (12 February). 22–24.

Rimmon-Kenan, S. (1983). *Narrative Fiction: Contemporary Poetics*. London: Routledge.

Rushdie, S. (1990). *Haroun and the Sea of Stories*. London: Granta Press.

Ryan, M-L. (1986). "Embedded narratives and tellability". *Style* 20. 319–340.

Ryan, M-L. (1991). *Possible Worlds, Artificial Intelligence, and Narrative Theory*. Bloomington, IN: Indiana University Press.

Ryan, M-L. (2006). "From parallel universes to possible worlds: Ontological pluralism in physics, narratology and narrative". *Poetics Today* 27.4. 633–674.

Ryf, R. S. (1977). "B. S. Johnson and the frontiers of fiction". *Critique* 19.1. 58–74.

Scruggs, C. (1985). "The two endings of *The French Lieutenant's Woman*". *Modern Fiction Studies* 31.1. 95–113.

Shklovsky, V. (1965) [1917]. "Art as technique". In *Russian Formalist Criticism*. Eds. L. T. Lemon and M. J. Reis. Lincoln, NE: University of Nebraska Press. 3–24.

Stephenson, S. (1991). "Language and gender in transit: Feminist extensions of Bakhtin". In *Feminism, Bakhtin, and the Dialogic*. Eds. D. M Bauer and S. J. McKinstry. Albany: State University of New York Press. 181–198.

Thackeray, W. M. (1963) [1848]. *Vanity Fair*. Boston, MA: Houghton Mifflin.

Verdonk, P. (2002). *Stylistics*. Oxford: Oxford University Press.

Verdonk, P. (2013). *The Stylistics of Poetry: Context, Cognition, Discourse, History*. London: Bloomsbury.

Warhol, R. (2005). "Neonarrative, or, How to render the unnarratable in realist fiction and contemporary film". In *A Companion to Narrative Theory*. Eds. J. Phelan and P. J. Rabinowitz. Oxford: Blackwell. 220–231.

Warhol-Down, R. (2010). "'What might have been is not what is': Dickens's narrative refusals". *Dickens Studies Annual: Essays on Victorian Fiction* 41. 45–59.

Waugh, P. (1984). *Metafiction: The Theory and Practice of Self-Conscious Fiction*. London: Routledge.

Werth, P. (1999). *Text Worlds: Representing Conceptual Space in Discourse*. Harlow, Essex: Longman.

6 Conclusion

This book has argued that discourse deixis makes a significant contribution to the workings of metafictional strategies—a contribution that has previously been critically under-acknowledged as well as theoretically under-explored and under-explained. It has extended theoretical insight into discourse deixis in literature and has provided detailed and intricate analyses of the function of discourse deixis in examples of metanarration, metalepsis, and disnarration in six metafictional texts. These analyses have added to critical understanding of these texts and have illustrated the role of discourse deixis in the creation of their metafictional interpretative effects.

Chapter 1 provided an overview of metafiction and the three metafictional techniques studied in this book. It reviewed the main contributions from prior literary theoretical and narratological work on metafictionality which provide a platform for the book's investigations. In particular, it drew together work on metafiction and work on unnatural narratology, illustrating the crossovers between the two, and the relevance of the latter to studies of metafiction as a genre. The chapter also briefly introduced discourse deixis and outlined its significance to expressions of metafictionality. The chapter closed with a proposal of the existence of a window of 'high metafiction', and an outline of the six works examined in this volume as examples of high metafiction.

Chapter 2 presented a model of discourse deixis in literature. It addressed some complexities within previous accounts, including the debated deictic value of definite reference and anaphora. It also outlined the particular discourse conditions of written literature and the impact of these conditions upon deictic operations. For example, the split discourse context and the nature of deictic projection were explored. This chapter identified and explained uses of discourse deixis which are specific to written literature, such as to refer to discourse participants in the contexts of their roles (e.g. as pseudo-authorial narrator, reader, etc.); to demarcate the boundaries of the ontological levels within the fiction (i.e. the storyworld and the extradiegesis) and signal the position of characters and narrators relative to these levels; to refer to a narrator's and/

or reader's textual deictic centre relative to the material text-continuum, and so on. The chapter closed by illustrating some of the ways in which metafiction thematises these and other discourse deictic relationships.

Having established the theoretical foundation of the investigation of metafictional techniques, Chapter 3 then examined the contribution of discourse deixis to metanarration. It offered a distilled typology of metanarration, drawing on and merging parts of the work of Fludernik (2003a), Genette (1980), Nünning (2005), Prince (1995 [1982]), and Wolf (2009), and prioritising the focus of metanarrative comments over other features (such as the narrative level from which the comment is being made, for example). As with each of the three central chapters of the book, examples of each type of the metafictional technique in question were analysed through a range of extracts from the selected works by Barth, Brophy, Coover, Fowles, Johnson, and Katz, here drawing out the contribution made by discourse deixis to the effects of metatextual, metacompositional, metadiegetic, metanarrative, and metadiscursive metanarration. These analyses also revealed discourse deixis to be significant in bridging implicit and explicit metanarration and endowing the former with intracompositional metanarrative implications.

Chapter 4 reviewed narratological approaches to the ontological structure of fiction and developed a model of metalepsis. This model builds on the work of a range of narratologists, including significant voices from unnatural narratology. The model presented in this chapter proposed the analytical value of distinguishing three types of metalepsis: metaleptic awareness, metaleptic communication, and metaleptic moves. This chapter examined discourse deixis in Barth, Brophy, Coover, Fowles, Johnson, and Katz via this categorisation to extend understanding of the discourse deictic mechanics of metalepsis in these fictions. This chapter also explored the potential analytical value and theoretical consistency of considering narration as metaleptic communication; of considering reading as a conceptual metaleptic move; and of considering pseudo-authorial narrators, and potentially second-person protagonists, as metaleptic counterparts of the author and reader.

Finally, Chapter 5 brought together previously studied types of disnarration to explore how far and in what ways discourse deixis contributed to their workings. Again, examples from Barth, Brophy, Coover, Fowles, Johnson, and Katz were investigated, analysing the range of discourse deictic operations which contribute to denarration, alternarration, negation and hypothetical focalisation, and narrative refusal and the antinarratable. Just as discourse deixis was shown to function to communicate the positioning of literary participants relative to the ontological levels of fiction in metalepsis in Chapter 4, this chapter demonstrated the role of discourse deixis in distinguishing different paths and segments of narrative in the acts of countering one path or segment with another, shifting between them or erasing them. This chapter also illustrated the ways in which some kinds of alternarration, unlike the other types of disnarration, may gain some of their meaning potential precisely through a crucial absence of discourse deixis.

These chapters have offered detailed investigations of a wide range of extracts across Barth's *Lost in the Funhouse* (1988 [1968]), Brophy's *In Transit: A Heroi-Cyclic Novel* (2002 [1969]), Coover's *Pricksongs and Descants* (2011 [1969], Fowles's *The French Lieutenant's Woman* (1996 [1969]), Johnson's *Christie Malry's Own Double-Entry* (2001 [1973]), and Katz's *The Exagggerations of Peter Prince* (2017 [1968]). These investigations have drawn on previous criticism in an attempt to see if discourse deixis can partially account for dominant interpretative impressions. They have also presented new analytical insights into the novels through this linguistic lens. For example, in exploring metanarration, Chapter 3 proposed that the perceived enigmatic quality of Coover's 'In a Train Station' could potentially be precisely because the text's metanarration remains implicit and without discourse deictic grounding in the text. In Chapter 4, the cyclic quality of Brophy's *In Transit* was shown to apply not only to the trajectory of the narrative plot but also to the ontological structure of the text. In addition, the use of the concepts of counterparthood and translevel identity in Fowles, examined chiefly via the pattern of discourse deictic pronoun references used by the speaking narrator in relation to his counterpart other or translevel self, allowed for a new account of the narrator's metaleptic moves in this novel and of the differences in their metafictional effects. Likewise, in Chapter 5, an extended analysis of the discourse deixis of the denarrated endings in Fowles's novel offers a new perspective on their different implications for interpretations of the novel's central themes of the control of the author-god, self-determinism and free will.

This book has also drawn new connections between the six fictional works under discussion. The density and range of the metafictional techniques these works have been shown to employ for their various interpretative ends, and the array of variably philosophical, ideological, and socio-political themes that their metafictionality serves, has supported the initial argument that these texts can be considered examples of 'high metafiction'. The discussions of these works have also been intended to draw further critical attention to Brophy's *In Transit* and Katz's *The Exagggerations of Peter Prince* and to signal the place they are owed alongside the likes of Fowles and Barth with regard to their literary significance.

When considering these texts together, several interesting areas of potential future research come to the fore which are beyond the scope of discourse deictic investigation. Each of these texts has a complex relationship with teleology. Most experiment in one way or another with trajectories towards endings (Groes, 2016). Both Barth and Brophy play with cycles as a means of exploring what might be considered a crisis of linearity and progression (Gillespie, 1975; Fogel and Slethaug, 1990), Brophy via a particularly feminist challenge to androcentric narratives (Andermahr, 2018). Relatedly, these texts all thematise the engagement and drives of the reader. In this light, the degree of voyeurism and/or brutal violence that percolates throughout these texts could be considered part of that thematisation, though it could also potentially be a reflection of cotemporaneous social or political concerns (cf. Darlington, 2014, on Johnson in this regard, for example). In addition to interrogating plot trajectories, these texts also all portray radical interpenetration across conventional ontological structures as part of their expressions of the epistemological and ontological crises which were identified by McHale (1987) as a distinguishing feature of postmodernist fiction.

Metaleptic collapse may, like alternarration, achieve its chaos and incoherence partially through the absence of discourse deixis which would otherwise serve to help to demarcate the boundaries of levels and to anchor positions relative to those boundaries. In addition to implicit metanarration, other strategies which reoccur in these texts also function without discourse deixis (as defined in this book, though for others, such as Stockwell, 2002, these strategies may be considered as entailing a discourse deictic element). Intertextuality is rife, for example, in Fowles's epigraphs, in Katz's introduction of other authors, and in many other embedded forms of intertextual direct quotation or subtle echoing. The contribution of intertextuality to metafictional effects is one area ripe for further study, for which Genette (1997) and Mason (forthcoming) promise to be highly useful.

Multimodality is also a prominent feature of Barth, Brophy, Katz, and Johnson, in particular. The graphological layout of the text is subject to extreme experimentation in these works. Illustrations are also a key feature: Katz's novel even finishes with a depiction of a series of highly stylised posters seemingly advertising variations of, or (non-existent) sequels to, his book. There is significant scope for critical investigation of multimodal metafictionality within high metafiction. The work of Gibbons (2014, 2012) on multimodality in much more recent metafictional experimentation offers a valuable approach to such an investigation.

This book has drawn on recent work in the field of unnatural narratology, particularly in discussing metalepsis and disnarration. Metafiction exploits many of the techniques studied within unnatural narratology, and so a greater symbiosis of work in the two areas promises to be both fruitful and interesting.

Lastly, this book, while offering advances in theory of discourse deixis, has stopped short of proposing a cognitive account of discourse deixis. As has been shown, discourse deixis regularly co-opts person, spatial, and temporal deixis in the service of discourse deictic reference. Person, spatial, and temporal deixis are all amenable to accounts based on an understanding of cognition as embodied—one of the fundamental principles of cognitive poetics. Some aspects of discourse deixis seem less directly amenable to an embodied, cognitive account. That said, as new work in cognitive grammar progresses, a deeper appreciation of the cognitive poetics of discourse deixis may be achievable. It is hoped that this book can contribute to work towards that goal.

References

Andermahr, S. (2018). "Both/And aesthetics: Gender, art, and language in Brigid Brophy's *In Transit* and Ali Smith's *How to Be Both*". *Contemporary Women's Writing* 12.2. 248–263.

Barth, J. (1988) [1968]. *Lost in the Funhouse: Fiction for Print, Tape, Live Voice*. New York: Doubleday.

Brophy, B. (2002) [1969]. *In Transit: An Heroi-Cyclic Novel*. Chicago, IL: Dalkey Archive Press.

Coover, R. (2011) [1969]. *Pricksongs and Descants*. New York: New American Library.

Darlington, J. (2014). "Cell of one: B. S. Johnson, *Christie Malry* and the Angry Brigade". In *B. S. Johnson and Post-War Literature: Possibilities of the Avant Garde*. Eds. J. Jordan and M. Ryle. Houndmills, Basingstoke: Palgrave Macmillan. 57–102.

Fludernik, M. (2003a). "Metanarrative and metafictional commentary: From metadiscursivity to metanarration and metafiction". *Poetica* 35.1–2. 1–39.

Fogel, S. and Slethaug, G. (1990). *Understanding John Barth*. Columbia, SC: University of South Carolina Press.

Fowles, J. (1996) [1969]. *The French Lieutenant's Woman*. London: Vintage.

Genette, G. (1980). *Narrative Discourse: An Essay in Method*. Trans. J. E. Lewin. Ithaca, NY: Cornell University Press.

Genette, G. (1997). *Paratexts. Thresholds of Interpretation*. Trans. J. E. Lewin. Cambridge: Cambridge University Press.

Gibbons, A. (2012). *Multimodality, Cognition, and Experimental Literature*. London: Routledge.

Gibbons, A. (2014). "Multimodality in literature: An analysis of Jonathan Safran Foer's 'A primer for the punctuation of heart disease'". In *Interactions, Images, and Texts: A Reader in Multimodality*. Eds. S. Norris and C. D. Maier. Boston, MA: Mouton De Gruyter. 371–380.

Gillespie, G. (1975). "Barth's *Lost in the Funhouse*: Short story text in its cyclic context". *Studies in Short Fiction* 12. 223–230.

Groes, S. (2016). *British Fictions of the Sixties: The Making of the Swinging Decade*. London: Bloomsbury.

Johnson, B. S. (2001) [1973]. *Christie Malry's Own Double-Entry*. London: Picador.

Katz, S. (2017) [1968]. *The Exagggerations of Peter Prince*. Singapore: Verbivoracious Press.

Mason, J. (forthcoming). *Intertextuality in Practice*. Amsterdam: John Benjamins.

McHale, B. (1987). *Postmodernist Fiction*. London: Routledge.

Nünning, A. (2005). "On metanarrative: Towards a definition, a typology and an outline of the functions of metanarrative commentary". In *The Dynamics of*

Narrative Form: Studies in Anglo-American Narratology. Ed. John Pier. Berlin and New York: Walter de Gruyter. 11–57.

Prince, G. (1995) [1982]. "Metanarrative signs". In *Metafiction*. Ed. M. Currie. London: Longman. 55–68.

Stockwell, P. (2002). *Cognitive Poetics: An Introduction*. London: Routledge.

Wolf, W. (2009). "Metareference across media: The concept, its transmedial potentials and problems, main forms and functions". In *Metareference Across Media: Theory and Case Studies*. Ed. W. Wolf. Amsterdam: Rodopi. 1–85.

Index

Alber, Jan 16–17, 108–113, 138, 140–141, 145–146, 148, 153
alienation 26–27, 59, 111, 126, 130–132, 136–137, 175, 199
alternarration *see* disnarration
anaphora 51–55, 75, 80–81, 117–118, 166, 168–174, 184, 193–194, 204–209, 220
antinarratable *see* disnarration
author-god 6, 22, 76, 78–81, 92–98, 119–120, 144–147, 176–179, 186, 193–194, 197, 222

Barth, John *see Lost in the Funhouse* (Barth)
Barthes, Roland 8, 19, 65, 78–79, 93, 95
Bell, Alice 17, 108–113, 138, 140–141, 145–146, 153
Benveniste, Émile 8, 36, 41, 132
Brophy, Brigid *see In Transit: An Heroi-Cyclic Novel* (Brophy)
Bühler, Karl 35–40, 46–47, 51

canonical situation-of-utterance 39–40, 44–49, 56, 87, 149–150
chapter titles 50, 52, 66, 68, 88–89, 136, 188, 212–213, 215
Chinese box 103–104, 151, 154
Christie Malry's Own Double-Entry (Johnson) 28–29, 49, 55–56, 71, 73–74, 76–80, 84, 88–89, 94–96, 98, 116–120, 129, 135–137, 147–148, 211–212, 215–216, 222–223
Coover, Robert *see Pricksongs and Descants* (Coover)
counterpart 113, 140–149, 153, 221; counterparthood 113, 140–149, 153, 221

Dannenberg, Hilary P. 104, 140, 161, 181–183, 188–192
definite article *see* definite reference
definite reference 41–44, 57–59, 114, 176–177
deictic centre 36–37, 41–50, 55–61, 72–74, 76–78, 80, 90, 97, 105, 118–119, 121, 123, 126, 132–135, 144, 150, 221; textual deictic centre 118–119, 121, 123, 133–135, 150, 221
deictic projection 44–48, 59–60, 72, 105, 120, 129–130, 204, 220
deixis 22–25, 35–61, 64–65, 68–70, 72–91, 94–99, 103, 105, 109, 112–153, 159, 161–162, 166–181, 184–186, 189, 191–198, 200, 202, 204–216, 220–224; *deixis am phantasma* 40, 45–47; *deixis im textraum* 47–48; *deixis im vorstellungsraum* 40, 46–47; *deixis in der sprechsituation* 47; *demonstratio ad oculos* 40, 44–46, 50
denarration *see* disnarration
diegesis *see* ontological levels
disnarration 1–2, 17–18, 21–22, 30, 78, 134, 154, 159–216, 220–223; alternarration 135, 140, 180–199, 221–222; antinarratable 161–162, 211–216, 221; denarration 161–180, 192–193, 197–198, 221; hypothetical focalisation 161, 199–211, 221; narrative refusal 161, 211–216, 221; negation 58, 77, 163–164, 173, 180–181, 199–211, 221

Emmott, Catherine 43, 54
Exagggerations of Peter Prince, The (Katz) 27, 71, 80–83, 119–125,

140–141, 148–153, 164–166, 168–172, 198, 212–216, 222
extradiegesis *see* ontological levels

Fludernik, Monika 16, 50, 64, 68–73, 85–86, 88, 91, 105, 109–110, 128, 132, 137–139, 143–144, 146, 221
Fowles, John *see French Lieutenant's Woman, The* (Fowles)
French Lieutenant's Woman, The (Fowles) 13, 20–21, 28–29, 55, 71, 78–81, 85, 87, 95–98, 126, 130, 136–137, 143–148, 172–180, 183, 190–195, 197, 204–211, 221–222

garden path 172, 180–199, 206
Genette, Gerard 20, 50, 52, 64–67, 73, 88, 92, 102–107, 109–110, 112, 127, 138, 142, 146, 161, 170–171, 199–200, 212, 221, 223

Herman, David 43–44, 92, 104–105, 111, 113–114, 126, 132, 137, 161–162, 199–207, 210
heteronomous 15, 93, 97, 210
high metafiction 5, 25, 220, 222–223
Hutcheon, Linda 2, 5–14, 28, 74, 79, 112, 172, 191–192
hypothetical focalisation *see* disnarration

immersion 4, 15, 19, 35–36, 55, 59, 69, 111, 113, 189, 196, 199–200, 210
intertextuality 19, 28, 35–36, 71, 95, 109, 136–137, 176–177, 194, 223
In Transit: An Heroi-Cyclic Novel (Brophy) 13, 27–28, 71, 74–76, 99, 130–134, 136–137, 141–142, 153–154, 183, 196–198, 221–223

Johnson, B. S. *see Christie Malry's Own Double-Entry* (Johnson)

Katz, Steve *see Exagggerations of Peter Prince, The* (Katz)

Levinson, Stephen 40, 44, 46, 48–54
Lost in the Funhouse (Barth) 5, 10–11, 23–26, 50, 53, 55, 73–74, 89–91, 97–98, 118–119, 121, 124–127, 130, 134, 153–154, 159, 166–167, 181, 184–186, 221–223; 'Autobiography: A Self-Recorded Fiction' 121, 124–125; 'Frame-Tale' 25–26; 'Life-Story' 25, 50, 53, 55, 73–74, 97–98, 124–127, 166–167; 'Lost in the funhouse' 23–26, 89–91, 118–119, 184–186; 'Night-Sea Journey' 26; 'Title' 124, 134, 159, 181, 184
Lyons, John 36–44, 46, 52, 54

McHale, Brian 6, 8–9, 12–13, 19–21, 28, 56, 74, 104–107, 110, 112, 114–115, 119, 127–128, 140, 145–146, 153, 159, 162, 164–165, 168, 174, 180–181, 187, 192, 196, 223
metaiepsis 2, 13, 17–18, 20–22, 27, 57–59, 61, 64, 66, 68, 73–76, 82–83, 89, 99, 102–153, 165, 167, 169, 191–193, 207, 212, 220–223; metaleptic awareness 73–76, 82–83, 89, 108–109, 115–122, 125–126, 131–135, 147–153, 168–169, 221; metaleptic collapse 110–111, 114–115, 124, 134, 153–154, 167, 180, 223; metaleptic communication 20–21, 108–109, 115, 121–138, 141, 149, 150–151, 153, 221; metaleptic moves 21–22, 108–109, 117, 120, 122, 128–130, 138–153
metanarration 2–3, 11, 17, 19–20, 22, 24–25, 59, 61, 64–98, 102, 110, 115, 117–123, 125–126, 128–129, 133–137, 141, 144, 147–148, 166–178, 184–187, 192–193, 197–198, 204, 210–216, 220–223; direct 69–72, 76, 89–94, 99; extracompositional 69–72, 89–95, 99, 221; indirect 69–72, 76, 89–94, 99; intracompositional 69–72, 89–95, 99, 221; metacompositional metanarration 68, 70, 76–81, 98, 121, 150, 166, 169, 173–176, 184–186, 191, 193–194, 208, 214, 216, 221; metadiegetic metanarration 81–85, 89, 98, 221; metadiscursive metanarration 68, 85–86, 91–98, 116, 121, 147, 174–175, 181, 197, 211–212, 221; metanarrative metanarration 85–91, 221; metatextual metanarration 73–76, 97–98, 121, 168–169, 173–176, 181, 190–191, 194, 211, 221
mimesis *see* realist

narrative refusal *see* disnarration
negation *see* disnarration
Nünning, Angsar 19, 64–73, 78, 80, 88, 92, 96, 104, 140, 221

ontological boundary 2, 13, 20–21, 25–26, 28, 56, 58, 72, 102–112, 119–123, 134, 139–143, 513, 167, 186, 195, 204, 220, 223
ontological hierarchy 13, 15, 30, 104–116, 123, 131, 143, 149–154, 171, 180–183, 186, 188, 197
ontological levels 2, 13, 15, 20–21, 27–28, 36, 56–58, 66, 68, 72, 79, 82, 88, 102–154, 160–161, 165–168, 179–187, 202, 212–213, 220–223; diegesis 20, 66, 90, 92, 103–108, 110, 119, 134, 138–141, 146, 148, 161, 163, 176–179; extradiegesis 20, 66, 72, 80, 103–108, 110, 119–120, 129, 134–135, 138–141, 148, 220; storyworld 2, 19–21, 24, 27, 47–49, 55–61, 67, 72–74, 77–86, 90–97, 105–106, 109–110, 115–118, 120–127, 132–139, 142–153, 159–168, 172, 174–175, 177–181, 183, 186–187, 189, 191, 195–214, 220

person deixis *see* deixis
Possible Worlds theory 107, 140, 160, 201
postmodernism 1–30, 102, 112, 164, 187, 190, 220, 222–223
Pricksongs and Descants (Coover) 10, 18–19, 25–27, 29, 83–89, 93–94, 129, 133–134, 137–138, 141, 186–190, 221–222; 'Babysitter, The' 186–190, 195; 'Elevator, The' 29, 186–188; 'In a Train Station' 93–94, 193, 222; 'Klee Dead' 86–89, 93; 'Magic Poker, The' 83–87, 89, 129, 133–134, 186–188; 'Panel Game' 26,

137–138, 141; 'Quenby and Ola, Swede and Carl' 18–19, 187–188
Prince, Gerald 21, 64–66, 92, 110–111, 159–162, 172, 181, 183, 186, 198–199, 212, 216

realist 4, 9, 16, 28–29, 78–79, 84, 92, 104–105, 112, 118, 128, 143, 147, 151, 160, 164–166, 173, 176, 178–179, 182, 188–190, 201–202, 204–206
reception figures 113, 138, 146, 149–153
Richardson, Brian 16–17, 91, 104, 161–165, 172, 180
Ryan, Marie-Laure 44, 91, 104–105, 109–111, 117, 121, 138–141, 143, 160, 181, 189–190, 192–193, 195

spatial deixis *see* deixis
split discourse context 48–49, 96, 136, 220
Stockwell, Peter 41–44, 50, 60, 88, 104, 130, 223
storyworld *see* ontological levels

temporal deixis *see* deixis
text-continuum 49, 72–73, 76–82, 97–98, 126, 135, 153, 173, 176, 179, 221
textual deictic centre *see* deictic centre
Thoss, Jeff 17, 102, 105–112, 115–121, 125–127, 138–139, 143, 153
translevel identity 113, 140–141, 144–149, 153, 189, 222
transworld identity *see* translevel identity

unnatural narratology 15–18, 111, 113, 115, 220–221, 223

Waugh, Patricia 2, 5–6, 11–13, 28–29, 112, 143, 176, 181, 193
Wolf, Werner 16–17, 64–65, 67–73, 76, 98, 105, 107–115, 138, 143, 146, 221